D1559367

Love and Death in
Renaissance Tragedy

.

Love
and Death

LOUISIANA STATE UNIVERSITY PRES

in Renaissance Tragedy

ROGER STILLING

BATON ROUGE

PR
658
.L63
S8

Designer: Albert Crochet
Type Face: VIP Palatino
Typesetter: Graphic World Inc.
Printer and Binder: Kingsport Press, Inc.

For permission to quote from T. S. Eliot's *Selected Essays*,
author and publisher gratefully acknowledge Faber and Faber, Ltd.,
London, and Harcourt Brace Jovanovich, Inc., New York.

Frontispiece Courtesy Folger Shakespeare Library, Washington, D.C.

LIBRARY OF CONGRESS CATALOGING IN PUBLICATION DATA

Stilling, Roger, 1938–
   Love and death in Renaissance tragedy.

   Bibliography: p.
   Includes index.
   1. English drama—Early modern and
Elizabethan, 1500–1600—History and criticism.
2. English drama—17th century—History and
criticism. 3. Love in literature. 4. Death in
literature. 5. English drama (Tragedy)—History
and criticism. I. Title.
PR658.L63S8   822'.051   74–27193
ISBN 0–8071–0188–5

For Janie Parkins Stilling
and Adam and Nora

Contents

Part III   Jacobean Reverberations

Acknowledgments

Special thanks go to Professor Philip W. Edwards, who guided the original version of this study to its final manifestation, a Trinity College, Dublin, doctoral dissertation; to teachers and friends at Trinity; and to friends and former colleagues in the English departments at University College, Dublin, and at Louisiana State University. I also appreciate the assistance of Les Phillabaum, Beverly Jarrett, and Martha Hall at the Louisiana State University Press.

To detail my wife Jane's contributions to this book would require still another book. Instead I offer this one to her and to our children.

Love and Death in Renaissance Tragedy

The Argument

This book attempts to cut through the conventional groupings of Elizabethan and Jacobean tragedy to reveal the presence of a single unifying motif,
with its own conventions and language, running through and linking the
major works of a dozen important playwrights from 1560 to 1640. This
motif is the opposition of love and death; the genre in which it is embodied
is the love tragedy taken in a larger definition than is customary, what I call
the tragedy of love and death. Historically the line begins—with many of
the genre's main features clearly in embryo—with *Gismond of Salern* in
1560. It ends with John Ford's tragedies in the 1630s.

Some idea of how often the love-death opposition occurs within these
dates may be suggested by a representative list of extracts, all of which in
some way embody the tensions I refer to:

> Ay, thus, and thus, these are the fruits of love.
> (Lorenzo, stabbing Horatio: *Spanish Tragedy*)

> If he forsake me not, I never die,
> For in his looks I see eternity,
> And he'll make me immortal with a kiss.
> (Dido, of Aeneas: *Dido of Carthage*)

> I will kiss thy lips.
> Haply some poison yet doth hang on them
> To make me die with a restorative.
> Thy lips are warm!
> (Juliet, in the Capulet tomb)

> The instances that second marriage move
> Are base respects of thrift, but none of love.
> A second time I kill my husband dead,
> When second husband kisses me in bed.
> (Player Queen: *Hamlet*)

1

Lechery, lechery! Still wars and lechery! Nothing
else holds fashion. A burning devil take them!
(Thersites: Troilus and Cressida)

Now do I see 'tis true. Look: here, Iago,
All my fond love thus do I blow to heaven—
'Tis gone.
Arise, black vengeance, from thy hollow cell!
(Othello)

ANNE: Pardon'd on earth, Soul thou in Heaven art
free;
Once more thy wife, dies thus embracing thee.

FRANK: New marry'd and new widowed; O, she's dead,
And a cold grave must be our nuptial bed.
(A Woman Killed With Kindness)

This very skull,
Whose mistress the duke poison'd, with this drug,
The mortal curse of the earth, shall be reveng'd
In the like strain, and kiss his lips to death.
(Vindice to Hippolito: Revenger's Tragedy)

ANTONIO: I'd have you first provide for a good husband,
Give him all.

DUCHESS: All?

ANTONIO: Yes, your excellent self.

DUCHESS: In a winding sheet?

ANTONIO: In a couple.
(The Duchess of Malfi)

Yes, and her honour's prize
Was my reward; I thank life for nothing
But that pleasure: it was so sweet to me
That I have drunk up all, left none behind
For any man to pledge me.
(De Flores, summing up: The Changeling)

Love is dead; let lovers' eyes,
   Lock'd in endless dreams,
   Th'extremes of all extremes,
Ope no more, for now love dies,
   Now love dies, implying
Love's martyrs must be ever, ever dying.
(Penthea's song: The Broken Heart)

And welcome, welcome! Die when thou hast lived,
Quicken with kissing: had my lips that power,
Thus would I wear them out.
(Cleopatra, to the dying Antony)

These extracts are, of course, merely distillations of what I believe to be the central forces and tensions of this whole group of tragedies. My intention is to unravel—by analysis of language, character, stage convention, and kinds of plot and story—the various strands and twists in the evolution of erotic themes and the love-death motif throughout the Elizabethan Jacobean period. The various terms and titles such as domestic tragedy, revenge tragedy, or the restricted idea of love tragedy—when I use these terms at all—I treat as kinds of love-death tragedy: *i.e.*, domestic tragedy treating love in terms of middle-class morality; revenge tragedy as tragedy in which hatred is strongly in the ascendant; love tragedy as love-death tragedy in which love is set, not against hate or middle-class principle, but against the loss or absence of love itself. Each kind relates to the others; each influences the others, for at the heart of the drama, uniting different conventions, are man and woman and the bond that unites the two, whether it be love or sexuality or—more usual—some potent mixture of the two; to these things, of course, add the forces of death—hatred, betrayal, loss.

The treatment of these subjects by the dramatists does show a traceable evolution, and, since I have had to stress relationships between play and play and interpret comparatively, it is roughly around this evolution that I have organized the individual chapters. Obviously, in the Elizabethan age, dating cannot be certain, but no key points depend on any very controversial chronology. The main features of the overall evolution do, in fact, depend less on precise dating than on placing Shakespeare's great contribution to this drama and the reaction of his followers to the dramatic world he gave them. Thus, in a sense this is a before/after study: first, the treatment of love in tragedy mainly before Shakespeare, ending with Shakespeare's own crystalization of the motif in *Romeo and Juliet* and the immediate influence of this play on John Marston; then the theme of the death of love in Shakespeare's profoundly disturbing middle tragedies; then the individual struggles of the Jacobeans to fit out dramatic fictions that would embody their sense of the post-Shakespearean universe. The main sign of Shakespearean influence, I might add, is the immense predominance in the Jacobean period of erotic motifs and love stories used for serious purposes. A brief précis will make certain general movements clear.

From 1560 to, say, 1599 we find the gradual development of love as a fit subject for tragedy. The distinctive thing about this early development is the cheerful, cheering romanticism of the portrayals. Women, even when they take their lovers sexually—as most of the early ones do—are seen without obtrusive moralizing. They—Gismond, Bel-imperia, Dido, Bethsabe, Juliet, Mellida—are all genuine heroines with whom one has to side precisely because their authors side with them themselves or present them with the kind of dramatic objectivity that makes prurient disapproval impossible. In these plays sexual love is a genuine good. It takes on an increasingly beautiful poetic language, and it has an instinctive and natural moral rightness. Those who love or who in some way promote love are set in distinct opposition to those who do not. Those who do not love are, indeed, usually the ones who hate and kill. As a usual corollary to this, any lover who turns killer has rejected love and to some degree failed his inner humanity. So goes this optimistic, naïve romanticism, the major monument of which is Shakespeare's revolutionary *Romeo and Juliet*. This play summed up the romantic tradition and passed its conventions and its attitudes on to the early John Marston, whose *Antonio and Mellida* plays are clearly written under the most powerful kind of influence—not borrowed phrases but a whole borrowed mythology of love. The particular key to this mythology is the idea of the romantic marriage. To Shakespeare this seemed one ideal way that spirit and flesh could unite, that earthly passions could aspire to spiritual status. Marston accepts this ethic along with the romantic plot, at least until that great turning date—1600. After that all was changed, and the change is vaguely foreshadowed in *Antonio's Revenge* when Antonio's mother leans strongly towards marriage with her husband's murderer. She is saved before the deed, but woman, as she was treated in most later plays, more often was beyond saving.

The second part of the book is concerned with the place of love in Shakespeare's great middle plays: *Hamlet*, *Troilus and Cressida*, and *Othello*. There is no easy way to capsulate the shifts within these plays, but several things are of the first importance. One is that in *Hamlet* the romantic synthesis of spirit and sexuality in the marriage for love is blown apart by Shakespeare's sudden, disturbing concentration on a story of betrayal, particularly adultery. The breakdown of love between man and woman in *Hamlet* heralds the breakdown of all sorts of social bonds. The breakdown also releases the field to distrust, suspicion, and murder, and much of the fascination of the play is centered on the way in which Shakespeare, using the huge but overwrought intelligence of Hamlet himself, traces out some of these connections. In Hamlet's mind all the vague discontents of the Jacobean age are organized and focused on adultery, particularly the adulterous woman, the new Eve. The Hamlet vision of evil, focused on the ambiguous figure of Gertrude, makes the naïve romantic view obsolete only five or so years after *Romeo and Juliet*; yet Hamlet's own mental and spiritual tremors show, I think, Shakespeare's dissatisfaction with Ham-

5   The Argument

let's as a total view, a dissatisfaction that operates even while Shakespeare seems to identify with it.

Troilus and Cressida seems to be an attempt to redefine the whole relation of the spiritual element in love to the sexual by freeing the problem from the mind of one character (as it was in *Hamlet*) and putting it forth in the wide panorama of one of the great myths of the medieval romance tradition. One of the minor themes of the first period of Elizabethan love tragedy—the rejection of courtly love and the abuses of the courtly vocabulary—is thus brought to the fore in this dramatization of the medieval tradition's greatest story of betrayal in love. The real point of the play, however, as far as the love story goes, is not that the play is a rejection of romantic love between woman and man—as *Hamlet* appeared to be—but that it is an examination of a kind of love that must fail because it has no genuine claim to permanence. Indeed, Shakespeare's position looks forward to that of such students of courtly love as C. S. Lewis and Denis de Rougemont in this day,[1] who find at the heart of the convention a positive side (courtly love as an idealistic attempt to give status to human affection) and a still more powerful negative side (the built-in transience necessitated by the symbolic and real adultery courtly love thrives on and the necessity for the lovers to remain outside larger social structures). One major development in Shakespeare's idea of love seems a special product of this more objective approach: individual betrayals by women no longer constitute grounds for the emotional rejection of the whole sex. Hamlet had condemned all women (and implicitly all humankind) in his mother's action, but when Ulysses asks Troilus "What hath she done, prince, that can soil our mothers?" (V. ii. 134),[2] he opens the way for Desdemona and, after her, such women as Cordelia, Hermione, Perdita, and Cleopatra.

Against this background it can be shown that *Othello* achieves a peculiar but significant reversal. Sexual betrayal ceases to be—as it is in the mythology of the medieval church—the signal mark of womanhood. Indeed, Shakespeare shows this kind of misogynous iconography to be mainly a fantasy of the diseased male imagination and the failure of love. His idea of love thus comes full circle, and he goes into *King Lear* with both a new romanticism and a much deeper consciousness of the precarious nature of human contentment.

1. C. S. Lewis, *The Allegory of Love*, Galaxy Books (New York: Oxford University Press, 1958 reprint of 1963 edition); Denis de Rougemont, *Passion and Society*, trans. Montgomery Belgion (Rev. ed.; London: Faber and Faber Ltd., 1962).
2. Except where noted, quotations from Shakespeare are from the New Cambridge Edition, ed. John Dover Wilson and Arthur Quiller-Couch (Cambridge University Press).

Section Three takes up the Jacobean responses to the drama of love and death. In play after play we find some version of the romantic, *Romeo and Juliet* pattern of love tragedy (Webster's *Duchess*) or the antiromantic, *Hamlet* pattern (*The Revenger's Tragedy*; Heywood's plays about adultery) or else (like *Troilus and Cressida*) plays in which the two viewpoints struggle to coexist (*The White Devil*, *The Changeling*, Ford's *'Tis Pity*). This bare outline admittedly oversimplifies, but in the context of detailed analyses it will provide some interesting configurations of influence and relationship. For after such plays as *Hamlet* and *Othello*, each of the important Jacobean tragedians defines or tries to define his view of the world in terms of the love-death conventions. Such things as the struggle of individual demands for self-realization against social pressures and the problem of betrayal in marriage against sterility in a loveless marriage form the framework for the post-Shakespearean psychological-symbolical drama. The study of the development of the conventions of love-death tragedy gives a specific and definite center from which the complex individualists of the Jacobean period (including the late Shakespeare) can be interpreted and compared, and to me it seems a more certain one than generalized discussion of non-dramatic moral literature and the seventeenth-century intellectual atmosphere. Such general issues should hardly be excluded, of course, but they should gain in meaning after one is conscious of a highly developed tradition for the dramatic representation of human love and sexuality. This, of course, is the purpose of this study, to explore the nature of this tradition and this dialectic by means of the critical analysis of specific, important, sixteenth- and seventeenth-century plays.

A preliminary point on tragic theory: it is customary to regard the tragic hero as—among other things—a man standing isolate and grand above his fellow men. This general view has always had great currency among the followers of Aristotle. A recent—and very influential— example may be found in Northrop Frye's *Anatomy of Criticism*: "The tragic hero is typically on top of the wheel of fortune, halfway between human society on the ground and the something greater in the sky. Prometheus, Adam, and Christ hang between heaven and earth, between a world of paradisal freedom and a world of bondage. Tragic heroes are so much the highest points in their human landscape that they seem the inevitable conductors of the power about them, great trees more likely to be struck by lightning than a clump of grass."[3]

3. Northrop Frye, *Anatomy of Criticism: Four Essays* (Princeton: Princeton University Press, 1957), 207.

It seems clear that in terms of love tragedy there is a strong tendency to break down this image of the lonely, almost epical, hero and bring him into close contact with the rest of the world. Obviously, the very fact that the hero becomes a lover brings him into relation with the beloved. But more than that, in most of the plays there is a sense of the pressure of society that is closer and more immediate than one associates with the traditional epic hero. Far from being ambitious and overweening and therefore evil as well as grand, the hero of the love tragedy is rarely ambitious in the old monkish sense, and the forces of evil must find different, usually social or psychological, embodiments. The point is that the old tragic heroic criteria are of little use in discussing the figures in these plays except where the writer deliberately evokes them as a source of tension. Some new theoretical basis is needed, therefore, and I would suggest Frye's ideas on comedy, on the comic Oedipus complex, on the struggle of Spring (the young generation) against Winter (the old),[4] of—in other words—life against death, as the source of it. Critics have often noted the strong admixture of the comic in such an influential play as *Romeo and Juliet*; this comic element has been cited as a sign that love is not to be taken seriously,[5] suggesting that nothing comic can be serious. Frye's work on comedy and its psychological and social significance has, of course, revealed the severe limitations of this critical view. It also suggests that what is really needed is a theory of New Tragedy to go with Old Tragedy, just as there is a similar grouping for comedy. The point would be that New Tragedy starts long before William Archer's century; it starts with some of Sophocles and most of Euripides. More important, it triumphs absolutely with the sixteenth century. So, far from being Old Tragedy, the tragedy of the English Renaissance was the birth (with all the pangs) of the modern.

4. Northrop Frye, "The Argument of Comedy," *English Institute Essays*, 1948: reprinted in Laurence Lerner (ed.), *Shakespeare's Comedies: An Anthology of Modern Criticism* (Harmondsworth: Penguin Books Ltd., 1967), 315–25.
5. F. M. Dickey, *Not Wisely but Too Well* (San Marino, Calif.: Huntington Library, 1957).

Part I

The Making of a Genre

1

Gismond of Salern: in Love

The progenitor of all the plays in this study is *Gismond of Salern: in Love*. It was written by five gentlemen of the Inner Temple, acted at the Inner Temple in 1567–1568, revised and printed in 1591, and most recently re-printed by J. F. Cunliffe in *Early English Classical Tragedies* in 1912. The 1591 editor himself made out what seems to me an irrefutable case for the play's subject: "'In poetry, there is no argument of more antiquity and elegancy than is the matter of love; for it seems to be as old as the world, and to bear date from the first time that man and woman was.'"[1] I put it forward as a preliminary justification for this study.

Mr. Cunliffe (from whose introduction the quote is taken) quotes another early critic on the play of *Gismond*: "'The tragedy was by them [the Inner-Temple gentlemen] most pithily framed, and no less curiously acted in view of her Majesty, by whom it was then as princely accepted, as of the whole honourable audience notably applauded: yea, and of all men generally desired, as a work, either in stateliness of show, depth of conceit, or true ornaments of poetical art, inferior to none of the best in that kind: no, were the Roman Seneca the censurer.'"[2] This is high praise, but Mr. Cunliffe quotes it only to introduce his own dispraise: "It seems almost sacrilege to suggest such a pitiful predecessor as this for *Romeo and Juliet*."[3] I cannot say I share the modern editor's embarrassment. There is obviously a gulf between

1. R. Wilmot, quoted in John W. Cunliffe (ed.), *Early English Classical Tragedies* (Oxford: Clarendon Press, 1912), lxxxvi. All quotations from *Gismond of Salern: in Love* are from this text.
2. William Webbe to R. Wilmot, quoted in Cunliffe, *Early English Classical Tragedies*, lxxxviii–ix.
3. Cunliffe, *Early English Classical Tragedies*, xc

11

the early play and the later, but the old play's survival and the Elizabethan interest in it demonstrate two things at least: that the theme
Shakespeare was to glorify had a tradition, and that this theme had an
inherent interest that enabled the play to survive the literary ragged-
ness of its authors. A remarkable number of the issues, images, and
characters which give later Elizabethan and Jacobean tragedies their
fascination find their first dramatic articulation in this play.

I shall begin the discussion of *Gismond* by considering its source in
Italian short fiction. The focus in this book is not often on sources; this
instance is important, though, because it offers the opportunity to note
certain significant aspects of the debt English drama owes the Italian
Renaissance, particularly certain basic dramatic devices and philosophical and psychological attitudes towards both the lighter and darker
sides of eros.

1.

In the Argument I mentioned the close relationship of much love tragedy to
the traditional patterns of comedy. Nothing better demonstrates this close-
ness than the source of *Gismond*, Boccaccio's *Decameron*. In Boccaccio's
magnificent work, farce sits cheek by jowl with tragedy and romance with
satire. Similar types of characters, of course, turn up in all the genres, and
the overall result is a kind of literary democratization, a very significant aspect of which is the relative equality of man and woman, even where the
man tries strenuously to deny it. George Meredith made a special point of
this equality in discussing the comic spirit.[4] It is no less significant in
tragedy; failure to deal with it adequately has obscured the extent to which
so much Renaissance drama has as its dynamic, not the progress from life
to death of a lightning rod of a hero, but the passionate interaction of person on person. It is typical of the Renaissance pattern that this very humanistic kind of tragedy should move from South to North. While England's
characteristic literary narrative was the monkish, masculine tale of the fall
of great men, Italy developed a literature that was social in a new way.
Boccaccio's great collection was a testament to the success of the new mode.
It is fitting, therefore, that the first of the line of tragedies that flower out
into *Romeo and Juliet* should be taken from Boccaccio—and not merely from
any story, but from one of the tales the author himself appears to give great

---

4. George Meredith, "An Essay on Comedy," reprinted in Wylie Sypher (ed.), *Comedy*
(Garden City, N. Y.: Doubleday Anchor Books, 1956), 14ff.

weight to. The story of Ghismonda is the first tragic tale in the *Decameron*, and Boccaccio's own beloved mistress Fiammetta tells it. The basic story is simple. The main characters are Tancred, an aging noble; his newly widowed daughter, Ghismonda; and a young man named Guiscardo. The motive force of the story is the sexual impulse of the two young people; the opposing force is the sexual conservatism of the old father. (One recalls Northrop Frye's analysis of New Comedy: "New Comedy unfolds from what may be described as a comic Oedipus situation. Its main theme is the successful effort of a young man to outwit an opponent and possess the girl of his choice. The opponent is usually the father [*senex*]"[5]).

Ghismonda loved her now dead husband, but she is still young, sensual, still desirous of life. Her father, who loves her, has no desire ever to part with her again. The forward motion of the action begins when she perceives that "the Prince . . . was at no pains to provide her with another husband, and deeming it unseemly on her part to ask one of him . . .[she] cast about how she might come by a gallant to be her secret lover."[6] It should be noted that, here and throughout the tale, Boccaccio betrays no conventional Gothic disapproval of her sexual initiative and fulfillment. It will be seen that his liberalism was not lost on the Gentlemen of the Inner Temple.

Ghismonda falls in love with the worthy but poor Guiscardo, communicates her affection to him, and soon they become clandestine lovers, meeting often in her bedroom. It is to this bedroom that Tancred comes one day. He finds her gone, naps at the foot of her bed wrapped in a curtain and awakes to find the pair making love only a few feet away. The opposing elements of the story are thus brought into the sharpest possible juxtaposition: impotent old age gapes on as sexual love is celebrated in bed; conventional authority is outraged by the free, joyful expression of the libido. The death motive is aroused by the erotic one. This opposition is by no means limited to one crucial scene; it determines the overall structure of the story. The desire for love follows on mourning to give Ghismonda renewed life. Then death—in the form of Tancred's vengeance—is aroused by the sight of love. Finally, out of the deaths inflicted or provoked by Tancred comes a renewed sense of the force and values of love.

We can also see the love-death opposition put to work as Boccaccio (and later the Gentlemen of the Inner Temple) probes the inner, psychological

5. Frye, "The Argument of Comedy," 315.
6. Giovanni Boccaccio, *The Decameron*, trans. J. M. Rigg (London: J. M. Dent & Sons Ltd., 1960 reprint of 1930 edition), I, 235.

structures of the story. Here, for instance, is Boccaccio's description of Tancred as he watches the love-making: "It so befell that Tancred awoke, and heard and saw what they did: whereat he was troubled beyond measure, and at first was minded to upbraid them; but on second thoughts he deemed it best to hold his peace, and avoid discovery, if so he might with greater stealth and less dishonour carry out the design which was already in his mind."[7] His first (and perfectly normal) reaction is to rebuke them. But as he continues to watch, his feelings become more sinister, secretive, deadly. The secret viewer becomes the secretive, twisted machiavel.

Boccaccio's interest goes deeper into psychological complexities, however. Love and hatred are mingled within Tancred's own heart:

> "I am distraught between the love which I have ever borne thee, love such as no father ever bare to daughter, and the most just indignation evoked in me by thy signal folly; my love prompts me to pardon thee, my indignation bids me harden my heart against thee, though I do violence to my nature. But before I decide upon my course, I would fain hear what thou hast to say to this." So saying, he bent his head, and wept as bitterly as any child that had been soundly thrashed.[8]

Tancred is on the verge here of mental breakdown. He loves Ghismonda, and yet finds he must hate her. Her nature is his nature, and so the emotion he feels not only turns against her, but against himself as well. There is nothing primitive about this kind of psychological perception, and it forms a rich legacy for Renaissance drama.

The same psychological intelligence shows itself in the handling of Ghismonda's side of the story, and here its influence is of tremendous importance in breaking down conventional, simplistic moral attitudes to what one might normally call sexual misbehaviour. First, Tancred—in his reproaches to her—tries to conceal his personal fury behind the mask of a more socially respectable issue: that Guiscardo is not of acceptable family rank. Ghismonda sweeps this aside with calm authority:

> "Consider a little the principles of things: thou seest that in regard of our flesh we are all moulded of the same substance, and that all souls are endowed by one and the same Creator with equal faculties, equal powers, equal virtues. . . . Pass in review all thy nobles, weigh their merits, their manners and bearing, and then compare Guiscardo's qualities with theirs: if thou wilt judge without prejudice, thou wilt

7. *Ibid.*, 237.
8. *Ibid.*, 238.

pronounce him noble in the highest degree, and thy nobles one and all churls."[9]

This again is a democratization of tragedy by the theme of love, showing how love cuts through externals to reach essences, those private, personal qualities that give personal relationships their force. Out of feelings like these of Ghismonda's comes the iconoclasm of Juliet's "What's in a name?" and "A rose by any other name. . . ." Ghismonda's speech and others in the story also make another point: that although both love and hatred may exaggerate the good or bad qualities of their object, the exaggerations of love come out of generosity. Hatred, even disguised as moralism, can only slander.

The final element in Ghismonda's philosophy that had great impact was her spirited defense of the sexual urge, based upon its important place in essential human nature. " 'It should not have escaped thee, Tancred, creature of flesh and blood as thou art, that thy daughter was also a creature of flesh and blood, and not of stone or iron; it was, and is, thy duty to bear in mind (old though thou art) the nature and the might of the laws to which youth is subject.' "[10] Animate flesh (life itself) is here set against inanimate stone and iron. And—cutting more closely at Tancred himself—we also see a vivid consciousness ("old though thou art") of the sterile, narrow vision of much of the wisdom of elders. Boccaccio's Ghismonda is here firing the first shots across the generation gap.

One or two further contributions from the *novelle* need mentioning. For instance, certain important shaping devices and symbolic confrontations were found very suitable to the love-death drama, and these help mold its characteristic form. One such is the revelation scene, such as that in which Tancred discovered the lovers. Dramatic fiction is an art form for the eye in a way that discursive fiction is not; one finds in later plays an increasing interest and inventiveness in the manipulation of scenes with unobserved observers. Often (we shall see this in *Dido, The Spanish Tragedy, Romeo and Juliet*, and numerous others) these are key turning points, showing the instant that love is transformed into hatred. At the very least, they give to a love scene a means of suggesting the gradual encroachment of death. The latent voyeurism of this is obvious, of course, and it does not take too great a leap of the imagination to perceive the relationship between scenes like

9. *Ibid.*, 240.
10. *Ibid.*, 239.

these in earlier Elizabethan love tragedies and Iago's snickering answer to Othello's demand for "ocular proof":

> . . . how satisfied, my lord?
> Would you, the supervisor, grossly gape on—
> Behold her topped?
>
> (*Othello*, III. iii. 396–98)

Another formal technique that becomes a notable convention in love tragedy is the symbolic death scene. In the plays of this line of development, the death of lovers is almost inevitably conducted in a manner that recalls and reinforces the erotic theme. For instance, in Boccaccio's story, when Guiscardo is murdered it is done by no ordinary means. Death is not sufficient for Tancred; because the heart is the symbolic seat of love, he must also cut the heart from the body. Ghismonda is given the bloody heart, and we see that this gesture of Tancred's is a powerful, almost totemic way of telling her that her love is dead. But she takes the motif one step further: "She bowed herself low over the cup; and, while no womanish cry escaped her, 'twas as if a fountain of water were unloosed within her head, so wondrous a flood of tears gushed from her eyes, while times without number she kissed the dead heart." [11] Then she puts the poison in and drinks down the mixture, gets into her bed and lays the dead lover's heart against her own, thus moving towards a symbolic reconciliation of the lovers in death. The need of the imagination for completed ends and balanced shapes demands such a resolution even if it means flying in the face of realism. It is an expression of an emotional need for shape and form in life itself, with death having its organic place in the process: "'As thou brookedst not that I should live with Guiscardo in privity and seclusion, so wherever thou mayst have caused Guiscardo's body to be cast, mine may be united with it in the common view of all.'" [12] In the end, the two are interred side by side in the same tomb: the final turn of the love-death theme—and one which reverberates throughout the Elizabethan-Jacobean era.

2.

We may now trace some of these reverberations in the first English love tragedy.

In terms of overall structure, of course, the love-death opposition is still

---

11. *Ibid.*, 242.
12. *Ibid.*, 243.

the prime organizing motif. The play opens after death has robbed Gismond of her first love; it comes to an emotional and thematic climax as her own beloved father robs her of her second; it ends with Gismond dying to her own epitaph:

> Loe here within one tōbe whear harbour twaine,
> Gismōda Quene, and Counte Palurine:
> she loued him, he for her loue was slayen,
> for whoes reuenge eke lyes she here in shrine.
>
> (V. iii. 45–48)

A final turn on the love-death theme completes the motif: Tancred himself feels the misery of having lost a beloved and finds himself traveling the same downward emotional path into negation that Gismond took:

> Shall not, alas,
> this spedy death be wrought, sithe I haue lost
> my dearest ioy of all?   (V. iv. 10-12)

More significant perhaps is the way the Gentlemen of the Inner Temple captured and elaborated on so many of Boccaccio's perceptions about the basic truths of the human heart, of love and hate and the complex, mysterious relationship between the two. For instance, they stress in one of Gismond's speeches the link between sexual love and the natural urge to fertility and fruition. We see this in the nature images with which she mourns the premature loss of her first husband:

> My Lord is gone, my ioy is reft away,
> that all with cares my hart is ouerfraught.
> In him was all my pleasure and delight:
> to him gaue I the frutes of my first loue:
> he with the cōfort of his only sight
> all cares out of my brest could sone remoue.
>
> (I. iii. 31-36)

Against the failure of fertility, nature responds with a consciousness of the passing of time, of the attracting purpose of beauty:

> This makes me in the silent night
> oft to record how fast my youth withdrawes
> it self away, how swift doeth rūne his race
> my pleasant life.
> . . . .
> . . . if I shold my pleasant yeres neglect
> of fresh grene youth frutelesse to fade away:
> whearto liue I? whearto hath nature decked
> me with so semely shape?   (II. i. 20–23, 26–29)

All these are embodied in traditional images of springtime and fertility. Nor, it should be stressed, are we to take Gismond's speeches as the rationalizations of youthful lust and folly. The Gentlemen seemed to anticipate this traditional moralistic reaction by having Tancred's own mature sister support Gismond's pleas:[13]

> But I see and perceiue
> that she hath not layed vp wth him in graue
> those sparkes of senses, wch she did receiue
> when kind to her bothe life and body gaue:
> nor with her husbandes death her life doeth ceasse:
> but she yet liues, and liuing she doeth fele
> such passions hold her tender hart in presse,
> as shew the same not to be wrought of stele, . . .
>
> (II. ii. 13–20)

The result is a cumulative and sensitive statement of the link between love, life, and nature that stands as a humane measure against which Tancred's death-haunted concepts of honor, morality, and revenge must be set.

I have already mentioned the pathological quality Boccaccio gives Tancred's revenge, but the Italian was—compared to the English authors of *Gismond of Salern*—a model of restraint. Boccaccio's Guiscardo had his heart cut out, but this is the only mutilation. The Gentlemen of the Inner Temple, sensing the element of the perverse in this act, augment it with further perversities—most probably under the influence of Seneca. The result is description that—for goriness—would not be out of place in *Thyestes*:

> After his breath was gone
> bereft thus from his brest by cruell force
> streight they despoiled him, and, not alone
> contented wth his death, on the dead corps,
> whom sauage beastes do spare, ginne they to showe
> new crueltie, and wth a swerd they pearce
> his naked belly, and vnrippe it soe
> that out the bowelles gush. Whoe can rehearse
> the dolefull sight, wherew^th my hart euen bledde?
> The warme entrailes were toren out of his brest
> w^thin their handes trēbling not fully dead:
> his veines smoked: his bowelles all to strest
> ruthelesse were rent, and throwen amidde the place:
> all clottered lay the blood in lompes of gore,
> sprent on his corps, and on his palëd face.   (V. i. 173–87)

---

13. This does, as Cunliffe suggests, rob Gismond of a certain dark glamor by giving her arguments respectability, but it gives her position, and therefore the idea of love itself, a moral force which it might have otherwise lacked.

What is notable here is the strong element of relish, of sheer enthusiasm for the task of killing implied in this description of the murderers, an enthusiasm compounded of the hatred of the object of vengeance and a wild Thyestean joy in the fact of his destruction. The emotional and poetical roots of this sadistic violence are worth seeking, for they form the basis for nearly all the treatments of jealousy and sadism throughout the period.

The portrait of Tancred is drawn with an acute sense of the dark ironies of his paternal situation. In the beginning, when Gismond is deeply distressed by the loss of her husband, Tancred appears to be the voice of dispassionate reason.

> TAN: Forgett therfore this vain and ruthefull care:
> and lett not teres yor youthfull beautie paire.
> GISM: Oh sir, these teres loue chalength as due.
> TAN: But reason sayeth they do no whit auaile.
> GISM: Yet can I not my passions so subdue.
> TAN: Your fond affections ought not to preuaile.
> GISM: Whoe can but plaine the losse of such a one?
>
> (I. iii. 51–57)

But it soon becomes clear that his philosophy is only a mask for his own pleasure at her return—thus making a point which persists throughout the romantic tragedy: the sinister egotism and concealed passion latent in certain kinds of emotional detachment. For, when Tancred is faced by his sister with Gismond's desire to remarry, his stoic facade breaks down completely and releases a flood of violently emotional rhetoric mingled with images of death:

> Yo^r wordes do slay my hart, as if the knife
> in cruell wise forthwith shold perce the same.
>
> . . . .
>
> Her late marriage hath taught me, to my grefe,
> that in the frutes of her desirëd sight
> doeth rest the only cõfort and relefe
> of my vnweldy age. For what delight,
> what ioy, what cõfort in this earth haue I,
> if my Gismonda shold depart from me?
> O daughter, daughter, rather let me dye
> some sodein cruel death, . . .
>
> (II. ii. 36–37, 53–60)

The reference to her previous marriage makes it clear that he had felt a rankling sense of loss, and out of this a kind of fatherly jealousy, throughout the course of her marriage. But the interesting thing is that such feelings on the part of the father take a form strangely like those of a husband.

When Tancred tells Gismond,

> And though yoᴿ husband death hath reft away;
> yet life a louing father doeth susteine,
> whoe (during life) to yow a doble stay
> as father and as husband will remaine,
>
>   (I. iii. 45–48)

he is in one sense being charmingly, even movingly, naïve. But this naïveté has its dark side. Tancred cannot be her husband, yet when he learns that she has a lover his vengeance is just as implacable and as symbolically appropriate as that of any Italianate cuckold. One thinks again of Frye's formulation of the psychological stresses behind New Comedy. But *Gismond* is New Tragedy, and Frye's *senex* succeeds in defeating the young man. Thus, where in comedy the victory goes to youth, to rebirth and life, in tragedy it is death and winter which triumph. Behind this pattern lie psychological realities which are still imperfectly understood. Why, for instance, does the father traditionally obstruct his daughter's love; why does he feel both in comic tradition and so often in life a pang at discovering that a daughter enjoys a sexual life of her own? Freud, of course, postulates a whole web of implicitly erotic relationships within the family group, only one of which, that of the mother and father, is explicitly sexual, the sexuality of the others existing primarily in the prohibitions which repress them.[14] It is difficult not to feel in this tragedy and later ones that some such intuition lies behind the presentation of the father as a jealous husband and the presentation of his vengeance as cruelty touched with erotic motivation.[15]

Certainly the poetry of the play shows death motive and love motive inextricably linked in Tancred's own mind. For instance, in the vocabulary of courtly love the word *relefe* implies the curing of emotional tensions or agonies by a physical means—the act of love.[16] It is revealing, therefore, to see

---

14. See, for a brief account, the Fourth Lecture of Freud's *Five Lectures on Psycho-Analysis* (1910), Vol. XI of *The Standard Edition of the Complete Psychological Works of Sigmund Freud*, trans. under the general editorship of James Strachey (London: Hogarth Press and the Institute of Psycho-Analysis, 1957), 40–48.

15. For a fuller discussion, see Ernest G. Griffin, "'Gismond of Salerne': A Critical Appreciation," *A Review of English Literature*, IV (April, 1963), 94–107.

16. As in Guishard's speech:
> "For I see plaine that she desireth no lasse,
> that we shold mete for to aswage our grefe,
> than I, if she could bring the same to passe,
> that none it wist: as it appereth by prefe
> of her gestures, which shewen me, alas,
> how she assentes that I shold haue relefe
> of my distresse, . . ."   (III. iii. 25–31)

Tancred using the same word in a strangely similar sense and in conjunction with that common metaphor for the passion of love—*fire*—here used in terms of vengeance:

> O great almighty Ioue, whome I haue heard to be
> the god, that guides the world as best it liketh thee,
> that doest wth thōder throwe out of the flaming skies
> the blase of thy reuenge on whom thy wrath doeth rise;
> graunt me, as of thy grace, and as for my relefe,
> that wch thow pourest out. . . .   (IV. ii. 1–6)

The identification becomes even stronger when appetite, another frequent metaphor for sexual desire, is used in connection with the desire to kill: "His slaughter and her teres, her sorrow and his blood/shall to my rancorous rage supplie delitefull foode"(IV. ii. 119–20). The root of the paradox is the apprehension that love and hate have similarities of process. In this play both unrequited love and hate are depicted as frustrations which must be relieved by action. And we see also that the two actions—the act of love and the act of hate—themselves, though totally obverse in intent, from the male point of view have obvious points of relationship. These similarities have been celebrated as far back as language itself by myriad puns on the phallic nature of almost every kind of weapon. Clearly this identification is a simple enough one, but it opens the way to a whole field of others from the idea of seduction-as-conquest to the identification of death with the moment of sexual fulfillment and to others much less obvious. The important thing in all of this, and the crux of so many of the problems in these plays, is the way love—which should be purely good and purely life-giving—has in the very biological, psychological, and linguistic modes of its expression this profound potential for the intrusion of the death motive.

3.

There is one other aspect of Tancred's vengeance that needs to be considered: its effect on the moral impact of the play. J. F. Cunliffe quotes from the dedication which R. Wilmot attached to his revised version of the play (1591): " 'There is nothing more welcome to your wisdoms than the knowledge of wise, grave, and worthy matters, tending to the good instructions of youths, of whom you are mothers.' " [17] And though the prefatory sonnets of the original authors were not so didactically inclined (the longest and most co-

---

17. Wilmot, dedication to *Tancred and Gismunda*, quoted in Cunliffe, *Early English Classical Tragedies*, lxxxvii–viii.

gent one did, in fact, stress pity for Gismond and her lover and suggest that fathers learn to treat their daughters "in kinder wise"[18], moralizing on love occurs in one form or another throughout the play, mainly in the choral sections. As one might expect, this moralizing is strongly antilove and, indeed, antilife. Cupid opens the play in the manner of a ranting Senecan ghost:

> This one hand beares vain hope, short ioyfull state,
> with faire semblance the louer to allure:
> this other holdes repentance all to late,
> warr, fiër, blood, . . .
> . . . .
>   I drink the louers blood,
> and eate the liuing hart within his brest.
>
>   (I. i. 5–8, 11–12)

The Chorus moralizes incessantly, at first in the general terms familiar from medieval and Tudor nondramatic tragedy:

> a) But happy is he, that endes this mortal life
>   By spedy death, . . .
>
>   (I. iii. Chore. 33–34)
>
> b) Whoes case is such, that frō his coate he may
>   behold afarre the chāge that chaūceth here,
>   how sone they rise, how sone they do decay
>   that leane their states on fortunes slipper sphere,
>   whoe liues alôwe, and feleth not the strokes
>   of stormes wth which the hyëst toures do fall,
>   ne blustring windes wth which the stoutest okes
>   stoupen full lowe, his life is surest of all.
>
>   (I. iii. Chore. 45–52)

Later, more directly concerned with women, the Chorus gives a series of *exempla* from the golden age. The following passages are typical:

> a) Quene Artemise thought not an heape of stones,
>   . . . .
>   a worthy graue wherin to rest the bones
>   of her dead Lord, for euer to abide:
>   but drank his hart, and made her tender brest
>   his tombe, . . .
>
>   (II. iii. Chore. 17, 19–22)
>
> b) The stout daughter of Cato Brutus wife
>   when she had heard his death, did not desire
>   longer to liue: and lacking vse of knife

---

18. *Gismond of Salern*, third prefatory sonnet, l. 14.

(a strange death) ended her life by fire,
and eate hote burning coles. O worthy dame!
O vertues worthy of eternall praise!

(II. iii. Chore. 29–34)

The choral interlude from which these are taken comes just after Tancred
has refused to allow Gismond to remarry. On the surface, the *exempla* seem
to be ironic criticisms of the failure of Gismond's sense of duty implied in
her desire to marry again. But even this simple irony proves to be double-
edged and ambiguous since Gismond does, in fact, at the end of the play
emulate the two women here named against her. One final piece of didac-
ticism is worth mentioning; it stands between Tancred's seizure of Guishard and the account of the subsequent murder. The passage suggests
that nothing but "blood" can come of "wicked love" and recommends chaste
and platonic "service" such as that of Petrarch:

So whilom did the learned Tuscane serue
his chast ladie, and glorie was their end.
Such ar the frutes, that louers doen deserue,
whoes seruice doeth to vertue and honor tend.

(IV. iv. Chore. 45–48)

Now, the striking thing about all of this moralizing is its human irrele-
vance. There is not a single passage quoted above which answers to the situation presented by Gismond's story. What she wants is to combine sexuality with honor; the means to this is marriage; this her father has denied
her. To answer this need the Chorus offers a symbol of love-as-sadism (the
perverse Senecan Cupid); generalized moralizing in the vocabulary of
politics (the wheel and the fall of princes); suicide as a virtue, and chastity
within the courtly love tradition. Of these, only the last—which, of a bad
lot, is the most humane—is in any manner a practical solution. But even
it is based on a social institution—the court of love—which was, as nearly
as one can tell, a dead horse by the mid-1560s. The other prescriptions are
either life-denying, absurd, or both. There is, in other words, nothing in
these moral orthodoxies which really has anything to do with Gismond,
particularly when they are set against the human reality of Lucrece's
speech on nature.

But it is at the death of the lovers that we see the full extent of the gulf
between the didactic and the fictional modes in this play. We never see
the lovers together on stage. We never hear them speak to each other; we
know nothing of the quality or character of their relationship other than
that they appear to enjoy sex together. The way in which they face death

is, therefore, revealing, just as is the way in which Tancred administers it. For within the orthodox moral framework of the play, the traditional and natural identification of the father with moral order and with the kind of precepts which the Chorus speaks is the natural and obvious one. Yet the father (the authority symbol) becomes a lunatic tyrant and the sexually immoral lovers face death in a manner that compels sympathy and admiration. The contrast between lovers and father is made plain in two separate confrontations, one between Tancred and Gismond and the other between Tancred and Guishard. In the face of Tancred's "fury of enkindled fire," Gismond refuses to plead for her life when called upon to explain herself, offering instead the calm rejection of life itself if it must be life without Guishard:

> But sithe it so hath settled in your minde,
> that neither he shall liue, nor yow will be
> the father, . . .
> . . . .
> alas vain is to ask what I can say
> why I shold liue: sufficeth for my part
> to say I will not liue and there to stay.
>
> (IV. iii. 71–73, 80–82)

Thus she, an illicit lover, falls into symbolic alignment with the virtuous wives cited by the Chorus in its critique of Brass Age morality.

Guishard's scene is, in many ways, even more important, for we have only his manner of losing life to show us how he valued love and to give us some indication of how we must value it. In response to Tancred's self-pitying, egotistical rage—

> Thyne, Palurine? and shall I so susteine
> such wrong? is she not myne, and only myne?
> Me leuer were ten thousand times be slayen,
> than thow shold iustly claime and vse for thyne
> her that is dearer than my self to me.
>
> (IV. iv. 49–53)

—the Gentlemen of the Inner Temple offer a lover who is almost a saint of selflessness (even pitying Tancred's mental disturbance) while at the same time, like Gismond, being a model of quiet and modest self possession:

> Sir, neither do your trickling teres delight
> my wretched soule, nor yet myne owne vnhap
> doeth greue my hart.   (IV. iv. 25–27)

The lover feels he must die well in order to justify and validate the love:

> and eke by death I ioy that I shall showe
> my self her owne, that hers was liuing here,
> and hers will be, where euer my ghost shall goe.
> Vse yow my life or death for your relefe,
> to stay the teres that moist yo' grefefull eyen:
> and I will vse my life and death for prefe
> that hers I liued and dye that liuëd myne.

(IV. iv. 42–48)

If we can ignore the stiff, unconvincing literary quality of the lovers' speeches, their very primitiveness makes them valuable. For even in such a simple prototype, we can see the seeds of the developing conflict between the freedom, power, nobility, and beauty which love brings to young lovers and the self-seeking, at times pathological, egotism, conservatism, and rigidity of established authority. The presentation of Gismond and Guishard is therefore quite plainly subversive to fixed ideas. Without recommending sexual unchastity, and indeed while specifically and reasonably favoring virtue, the authors portray characters who engage in an illicit love affair and emerge as humane and sympathetic.

The reason for this reversal is probably that no area of moral thought and action is more personal and, consequently, less amenable to generalized prescription than that of love and sex. Some critics—possibly because their own medium is closer to moral philosophy (both prose, both didactic) than to dramatic poetry—are taken in by the moralizing and attribute to it far more weight than it will bear. One instance is to be found in an article by Irving Ribner: "But when Wilmot and his friends approached the story, they cast it into a Senecan mold and retold it in terms of a Senecan morality with retribution for sin as a dominant motif. Gismunda suffers because of the sin of lechery." [19] This emphasis primarily on the choral interludes is, it seems to me, misplaced. Even in a relatively primitive drama like *Gismond*, D. H. Lawrence's dictum "Never trust the artist. Trust the tale" would appear to hold true. In the consideration of the more complex and difficult drama to come, it must be considered gospel.

19. Irving Ribner, "Then I Denie You Starres," in *Studies in the English Renaissance Drama in Memory of Karl Julius Holzknecht*, ed. J. W. Bennett, Oscar Cargill, and Vernon Hall, Jr. (New York: New York University Press, 1959), 271.

2   The Spanish Tragedy

One important aspect of *Gismond* is the way in which it incorporates a study of hate into a love story. Of *The Spanish Tragedy* one could say that its distinctive characteristic is the incorporation of love into a powerful story of hatred. Indeed, in his treatment of the tale Kyd seems to insist that this doubleness is a necessary part of his dramatic strategy. The opening section, with its Hades and ghosts, is built around ironies of eros and thanatos. Don Andrea explains his own predicament in just these terms:

> For there in prime and pride of all my years,
> By duteous service and deserving love,
> In secret I possess'd a worthy dame,
> Which hight sweet Bel-imperia by name.
> But in the harvest of my summer joys
> Death's winter nipp'd the blossoms of my bliss,
> Forcing divorce betwixt my love and me.[1]   (I. i. 8–14)

Such was his earthly situation. Because of it the rulers of the underworld send him to act as Chorus to the play of love and death that springs out of his own ambiguous situation.

The surface whimsy of this opening exchange masks its seriousness. Kyd is announcing that he has two themes in mind and that they are interrelated in art as in life. This remark of Philip Edwards points the direction to be followed. With the meeting of Bel-imperia and Horatio, "character and plot are married, and the action drives forward on its twin pistons of love and revenge."[2] This interplay of love and revenge also organizes the sym-

---

1. Thomas Kyd, *The Spanish Tragedy*, ed. Philip Edwards, the Revels Plays (London: Methuen & Co. Ltd., 1959). All quotations from the play are from this text.
2. Philip Edwards, "Introduction," *The Spanish Tragedy* (the Revels Plays), liv.

bolism and moral values of the play. Kyd criticism has been predominantly one-sided, stressing mainly the death motive—the revenge plot and the character and moral status of the avengers.[3] But to judge the hatred, the lust for revenge, without its complicating and complementing opposite is to lose an influential source of richness in the play, for it is more in Kyd's complex sense of the dramatic and emotional potential of his material and his ability to exploit that material than in any pioneering of themes or subject matter that we see his distinctive genius. The critical problem is, therefore, to show how Kyd works with great care to establish a coherent framework for the study of hatred by establishing in the midst of hate a sense of love.

1.

The forward action of *The Spanish Tragedy* falls into two major parts: the first concerns the love of Bel-imperia and Horatio and the jealousy and machinations that lead to Horatio's death, the second mainly Hieronimo's madness, his alliance with Bel-imperia and their bloody vengeance. In both parts, the conflict of love and death exists as a theme and a source of metaphor, although in each the manifestations differ. In the first part Kyd develops the theme of love in terms of love's beauty, love's healing qualities, love's place and value as creator of human bonds; in the second we see how the violent frustration and negation of love lead in turn to more violence, though so complex is Kyd's handling of his themes that one line of development hardly exists without the other.

In this section I deal with the first part of the play, which for clarity can be divided into three major scenes or groups of scenes: (a) the long and complicated Act I. iv in which the male rivals are set in patterns of opposition around Bel-imperia; (b) the counterpointed first and second scenes of Act II, in which flawed ideas of love are set against a natural and beautiful one; and (c) Act II. iv—the brilliantly orchestrated murder of Horatio in the bower. The focus of Act I. iv is unquestionably Bel-imperia, and one could argue that she is the first genuinely seductive heroine to take the Elizabethan stage. In her, the bold presentation of female sexuality is established early. We have learned already that she had been enjoying a sexual relationship with Andrea before his death. The point is made stronger by the nature of

---

3. In particular, Fredson T. Bowers, *Elizabethan Revenge Tragedy, 1587–1642* (Princeton: Princeton University Press, 1940).

her first appearance, which—coming as it does after three scenes devoted mainly to public pomp and splendor—has a certain quiet provocativeness. She is seen alone with Don Horatio; they talk of her dead lover; the two on stage are united by their temporary isolation where previously all had been bustle and crowds. They are further united by their mutual love for Don Andrea. No words of love pass between them at this first meeting, but a token does change hands; Bel-imperia gives Horatio the scarf which Andrea had worn to battle. The mantle of the dead man passes by means of one of the great Romance symbols to the one most worthy to succeed him.

The tone of this exchange is decorous and calm, much more melancholy than sensual. Bel-imperia keeps well within the limits of courtly respectfulness:

> For 'twas my favour at his last depart.
> But now wear thou it both for him and me,
> For after him thou hast deserv'd it best.
> But for thy kindness in his life and death,
> Be sure while Bel-imperia's life endures,
> She will be Don Horatio's thankful friend.   (I. iv. 47–52)

And Horatio's answer is pitched to the same key: "And, Madam, Don Horatio will not slack/Humbly to serve fair Bel-imperia" (I. iv. 53–54). The two are linked therefore by this poetic unity, the unity of souls being suggested by the consistency of tone, the impression of unspoken communication residing in the spoken. I stress this aspect for two reasons. First, exchanges such as this and later ones demonstrate how far the dramatists had come since *Gismond* in their ability to depict close personal relationships, to write poetry that is also genuine dialogue. The second reason springs from the first. Bel-imperia is also being courted by the captured Portuguese prince who in dubious circumstances killed her first lover. The gulf between Prince Balthazar and Bel-imperia is created first of all from this fact, but it is maintained, made dramatically alive, by a radical shift in the tone of conversation when the two are together. Where Horatio had spoken the language of courtly service with obvious sincerity and honesty, Balthazar speaks it in a way which empties it of meaning. The result is the kind of distancing effect pointed out by Wolfgang Clemen[4] and demonstrated by such a dialogue as the following:

LOR: But here the prince is come to visit you.
BEL: That argues that he lives in liberty.

4. Wolfgang Clemen, *English Tragedy Before Shakespeare*, trans. T. S. Dorsch (London: Methuen & Co. Ltd., 1961), 104–105.

BAL: No madam, but in pleasing servitude.
BEL: Your prison then belike is your conceit.
BAL: Ay, by conceit my freedom is enthrall'd.
BEL: Then with conceit enlarge yourself again.

(I. iv. 79–84)

The stichomythia does here what it did in the first act of *Gismond* (I. iii. 51–57), underlines a lack of contact which later becomes aggravated into open enmity.

The scene ends with a piece of stage action that reinforces the effects made in the first part. Bel-imperia drops a glove in leaving. A contest ensues between the male rivals, a duel reduced to social proportions which Horatio wins by retrieving the glove. He then receives it as a further token of favor. Five quick lines complete the action:

HOR: Madam, your glove.
BEL: Thanks good Horatio, take it for thy pains.
BAL: Signior Horatio stoop'd in happy time.
HOR: I reap'd more grace than I deserv'd or hop'd.
LOR: My lord, be not dismay'd for what is past, . . .

(I. iv. 100–104)

The very briskness of it, the quickness with which Bel-imperia and Horatio respond to each other and exclude the other two, the first hint in Balthazar's line of his looming jealous reaction indicate that with Kyd, English tragedy was as ready to deal dramatically with the subtleties of love as the comedies of Lyly and his followers.

The gulf opened in Act I. iv widens rapidly in the first two scenes of Act II. On one hand we have Bel-imperia and Horatio coming closer together and on the other the closer alliance of Balthazar and Bel-imperia's brother Lorenzo.

From the start Kyd draws Balthazar as a courtly fool. The questionable nature of his triumph over Andrea and the exaggerated quality of his courtly rhetoric mark him as one even before we learn that he has fallen in love with Bel-imperia. His first conversation with her (a part of which has already been quoted) confirms the first impression. Kyd gives him language which can be nothing else than a parody of the abuses of customary Romance speech and emphasizes this by having the other characters intensely conscious of his absurdity. His keynote is unreality, embodied in a ridiculous, transcendental love rhetoric which seems all the more nonsensical in comparison with the earthy realism and calm lyricism of Bel-imperia and Horatio. With the latter, Kyd penetrates to what is true and beautiful in courtly language. He gives

Balthazar what is patently false and untrue. The answer Balthazar makes to Bel-imperia's witticism—"A heartless man and live? A miracle!" (I. iv. 88)— is typical: "Ay lady, love can work such miracles" (I. iv. 89). His final plea is another example:

> Yes, to your gracious self must I complain,
> In whose fair answer lies my remedy,
> On whose perfection all my thoughts attend,
> On whose aspect mine eyes find beauty's bower,
> In whose translucent breast my heart is lodg'd.
>
> (I. iv. 93–97)

All the cliché terms—"gracious self," "complain," "fair answer," "reme- dy," "perfection," "beauty's bower," "translucent breast"—are dutifully and stiffly trotted out. Bel-imperia calls them "words of course" (I. iv. 98), and just before this speech of Balthazar's, Lorenzo has told him to "let go these ambages" (I. iv. 90). Both characters point to the fact that Balthazar's love language has no roots in profound emotion.

Balthazar's emotional facility is not at this point dangerous, but the dog- gedness with which Kyd keeps Balthazar talking as he does dramatizes the relationship between shallow, self-regarding language and shallow, self- regarding emotions and the potential danger of the combination of the two. That Balthazar is self-obsessed is shown by the luxuriant self-humiliation of the speech which opens Act II:

> Yet might she love me for my valiancy,
> Ay, but that's slander'd by captivity.
> Yet might she love me to content her sire,
> Ay, but her reason masters his desire.   (II. i. 19–22)

When Kyd moves Balthazar into the more serious realms of love and death, his stiff jog-trot rhythms express perfectly the facile and superficial logic by which he moves to his very dangerous decision:

> Both well, and ill: it makes me glad and sad:
> Glad, that I know the hinderer of my love,
> Sad, that I fear she hates me whom I love.
> Glad, that I know on whom to be reveng'd,
> Sad, that she'll fly me if I take revenge.
> Yet must I take revenge or die myself,
> For love resisted grows impatient.   (II. i. 111–17)

In other words, Kyd uses Balthazar here to suggest that a man with so lim- ited a feeling for love and the language of love will have a similarly superfi- cial understanding of the meaning of death. Diction points to morality, and the study of one becomes the study of the other.

These comments apply as well to Lorenzo's very different style; his speech is direct and vivid, but its very precision indicates a kind of moral insufficiency. He is supremely confident and seems supremely knowledgeable:

> Let's go my lord, your staying stays revenge.
> Do you but follow me and gain your love:
> Her favour must be won by his remove.   (II. i. 134–36)

But the third line above marks him an ignoramus about the nature of love, as the story proves. Like Balthazar he is profoundly egocentric, and his egocentrism finds outlet in the need to manipulate and dominate. This trait dominates his concept of love:

> My lord, though Bel-imperia seem thus coy,
> Let reason hold you in your wonted joy:
> In time the savage bull sustains the yoke,
> In time all haggard hawks will stoop to lure,
> In time small wedges cleave the hardest oak, . . .
>
> > (II. i. 1–5)

To him love is a process of humbling the loved one, bringing her to heel; but this combination of brutality and pragmatism results in a self-defeating blindness to the irrational strength of the bond that love can form. The Lorenzo point of view has its local victories (with Iago, for instance), but—in Elizabethan romantic tragedy—no staying power, no lasting value.

Set against the obtuse self-love of these two, Horatio and Bel-imperia seem ideal lovers. The chief note of their relationship is quiet but sensuous decorum. The result is some poetry of quiet, beautiful joy. After war and loss come the still moments of calm and happiness, expressed in images of the sea and of music. Bel-imperia says:

> My heart, sweet friend, is like a ship at sea:
> She wisheth port, where riding all at ease,
> She may repair what stormy times have worn,
> And leaning on the shore, may sing with joy. . . .
>
> > (II. ii. 7–10)

They arrange to meet in Hieronimo's bower, a place which is itself a stage metaphor carrying all the Elizabethan connotations of pastoral peace and safety ("The court were dangerous, that place is safe" [II. ii. 44].) and Edenic love and sexuality. Kyd seems very much involved in his writing here, for the verse is natural and limpid enough to approach the Shakespearean:

> Our hour shall be when Vesper gins to rise
> That summons home distressful travellers.
> There none shall hear us but the harmless birds:
> Happily the gentle nightingale

> Shall carol us asleep ere we be ware,
> And singing with the prickle at her breast,
> Tell our delight and mirthful dalliance.
> Till then each hour will seem a year and more.
>
> (II. ii. 45–52)

Such details as the "distressful travellers" and the gentle nightingale "sing-ing with the prickle at her breast" complicate and give resonance to the calm lyricism of Bel-imperia's description by hinting that their love is not (and is not to be) unalloyed happiness.

This point is made in a much stronger manner by the brilliant staging of the scene. Shortly before the lovers speak the lines just quoted, Lorenzo and the rejected Balthazar have been shown creeping into a secret vantage place above the lovers. As Bel-imperia and Horatio speak of love, the two watchers—death personified—are driven, like Tancred, into a state of re-vengeful fury. Their unheard threats counterpoint the lovers' exchanges, enveloping them in a miasma of morbid, sadistic hatred. As the lovers speak, Lorenzo intones his curses:

> Watch still mine eyes, to see this love disjoin'd,
> Hear still mine ears, to hear them both lament,
> Live heart, to joy at fond Horatio's fall.   (II. ii. 21–23)

Kyd thus makes a powerful theater image out of what was a nondramatic voyeur scene in *Gismond*. The gain by this kind of stagecraft is multifold. In this context I would list three main ones (for others see Philip Edwards and Anne Righter[5]): the direct visual involvement of the audience; the empha-sis on the frustration felt by Balthazar, who can only see, while Horatio and Bel-imperia touch; and the impressiveness of the audience's realization (they being able to see and hear both killers and lovers) that the expecta-tions of love are to be balked by death.

The first part of the play comes to its climax in the very powerful murder scene in the bower. In this scene Kyd merges all the possible implications and ironies of the love-death antithesis. He first induces a sense of forebod-ing and mystery which arises naturally out of the precarious secrecy of the lovers' affair and the tension which attends the anticipation of lovemaking, as well as any premonition of danger:

> BEL: I follow thee my love, and will not back,
>   Although my fainting heart controls my soul.
>
> (II. iv. 6–7)

---

5. Phillip Edwards, *Thomas Kyd and Early Elizabethan Tragedy* (London: Longmans, Green & Co., 1966), 31–33; Anne Righter, *Shakespeare and the Idea of the Play* (London: Chatto & Windus, 1962), 70ff.

Then references to the song of the nightingale lead us into the gentle ambiguities of the love-war relationship, of the relationship between Mars and Venus, of darting kisses like spears, and finally the doubleness of the idea contained in the word *yield*:

> BEL: Nay then, to gain the glory of the field,
>   My twining arms shall yoke and make thee yield.
>
>   (II. iv. 42–43)

All this would, of course, be acted out as it is spoken, thus bringing the ever-increasing intimacy of physical contact between the lovers to its penultimate moment. This moment itself is graced by the sensitive, dramatic use of the most fundamental of all the loving versions of the love-death antithesis, the death of the ego in the moment of passion:

> BEL: O let me go, for in my troubled eyes
>   Now may'st thou read that life in passion dies.
> HOR: O stay awhile and I will die with thee,
>   So shalt thou yield and yet have conquer'd me.
>
>   (II. iv. 46–49)

Kyd exploits all the bitterly ironic poetic and dramatic paradoxes of the situation. It is at this moment that the lovers make their shocked discovery of the murderers and the murder itself is executed. Appropriately enough it is staged as a deliberate and gross verbal and physical parody of the act of love. As Lorenzo thrusts home he says: "Ay, thus, and thus, these are the fruits of love" (II. iv. 55). This is a crowded moment but a very important one, for, as in *Gismond*, the moment of death is the moment when each character reveals himself fully in relation to the idea of love. The final words of Bel-imperia, for instance, put the stamp of authenticity on her love by showing its essential selflessness:

> O save his life and let me die for him!
> O save him brother, save him Balthazar:
> I lov'd Horatio but he lov'd not me.   (II. iv. 56–*58)*

One cannot help but think of Coleridge's cryptic lecture note on love: "With love, pure love, the anxiety for the safety of the object—the disinterestedness by which it is distinguished from the counterfeits of its name."[6] By the same token, Lorenzo's and Balthazar's responses reveal the full egocentrism of their natures: Lorenzo in terms of his preoccupation with status— "Although his life were still ambitious proud,/Yet is he at the highest now

---

6. Samuel Taylor Coleridge, *Shakespearean Criticism*, ed. Thomas Middleton Raysor, Everyman Library, Vol. I (2nd ed.; London: J. M. Dent & Sons Ltd., 1960), 8.

he is dead" (II. iv. 60–61)—and Balthazar (wildly imagining that his deed demonstrates profound affection) in terms of his lunatic insensitivity. He insists to the end: "But Balthazar loves Bel-imperia" (II. iv. 59).

2.

The remainder of the play is dominated by Hieronimo's revenge, but the reverberations of the first part are never lost, particularly since Hieronimo's revenge has its roots in the first part and the revenge theme itself proceeds side by side with another version of the love theme, that of the Enforced or Arranged Marriage. It is primarily to this latter theme that I now turn.

The "enforced marriage"[7] (to use the term given the practice by George Wilkins, the author of a seventeenth-century tragicomedy on the subject) or the "arranged marriage"[8] (the term used by William Empson) becomes with Kyd's play one of the leading minor motifs in Elizabethan and Jacobean tragedy. The central characteristic of this convention (in society and in drama) is that such a marriage normally victimizes the woman involved, and, indeed, the practice could probably not have arisen without a widespread feeling among males that women were chattel. Therefore, any betterment in the status of women would undermine the conventions of male dominance; certainly the idea of romantic love would do so, since love implies the acceptance and celebration of the beloved's individual humanity. Furthermore, the marriage for financial, social, or political reasons is a direct denial of the romantic marriage, the marriage for love, an institution not directly involved in this play but one standing in the wings, as it were, since most of the plays taken up in this study deal directly with it. In essence the Arranged Marriage in *The Spanish Tragedy* stands in the same relation to the lovers as Tancred's denial of his daughter's desire to wed did to Gismond and Guishard, since both actions are negative, frustrate a very powerful natural force, and end in disaster.

In *The Spanish Tragedy* the Arranged Marriage motif is muted but very powerful, particularly since it has its roots in the very peace treaty which ends the war between Spain and Portugal and its end at the instant of Hieronimo's and Bel-imperia's vengeance. The first scene in which it is ex-

7. George Wilkins, *The Miseries of Enforced Marriage*. This play may be found in Robert Dodsley (ed.), *A Select Collection of Old English Plays*, revised and enlarged by W. Carew Hazlitt, IX (4th ed.; London, 1874–1876).
8. William Empson, "*The Spanish Tragedy*," *Nimbus*, III (Summer, 1956); reprinted in *Elizabethan Drama: Modern Essays in Criticism*, ed. R. J. Kaufmann, Galaxy Books (New York: Oxford University Press, 1961), 66.

plicitly mentioned (it is implicit in Balthazar's early protestations of love) is Act II. iii, where it is significantly sandwiched between the scene in which Prince Balthazar and Lorenzo murderously observe Bel-imperia and Horatio exchanging their first love vows and that in which they murder Horatio. The ironic implication of the juxtaposition is clear: that the Arranged Marriage, carried on at a high diplomatic level, is to be closely associated with the murder of Horatio. Nor is this just a symbolic association; whether Castile or the king knew about the murder or not (and there is nothing in the text to suggest they do), it is a necessary step in the progress which will end in a state wedding. The actions of Lorenzo—the most dedicated, self-conscious *politician* of the group—make it clear that he realizes this fact; his downfall is that he expects no trouble in bringing his sister to his way of thinking, his same high valuation of political advancement.

In any case, although Castile and the king cannot be convicted of premeditated murder (as William Empson would convict Castile[9]), they are implicated in it by their casual acceptance of the clichés of male dominance. Their colossal sense of their own importance makes it impossible for them to take Bel-imperia seriously as a free agent with her own mind and heart. Castile's complacency on the matter is almost amusing; the repeated *I* and the verb *stoop* give him away in this passage:

> Although she coy it as becomes her kind,
> And yet dissemble that she loves the prince,
> I doubt not, I, but she will stoop in time.
> And were she froward, which she will not be,
> Yet herein shall she follow my advice,
> Which is to love him or forgo my love.   (II. iii. 3–8)

The final threat is more serious, however, because it betrays the superficiality of his idea of love. Castile never considers the possibility that his daughter could not love Prince Balthazar and neither does the king, who on the spot commits her to the marriage. Their ignorance of the power of love, combined with the unthinking exercise of their own self-will over the fortunes of a daughter, puts them in the same category as Tancred and Shakespeare's old Capulet. Indeed, so often do the Elizabethans use this character type as an agent of death in love tragedies that one can only conclude that it is at least partly intended as a foil to the ever-increasing belief in the sanctity of personal affairs, particularly for women. Such must be the conclusion here at any rate. The ironies are too strong to suggest otherwise.

9. *Ibid.*, 60–63.

How ominous, for instance, the king's innocent words sound in the larger
context in which Kyd has placed them:

> Now brother, you must take some little pains
> To win fair Bel-imperia from her will:
> Young virgins must be ruled by their friends.
> The prince is amiable and loves her well,
> If she neglect him and forgo his love,
> She both will wrong her own estate and ours: . . .
>
> (II. iii. 41–46)

The king's philosophy is Lorenzo's philosophy precisely, and the vigorous
Lorenzo pushes the idea of "some little pains" to its ultimate logical conclusion. Lorenzo says as much to Bel-imperia in explaining why he killed Horatio and spirited her into seclusion; he had, he says falsely, been sent
ahead of the king and Castile to Hieronimo and found Bel-imperia with
Horatio:

> Why then, remembering that old disgrace
> Which you for Don Andrea had endur'd,
> And now were likely longer to sustain,
> By being found so meanly accompanied,
> Thought rather, for I knew no readier mean,
> To thrust Horatio forth my father's way.   (III. x. 54–59)

The patronizing tone, the heavy implication that the name of honor is
worth more than a human life, the inability or unwillingness to imagine
that her lovemaking is anything more than transient lust, the expectation
that she will calm down and see things his way: all these are present in this
short speech as in the whole scene. Bel-imperia gulls her brother fatally by
seeming to fall in with his stereotype of woman, by playing the ironist and
appearing to acquiesce in the political marriage. Hieronimo, fighting down
bouts of madness, plays the same kind of game and the two come together
to subvert the marriage feast and, in so doing, orchestrate the final love-
death ironies.

There is a definite implication that the last acts of this play are meant to
represent the paradoxical triumph of love over death, through revenge. In
the first two acts, Lorenzo and Balthazar were the hunters, pouncing at a
climactic moment to substitute a death act for a love act. In the last half of
the play, Horatio's lover and his father, drawn into conjunction by their
mutual love for the murdered man, are the hunters, coming together over a
series of carefully counterpointed scenes to substitute a second death for a
second act of love, the expected marriage of Bel-imperia and Balthazar. The

symmetry of the design is striking and—particularly when we consider how many times in Elizabethan tragedy this reversal occurs—requires a name, if only to acknowledge that the motif exists as a repeated complement to the Arranged Marriage theme. My suggestion would be the Fatal Wedding or Deadly Nuptial.

Kyd's use of Deadly Nuptial symbolism is vivid. Act III ends in a prophetic dumb-show (staged by Revenge for Andrea's benefit) in which the symbolic qualities of red and black, of light and dark, and of marriage and murder are used to effect a deepening of the dramatic mood within the context of the love-death theme:

> The two first, the nuptial torches bore,
> As brightly burning as the mid-day's sun:
> But after them doth Hymen hie as fast,
> Clothed in sable, and a saffron robe,
> And blows them out and quencheth them with blood,
> As discontent that things continue so.   (III. xv. 30–35)

Andrea's gloss introduces the idea of the triumph of love:

> Sufficeth me, thy meaning's understood,
> And thanks to thee and those infernal powers
> That will not tolerate a lover's woe.   (III. xv. 36–38)

Taken together these lines could be seen as the author's commentary on the whole action of the play.

For his final turn on the theme, Kyd uses the special conventions of his own trade and of this evolving genre of love tragedy. He makes Hieronimo the author, director, and star of a play of passion and death—the tragedy of Soliman and Perseda—wherein Balthazar plays a part that parallels his role in *The Spanish Tragedy* and Hieronimo plays one not unlike that of Lorenzo:

> HIER: *Let not Erasto live to grieve great Soliman.*
> BAL: *Dear is Erasto in our princely eye.*
> HIER: *But if he be your rival, let him die.*
> BAL: *Why, let him die, so love commandeth me.*
>   (IV. iv. 45–48)

The conclusion of the play finds both Balthazar and Lorenzo murdered, Bel-imperia dead by suicide, and Hieronimo explaining the meaning of his revenge in terms of the love-death relationship:

> The cause was love, whence grew this mortal hate,
> The hate, Lorenzo and young Balthazar,
> The love, my son to Bel-imperia.   (IV. iv. 98–100)

This is baldly stated, and it presents in outline the thematic structure which gives the play's ironic, deadly ending its considerable resonance. Hieronimo's play of love and death is ostensibly an ornament to a royal marriage. It proves to be no gesture of love, however, but an act of death revenging the death of love. Already then, in this the second of the plays on love and death, we find the dramatist seeking fresh levels of significance in the opposition of these two great ultimates and the genre itself finding its basic formal and intellectual principles.

3.

I would put forward two final points as a means of moving to a larger interpretation. First, there is one line of imagery which connects Andrea, Horatio, Bel-imperia, Horatio's mother Isabella, and Hieronimo and excludes— except as enemies—all the others. This is nature or pastoral imagery. I have already mentioned its intimate connection with the love poetry of Bel-imperia and Horatio. It is also the imagery of the "fields of love" (I. i. 42) which Don Andrea sees after death, with their "green myrtle trees and cypress shades" (I. i. 44). These are linked with the earthly field of love, the love bower in which Horatio and Bel-imperia meet and Horatio dies. Hieronimo's wild laments associate the bower with life and pleasure, and he refers to his son as "Sweet lovely rose, ill-pluck'd before thy time" (II. v. 46). Somewhat later he makes reference to the participation of nature in his own mourning:

> The blust'ring winds, conspiring with my words,
> At my lament have mov'd the leaveless trees,
> Disrob'd the meadows of their flower'd green,
> Made mountains marsh with spring-tides of my tears, . . .
>
> (III. vii. 5–8)

The mad Isabella's frenzy takes the ironic form of vengeance upon nature itself. Cutting down the arbor, she says:

> Down with these branches and these loathsome boughs
> Of this unfortunate and fatal pine:
>
> . . . .
>
> I will not leave a root, a stalk, a tree,
> A bough, a branch, a blossom, nor a leaf,
> No, not an herb within this garden plot—
> Accursed complot of my misery.
> Fruitless for ever may this garden be, . . .
>
> (IV. ii. 6–7, 10–14)

The full relationship of all these symbols is made clear through her frenzied identification of herself and her son (and by implication Hieronimo and Bel-imperia) with nature through the larger idea of sexual love as a creative force:

> And as I curse this tree from further fruit,
> So shall my womb be cursed for his sake,
> And with this weapon will I wound the breast,
> > *She stabs herself*
> The hapless breast, that gave Horatio suck.
>
> (IV. ii. 35–38)

Her suicidal madness points up the power of her love for her son, and her self-inflicted death identifies her still more closely with those others who have lost their taste for life because of the violent loss of a loved one.

In other words, all the sympathetic characters are unified by the bond of love, whether it be erotic or familial, and by the imagery of nature. In this we may see a development of the tentative use of nature imagery and the idea of nature in *Gismond*. Such a grouping also helps make one final puzzle reasonably clear; Castile's death and his relegation to eternal torture find their logic in the fact that he is a man who attempted to meddle for extrapersonal reasons in an area of his daughter's life which was her own closest concern. This made him one of the forces of death, and it is this that he pays for with his life.

My final point concerns the wider application of these ideas in terms of the development of the revenge play. Most critics have tended to treat the idea of vengeance in a vacuum, as if it arose from emotional nullity, a zero degree of feeling. The result has been that arguments about the moral emphasis of the revenge drama often have been sidetracked into somewhat sterile, abstract discussions of Elizabethan ideas of revenge divorced from a full response to the whole of the dramatic poetry and action. This passage from Fredson Bowers's *Elizabethan Revenge Tragedy* shows how tenuous the connection between abstract theory and emotional response really is:

> Under these circumstances—and the evidence of the tragedies bears out the theory—the revenger of the drama started with the sympathy of the audience if his cause were good and if he acted according to the typically English notions of straightforward fair play. It was only, as with Hieronimo (although this example may seem the most debatable of the many available), when he turned to "Machiavellian" treacherous intrigues that the audience began to veer against him.[10]

10. Bowers, *Elizabethan Revenge Tragedy*, 40.

This seems very shaky to me, as anything resting on so fragile a moral foundation as "typically English notions of straightforward fair play" must inevitably be. This is one reason why love must have a part in any discussion of plays about hate. It is only love which makes hatred meaningful, whether it is set in opposition to hatred or shown in the process of becoming hatred. In *The Spanish Tragedy*, as in *Gismond*, love and hate are seen in both of these contexts. Acknowledgment of this brings us down on the side of those critics for whom Hieronimo remains a compelling, sympathetic figure. Professor Edwards puts it perfectly:

> There can be no doubt that the audience is on his side, whatever the Elizabethan preachers and moralists said about private revenge. We are in a different place from the preacher's auditory.
> . . . .
> Hieronimo's voice is the voice of protest against criminal cruelty, the voice of real sorrow and love.[11]

What is said here of Hieronimo is equally true of all his associates, and it is these associations, these bonds, that make it true of Hieronimo.

11. Edwards, *Thomas Kyd*, 38–40.

3   The Tragedy of Dido, Queen of Carthage

Exploring the patterns of love and death in Marlowe's *Dido* requires a slightly different approach from that used for *Gismond* and *The Spanish Tragedy*. In this play there is no villian embodying the death motive within himself. Instead there are two somewhat battered lovers who carry the seeds of both love and death within themselves. The substance of the play is primarily character, and the love-death imagery is put to a variety of new and arresting uses in showing the inner and outer workings of heart and mind.

In this context, three things merit special attention. First, by focusing on Aeneas' state of mind when he lands at Carthage and meets Dido, Marlowe can show how the death of those one loves can incapacitate a person for life itself, make him live a living death. Second, Marlowe can also show that erotic love carries in it the power to revivify. In the process he sets the groundwork for the kind of transcendent romantic rhetoric that one finds in *Romeo and Juliet*, for no one before Marlowe had let the music of sexuality flow with the beauty and urgency it does in this play. Third, because there is no bloody villain in this story, Marlowe can put his death imagery to use in another area; the death of love can be seen as a process operating from within, not just from without. This too was an innovation in English drama, and the specific premise behind this version of the death of love (that is, the battle in the male's mind between devotion to duty and devotion to emotion) clearly looks forward to one of the greatest of love tragedies—*Antony and Cleopatra*.

The first thing to discuss is Marlowe's use of love and death images to tie the background story of the fall of Troy to the foreground story of the love of Dido and Aeneas. The nexus will be Aeneas' own tortured spirit.

41

1.

One of the great moments of psychological insight in *Doctor Faustus* is this:

FAUSTUS: Where are you damned?
MEPHIS: In hell.
FAUSTUS: How comes it then that thou art out of hell?
MEPHIS: Why this is hell, nor am I out of it.[1]

(I. iii. 74–76)

The particular phrasing does not occur in *Dido*, but the condition is given lengthy analysis. Aeneas' mind, when he reaches Carthage, is a hell of dreadful, unmanning images, and these remembered scenes have great effect on his actions in Carthage.

The images emerge most strongly when Aeneas tells his own story and the story of the fall of Troy, and they gain much of their power from the close linking of love and death, in this case violent murder and a peculiar, partly suppressed eroticism. Take, for instance, this passage describing the first sights to meet Aeneas' eyes after the alarm in Troy had sounded:

> Young infants swimming in their parents' blood,
> Headless carcasses piled up in heaps,
> Virgins half-dead, dragged by their golden hair
> And with main force flung on a ring of pikes,
> Old men with swords thrust through their agèd sides,
> Kneeling for mercy to a Greekish lad,
> Who with steel pole-axes dashed out their brains.

(II. i. 193–99)

The dominant theme is death. But—as in the description of Tancred's murder of Guishard—it is death with the special kind of violence that we name for the Marquis de Sade. The victims who people Aeneas' memory are not merely killed; they are violated and mutilated. And subtle erotic associations occur throughout, from the explicit phallic cruelty of "Virgins half-dead, dragged by their golden hair/And with main force flung on a ring of pikes," to the symbolism of fertility grossly negated ("Young infants swimming in their parents' blood, . . .") and brief evocations of generational or Oedipal violence:

> Old men with swords thrust through their agèd sides,
> Kneeling for mercy to a Greekish lad,
> Who with steel pole-axes dashed out their brains.

<hr />

1. Quotations from Marlowe's plays are from *The Complete Plays of Christopher Marlowe*, ed. Irving Ribner (New York: Odyssey Press Inc., 1963).

This vision of horror is intensified when he is forced to watch the destruction of those who are bound much more closely to him by bonds of loyalty and love. The rape of Cassandra is an instance:

> We saw Cassandra sprawling in the streets,
> Whom Ajax ravished in Diana's fane,
> Her cheeks swollen with sighs, her hair all rent,
> Whom I took up to bear unto our ships.
> But suddenly the Grecians followed us,
> And I, alas, was forced to let her lie.   (II. i. 274–79)

This is a powerful scene, and the source of its power is the violent merging of eroticism and violence, the rape being an act of war as well as an act of sex. The final horror, of course, and the one that seems to linger largest in Aeneas' own mind, is that he himself is helpless to aid her. He must look and pass on.

The deaths of Priam and Hecuba offer an interesting example of how the conjunction of love and death images may shape a long narrative passage and one that is not explicitly erotic. The rape of Cassandra seems to be an expansion of the two lines concerning the "virgins half-dead"; the following lines expand the theme of generational violence but give it a very personal coloration:

> He [Pyrrhus], with his falchion's point raised up at once,
> And with Megæra's eyes, stared in their face,
> Threat'ning a thousand deaths at every glance.
> To whom the agèd king thus, trembling, spoke:
> 'Achilles' son, remember what I was,
> Father of fifty sons, but they are slain;
>
> . . . .
> O, let me live, great Neoptolemus!'   (II. i. 229–34, 239)

The basic image: the young man towering furious and dominant over the old, with the old man appealing to the most basic love relationship known to man, that of the family. We note how Priam calls Pyrrhus "Achilles' son," to try to arouse this central source of human fellow-feeling and turn it to the cause of life, and how he refers to his own slain family. Pyrrhus here, however, is the very incarnation of the death motive, not merely killing but making a mocking game out of it:

> Not moved at all, but smiling at his tears,
> This butcher, whilst his hands were yet held up,
> Treading upon his breast, struck off his hands.
>   (II. i. 240–42)

Then follows a further development of the love-death theme. As Pyrrhus moves to finish Priam, Hecuba makes a futile attempt to play the self-sacrificial role of a Bel-imperia:

> At which the frantic queen leaped on his face,
> And in his eyelids hanging by the nails,
> A little while prolonged her husband's life.
> At last the soldiers pulled her by the heels
> And swung her howling in the empty air, . . .
>
> (II. i. 244–48)

And Priam in turn attempts to play the hero:

> Whereat he lifted up his bed-rid limbs,
> And would have grappled with Achilles' son,
> Forgetting both his want of strength and hands,
> Which he disdaining, whisked his sword about,
> And with the wind thereof the king fell down.
> Then from the navel to the throat at once
> He ripped old Priam, . . .   (II. i. 250–56)

In these two vignettes we have tightly compressed images of the battle of love versus death, miniatures painted to demonstrate the lover's instinctive urge in time of danger to self-forgetfulness and self-sacrifice. The absurd futility of both efforts only heightens the instinctive nobility of them, and this futile nobility sharpens our awareness of the fragility of love in the face of fully armed, fully determined death.

This then is the world of Aeneas' memory, a world where death has triumphed over love, and the most personal and terrible image for Aeneas is the loss of his own family:

>   . . . I got my father on my back,
> This young boy in mine arms, and by the hand
> Led fair Creusa, my belovèd wife.
> When thou, Achates, with thy sword mad'st way,
> And we were round environed with the Greeks,
> O there I lost my wife, and had not we
> Fought manfully, I had not told this tale.
> Yet manhood would not serve.   (II. i. 265–72)

This gives very personal expression indeed to one of the major themes of the play: the relation between love and manhood. A man is defined not just as a fighter, even in wartime. He is also a son, a husband-lover, a father—all these being relationships of love, and all linked in some way with primal sexual bonds. Aeneas fails in all these but one. He does save his son, and his son serves throughout as a symbolic reminder of the past and the future that must come from that past. At this point, however, the theme is definitely failure and the deadening effects of failure. The theme, as Aeneas puts it, is "manhood would not serve."

To stress this, Marlowe, throughout Act II, emphasizes the daunting pressure of the death-haunted past on Aeneas in the present. He sees gruesomely ironic wish-fulfillment visions: "Achates, see! King Priam wags his hand!/He is alive! Troy is not overcome!" (II. i. 29–30). He shrinks from places of honor and authority:

> This is no seat for one that's comfortless.
> May it please your grace to let Æneas wait,
> For though my birth be great, my fortune's mean,
> Too mean to be companion to a queen.   (II. i. 86–89)

A moment later he cries out: "This place beseems me not. O, Pardon me" (II. i. 94). When finally forced to take his place by Dido, he goes on and on in the same vein:

> In all humility, I thank your grace.
>
> . . . .
> And who so miserable as Æneas is?
>
> . . . .
> O Priamus! O Troy! O Hecuba!   (II. i. 99, 102, 105)

And Dido's request to hear his story turns his soul and limbs to jelly:

> A woeful tale bids Dido to unfold,
> Whose memory, like pale death's stony mace,
> Beats forth my senses from this troubled soul
> And makes Æneas sink at Dido's feet.   (II. i. 114–17)

He is clearly a man who is unmanned by the loss of virtually all those people whom he valued and in whose love he defined himself. And it is in this context that Dido, who brings love as a restorative, a life-giving force, has her central importance. Even before being touched by Cupid, she seems to know by instinct that she has something significant to give Aeneas. Thus, the immediate attempts to rescue him from the shadows of his losses and his failure by giving him back himself:

> Warlike Æneas, . . .
>
> . . . .
> Brave prince, . . .
>
> . . . .
> Sit in this chair and banquet with a queen.
> Æneas is Æneas, were he clad
> In weeds as bad as ever Irus ware.
>
> . . . .
> Remember who thou art. Speak like thyself.
> Humility belongs to common grooms.

. . . .
What, faints Æneas to remember Troy,
In whose defence he fought so valiantly?
Look up and speak.   (II. i. 79, 81, 83–85, 100–101, 118–20)

These are the gestures of love, and they prepare for another of Marlowe's central themes: the life-giving generosity of eros.

2.

Love as life-giver: this is a central motif in romantic tragedy. Marlowe's contribution to Elizabethan romanticism is great indeed and is not at all mitigated by his consciousness of the comedy, and the violence and death, that can attend erotic love.

For one thing, love is seen as a force which can break through deadening conventional ties and restraints. Dido's relationship with Iarbas is certainly deadeningly conventional and restrained. When Iarbas pleads his love, Dido only condescends to him, accepting him in theory but standing apart in practice. Iarbas has become an old story, tedious and complaining (as he himself is fearfully beginning to realize):

How long, fair Dido, shall I pine for thee?
'Tis not enough that thou dost grant me love,
But that I may enjoy what I desire.
That love is childish which consists in words.   (III. i. 7–10)

Her answer comes more from boredom and duty than the love he looks for:

Iarbas, know that thou of all my wooers—
And yet have I had many mightier kings—
Hast had the greatest favors I could give.
I fear me, Dido hath been counted light
In being too familiar with Iarbas,
Albeit the gods do know no wanton thought
Had ever residence in Dido's breast.   (III. i. 11–17)

The damning lines are, of course, the last two.

Set against this aridity of emotion, Marlowe then gives a comic allegory of the growth of a real sexual passion, that for Aeneas. Cupid embodies everything capricious, childlike (though not necessarily innocent) and erotic in love:

DIDO: How lovely is Ascanius when he smiles.
CUPID: Will Dido let me hang about her neck?
DIDO: Ay, wag, and give thee leave to kiss her too.
CUPID: What will you give me now? I'll have this fan.
DIDO: Take it, Ascanius, for thy father's sake.
                                                            (III. i. 29–33)

And the very fact that Cupid is masking as Aeneas' son Ascanius deepens the erotic symbolism of the passage. For what is lacking in Dido's feelings (if such they can be called) for Iarbas is what is here developing in her for Aeneas: a complex of emotions rising out of some center where erotic desire and the maternal instinct are fused. Reading these passages, one recalls her lament at the end of the play: "Had I a son by thee, the grief were less,/ That I might see Æneas in his face" (V. i. 149–50). Iarbas, then, is satisfactory in the abstract, but Marlowe shows here that the true life of the feelings grows out of instincts more fiery, primitive, and more potentially fruitful than mere abstractions.

Marlowe's acuteness on the matter of love's growth is one of the unacknowledged reasons for the importance of the play. Having dispensed with the conventional rival lover of love tragedy, he goes on to delineate another way in which convention can block openness of emotion—in this case the restraints that the fearful, self-protective part of the ego sets up to militate against the desire for surrender into love. The result is some spirited insight into the complexity of human mental life. For instance, in private Dido spills out a flood of images of ecstasy and adoration:

> I'll make me bracelets of his golden hair;
> His glistering eyes shall be my looking-glass,
> His lips an altar, where I'll offer up
> As many kisses as the sea hath sands.
> Instead of music I will hear him speak.
> His looks shall be my only library,
> And thou, Æneas, Dido's treasury,
> In whose fair bosom I will lock more wealth
> Than twenty thousand Indias can afford.   (III. i. 84–92)

But Aeneas' arrival shuts off the fountain in favor of prudence, the playing of the correct social role—in a word, the denial of the personal:

> O, here he comes! Love, love, give Dido leave
> To be more modest than her thoughts admit,
> Lest I be made a wonder to the world.   (III. i. 93–95)

Likewise, the terrific imaginative energy of the passage beginning "I'll give thee tackling made of rivelled gold" is caught up sharply by the fear of giving away too much. Like Juliet, Dido would fain dwell on form:

> ÆNEAS: Wherefore would Dido have Æneas stay?
> DIDO: To war against my bordering enemies.
> Æneas, think not Dido is in love,
> For if that any man could conquer me,
> I had been wedded ere Æneas came.
>   (III. i. 133–37)

The tone is comic, but the psychological perceptions are sharp. Denial of love masks love, and Dido's fear of giving away too much looks forward to the end of the play when she must pay in anguish for the fulfillment she is moving towards.

In the romantic tradition, however, heroines are not long bound by convention. Like Gismond and Bel-imperia before her, and Juliet after, she does not shy from taking the initiative in love matters. And as she does, Marlowe marshals a whole range of erotic imagery and reference behind her until the whole natural and supernatural scene is supporting her conquest. The impetus to the scene is the hunt, and Dido—as she dresses for it—becomes both the huntress and protector: huntress in the aggressiveness of her seduction of Aeneas, and protector in that she is identified by her new dress with the Venus who had earlier appeared to Aeneas. Achates himself points out the likeness both in appearance and function:

> As I remember, here you shot the deer
> That saved your famished soldiers' lives from death,
> When first you set your foot upon the shore,
> And here we met fair Venus, virgin-like,
> Bearing her bow and quiver at her back.   (III. iii. 51–55)

The hunt itself is referred to as "gamesome sport" (III. ii. 89), a double-edged phrase equally applicable to the killing of animals and the loving of men and women. The deep woods setting furnishes the same kind of sympathetic nature symbolism that the bower did for the lovers in *The Spanish Tragedy*. The storm which arises is an outer reflection of the emotional storm that has already caught up Dido and is about to do the same to Aeneas. The final note in this large orchestration of love images is the cave that Dido and Aeneas enter when fleeing the storm. It is a symbolic womb, dark, private, protective: the direct opposite of the dangers of the open sea and the public quest that Aeneas has for the moment abandoned but will return to. Thus, for one moment, all nature is poetically organized to foster Dido's hopes and her gift of love.

We should, however, pause to ask what kind of gift this love is, what Marlowe sees as its main characteristics, virtues, and limitations. For the paradox of the play is that Aeneas must leave behind something that does unquestionably have great value.

The answer, it seems to me, can be given under two related categories: first, love as a creative force in language; second, love as enricher of the human spirit. Take, for instance, a passage already referred to:

> I'll make me bracelets of his golden hair;
> His glistering eyes shall be my looking-glass,

> His lips an altar, where I'll offer up
> As many kisses as the sea hath sands.
> Instead of music I will hear him speak.
> His looks shall be my only library,
> And thou, Æneas, Dido's treasury,
> In whose fair bosom I will lock more wealth
> Than twenty thousand Indias can afford.   (III. i. 84–92)

What we see here are the first attempts in English tragedy at a truly luxuriant, even heroic, love rhetoric—a revolutionary language of the private self equal in force to anything that the public world can inspire. The beloved becomes for the lover an inspiration to artistic creation (the bracelets), a means of exploring the self (the looking glass), a source of beauty and wisdom (music and the library). The final lines sum up and organize the whole passage in what could be termed the motif of "love's wealth." This phrase was used by John Russell Brown to help define aspects of love in Shakespeare's comedies.[2] It is no less applicable (as I shall show) to Shakespeare's tragedies, but Marlowe's *Dido* gives the theme much of its first impetus.

Dido's erotically charged imagination succeeds in the primal poetic act: she gives to the inanimate things of the world a richly sensuous, even erotic, life. Another relevant passage:

> I'll give thee tackling made of rivelled gold,
> Wound on the barks of odoriferous trees,
> Oars of massy ivory, full of holes
> Through which the water shall delight to play.
> Thy anchors shall be hewed from crystal rocks
> Which, if thou lose, shall shine above the waves;
> The masts whereon thy swelling sails shall hang,
> Hollow pyramidès of silver plate; . . .   (III. i. 115–22)

The gold clings to the bark of odoriferous trees; the water plays in the orifices of the oars; the sails swell like pregnant women. Even dour Achates, who later in the play is the chief human spokesman against eros, is transformed—against all customary logic—into a figure of great erotic attractiveness:

> Achates, thou shalt be so meanly clad
> As sea-born nymphs shall swarm about thy ships
> And wanton mermaids court thee with sweet songs,
> Flinging in favors of more sovereign worth
> Than Thetis hangs about Apollo's neck, . . .   (III. i. 127–31)

2. John Russell Brown, *Shakespeare and His Comedies* (London: Methuen & Co. Ltd., 1957), 45.

The point that Marlowe makes here, it seems to me, is that love and the highly charged language of love confer value to giver and receiver alike. And further—that life without this very human ability to confer value and to heighten appreciation would be very bleak indeed.

To return to the hunt/seduction scene: Aeneas at the beginning is still the humble, shaken, unmanned figure of the second act. Having failed consistently to respond to hint after hint of Dido's love for him, he is finally faced with the explicit statement of it. His response is: "Æneas' thoughts dare not ascend so high/As Dido's heart, which monarchs might not scale" (III. iv. 32 –33). But she, both before this moment and after it, will not accept his valuation of himself. She, in the generosity of love, has much more to confer upon Aeneas—a new image of himself:

> The man that I do eye where'er I am,
> Whose amorous face, like Pæan, sparkles fire,
> Whenas he butts his beams on Flora's bed.
> Prometheus hath put on Cupid's shape,
> And I must perish in his burning arms.   (III. iv. 17–21)

Then "a crown and kingdom" at his command, jewels to seal their vows, golden bracelets, her wedding ring, and, finally, herself. By means of all these gifts she gives him the greatest one, his manhood, his heroic conception of himself. The irony is, of course, that in giving him his identity again, she has given him back his past. As much as she would like to see Aeneas new baptized "The king of Carthage, not Anchises' son" (III. iv. 59), she is asking the impossible. Dido herself has just one love, one object of inspiration. Aeneas has two, one living in the present, the other living in the memory. It is to this conflict and its effects on the pair that I would now turn.

3.

We can define the downward movement of the tragedy by recalling John Donne:

> What ever dyes, was not mixt equally;
> If our two loves be one, or, thou and I
> Love so alike, that none doe slacken, none can die.[3]

Donne here gives us a positive ideal: the ideal of complete mutuality as the

---

3. John Donne, "The Good-Morrow," in *John Donne: Complete Poetry and Selected Prose*, ed. John Hayward (London: Nonesuch Press, 1962), 3.

source of an undying love. Marlowe gives us the reverse of this: the death of love by a failure of mutuality.

This failure is subtly suggested at the very outset of the affair between Dido and Aeneas. The pull of the quest Aeneas is engaged in is strong from the very start; his first requests to her are for ship's tackling with which to proceed. But even in the cave, in the midst of succumbing to Dido, Aeneas makes her an oath of fidelity notable mainly for the strange undercurrent of tentativeness in its language:

> If that your majesty can look so low
> As my despisèd worths that shun all praise,
> With this my hand I give to you my heart
> And vow by all the gods of hospitality,
> . . . .
> Never to leave these new-uprearèd walls,
> Whiles Dido lives and rules in Juno's town,
> Never to like or love any but her.   (III. iv. 40–43, 48–50)

The "gods of hospitality" are strange gods by which to swear eternal love. Equally strange are the last three lines, where covert tendencies in the language undercut overt meanings. "Never to leave" is hedged by "while Dido lives and rules," and the hesitation over "like or love" is patently equivocal. However, these are but minor verbal signs of a division in Aeneas' mind and heart that remains permanent from this point in the play onward. The result: Dido acts from a single-minded, single-hearted devotion; Aeneas from a heart that is divided against itself, though often the division is below the level of consciousness (as it appears to be here). Marlowe's use of this situation shows that there are two kinds of love tragedy—those in which the lovers die and those in which the love itself fails, a process of inner destruction by conflict, hypocrisy, betrayal.

The inner conflict in Aeneas emerges as an ideological battle between rival conceptions of manliness. On one side is the Aeneas who is reborn through Dido's love, the Aeneas whose strength comes from his private fulfillment. Set against this Aeneas, but rising out of him, is Aeneas as traditional public hero. To Dido, Aeneas is primarily an erotic hero "like Pæan," sparkling fire and "butting his beams on Flora's bed." But in Aeneas' own mind another image intrudes: the man among men, pitted against the outer world. Thus, the cruel paradox: having furrowed Dido, he cannot rest until he has "furrowed Neptune's glassy fields" (IV. iii. 11).

This alternate image is the product primarily of the military mind. Those traditional bluff soldiers Achates and Ilioneus (whose most interesting de-

scendants are Iago and Enobarbus) define the hero in distinctly antiromantic terms. Love is no source of value; it is a trap, a sickness:

ACHATES: This is no life for men-at-arms to live,
           Where daliance doth consume a soldier's strength,
           And wanton motions of alluring eyes
           Effeminate our minds, inured to war.
ILIONEUS: Why, let us build a city of our own,
           And not stand lingering here for amorous looks.
           Will Dido raise old Priam forth his grave
           And build the town again the Greeks did burn?
                                          (IV. iii. 33–40)

Men among men define manhood by the ability to make war, not love, and
this is what Aeneas' lieutenants make him feel here, though only with
some difficulty:

           Grant she or no, Æneas must away,
           Whose golden fortunes, clogged with courtly ease,
           Cannot ascend to fame's immortal house
           Or banquet in bright honor's burnished hall, . . .
                                          (IV. iii. 7–10)

Womanhood is rejected; sensual pleasure is purged; the call of the abstract
idea of fame is invoked. Then, however, comes the call from that private
side:

           Yet Dido casts her eyes like anchors out,
           To stay my fleet from loosing forth the bay.
           'Come back. Come back,' I hear her cry afar,
           'And let me link thy body to my lips,
           That, tied together by the striving tongues,
           We may as one sail into Italy.'   (IV. iii. 25–30)

The force and sensual vigor of the image of the striving tongues shows how
powerful the personal attraction of Dido really is, but the tide of feeling
swings back to the Achates point of view: "I may not dure this female
drudgery./To sea, Æneas! Find out Italy!" (IV. iii. 55–56).

We have here the classic (almost cliché) sentiments of the eternal sex war
given mythic status. But one question must be asked: given the seemingly
irresistible force of the heroic image evoked here, why does Marlowe
embarrass both Aeneas and Achates in a losing battle with Dido, in which

both heroes are shamed into lies and equivocations. First, she faces Aeneas and he collapses:

DIDO: Is this thy love to me?
AENEAS: O princely Dido, give me leave to speak.
          I went to take my farewell of Achates.

                                                    (IV. iv. 16–18)

Achates fares even worse:

DIDO: How haps Achates bid me not farewell?
ACHATES: Because I feared your grace would keep me here.
DIDO: To rid thee of that doubt, aboard again.

                                                    (IV. iv. 19–21)

Dido's wit and strength here are as impressive as Aeneas' and Achates' are not. The reason for this, I think, is that Marlowe wished to do more than merely dramatize an Odysseus-like escape from a Circean erotic witch, thus confirming without reservation the bluff soldier image of love. The personal bond must have its place, and its place here—in direct personal confrontation—is very powerful indeed, for we are made to realize that to talk of an abstraction like "fame" and yet to try to slip away without a good-bye to one who loves him does not a hero make, just a sneak. The one ethical good in the whole episode is that we see that Aeneas has at least enough human feeling in him to feel like a fool.

It is plain after this episode that this unmutual love runs the strong danger of strangling itself in petty deceits and self-deceptions. Dido's trust is shaken. Even as she praises Aeneas for staying, she tries to trap him by external impediments: hiding his son, stealing his ship's gear. Aeneas, on the other hand, persuades himself that he can cheat destiny by making Carthage a new Troy. Both are deceiving themselves, and both seem smaller because of this. Where Marlowe's genius exerts itself is in showing how the simultaneous acknowledgment of their love and its value and the inevitability of their separation saves them from smallness. Thus, when Aeneas goes to leave for the second and final time, he can face Dido's poignant, deeply felt question:

Why are thy ships new-rigged? Or to what end,
Launched from the haven, lie they in the road?
Pardon me, though I ask. Love makes me ask.   (V. i. 88–90)

And he can answer it with feeling and without a self-protective lie:

> O, pardon me if I resolve thee why.
> Æneas will not feign with his dear love.
> I must from hence.   (V. i. 91–93)

Dido responds to the new tone here with a new level of perception: "These words proceed not from Æneas' heart" (V. i. 102), and Aeneas gives an honest and painful answer: "Not from my heart, for I can hardly go./And yet I may not stay" (V. i. 103–104). All of Marlowe's tact and good sense are operating here. The quietness and simplicity of Aeneas' language in this scene make an effective contrast to his earlier windiness ("Swell, raging seas. Frown wayward destinies" [IV. iv. 57].) and evasiveness. The psychological insight is also powerful. Aeneas' earlier heroic supermasculine bombast was dishonest because it expresssed only one side of a more complex mind and because it was an attempt to deny a human bond that was very palpably there, an attempt to escape that bond painlessly. Here, however, Aeneas accepts the pain because he accepts what his heart tells him, that there is great value in the heroic quest he must now follow, but that there is also great value in the private, personal bond being abandoned. Were it any other way, were Aeneas the pure *heroic* man, he would not be Aeneas, but merely Achates.

The manner of Dido's end is as significant as that of Aeneas' departure. With it Marlowe pushes forward the exploration of a kind of dramatic occasion that lies directly at the heart of the Elizabethan tragic effect: the moment when the heart must face the loss of its very reason for being. The classic instance is Lear's terrible speech over Cordelia's body:

> No, no, no life!
> Why should a dog, a horse, a rat have life,
> And thou no breath at all? Thou'lt come no more,
> Never, never, never, never, never!
> Pray you, undo this button. Thank you, sir.
> Do you see this? Look on her! Look —her lips!
> Look there, look there!   (V. iii. 305–11)

The whole force of the play is distilled here in the moment of loss and the strange but compelling illusion that despairing love and futile hope create just as he dies himself. Before Marlowe only Kyd had successfully used such moments of frenzy with the same effect. Thus, as Dido watches Aeneas leave we have a passage of real power and complexity. The mingling of love and despair produces first a wish-fulfilling daydream:

O Anna, fetch Arion's harp
That I may tice a dolphin to the shore
And ride upon his back unto my love.   (V. i. 248–50)

But even in the midst of hysteria, the generosity of her emotion still operates:

Look, sister, look! Lovely Æneas' ships!
See, see, the billows heave him up to heaven,
And now down falls the keels into the deep.
O sister, sister, take away the rocks.
They'll break his ships. O Proteus, Neptune, Jove,
Save, save Æneas, Dido's liefest love.   (V. i. 251–56)

Her instinctive prayer for his safety is a denial of selfish egotism even when egotism is to be most expected.

4.

The story of Dido is in one sense the story of love defeated; Aeneas does abandon Dido and pursue his destiny in the outside world. Despite this, however, the play is not—as I've tried to suggest—antiromantic in total effect. Marlowe was—like many of his contemporaries—a man large enough to manage a variety of viewpoints, visions, and ideas without being tied down to a simple stand on any of them, to anything but the story in which these points of view encounter each other. What is incontrovertible, however, is that although he acknowledges what his story demands he acknowledge—the final force of the heroic quest—it is the world of eros that calls forth the greatest imaginative, poetic excitement from him. This can easily be seen by comparing the vivid language of Dido's "rivelled gold" speech with any of Aeneas' heroic speeches. The result of this circumstance is paradoxical and significant: Marlowe—through Dido—gives to love in tragedy a language transcendent in its urge and heroic in its energy and beauty. Two instances should make my point. In the first, love creates—or re-creates—paradise on earth, one so fine the gods are jealous:

Heavens, envious of our joys, is waxen pale,
And when we whisper, then the stars fall down
To be partakers of our honey talk.   (IV. iv. 52–54)

In the second, the poetry of eros creates the condition of godhood itself:

If he forsake me not, I never die,
For in his looks I see eternity,
And he'll make me immortal with a kiss.   (IV. iv. 121–23)

This is hubris unquestionably, but its appeal was powerful, for echoes of it are heard throughout Elizabethan and Jacobean tragedy.

4   The Love of King David and Fair Bethsabe

Inga-Stina Ekeblad has made out an excellent case for considering George Peele's biblical chronicle play in the context of Elizabethan Ovidian erotic poetry, noting particularly the obvious Ovidian character of the love imagery and the similarity of the basic opening situation to the Ovidian myths of bathers observed. Peele, she says, is giving us more than merely a *de casibus* play on David's sins of the flesh and divine punishment. "He is also out, in the Ovidian fashion, to show us the beauties of the flesh and of the senses —'the *Love* of King David and *Fair* Bethsabe'—and he does it through the very texture of his poetry."[1]

Miss Ekeblad's remarks clearly suggest that Marlowe's *Dido* and *David and Bethsabe* might be linked to each other through the nature and quality of their verse, as well as their themes. But Peele's play has an explicit moral concern inappropriate to Marlowe's. The biblical source was deeply moral as well as erotically suggestive, and Peele passes this quality on to his play. If the verse of Marlowe's play enriches the Elizabethan dramatists' range of erotic vocabulary (of feelings as well as words), Peele's play adjusts the direction of it. Marlowe's lovers were people in a psychologically impossible yet morally neutral situation. The personal forces which brought them together were not equal to the historical ones which drove them apart, but the question of good and evil in love hardly arises. In *David and Bethsabe*, however, Peele had two tales, one showing sexuality exerting itself as a purely evil force and the other showing it being redeemed. This allowed for a new complication in the treatment of eroticism, and Peele took full advantage of it by integrating with David's story that of Amnon and Thamar. The

---

1. Inga-Stina Ekeblad, "*The Love of King David and Fair Bethsabe*: A Note on George Peele's Biblical Drama," *English Studies*, XXXIX (April, 1958), 62.

previous romantic tragedies had made evil a force outside of love which crushed inward on the lovers. In *David and Bethsabe* Peele explores some of the ways that evil evolves within love itself.

1.

The first thing to emphasize in *David and Bethsabe* is the interplay referred to above between the two separate but related erotic affairs. In the first, King David uses his political power to urge his desires on a married woman. In the second, David's son uses his similar, though lesser, power, augmented by trickery and violence, to possess his own half sister. The ordering of these early scenes makes it clear that the audience was meant to find them mutually illuminating. The seduction of Thamar comes just after the seduction of Bethsabe and just before the scene in which Urias is called back for the unsuccessful attempt to trick him into bed with Bethsabe—during, in other words, the period of David's fullest moral decline. Yet, in the end Amnon dies whereas David, in spite of a similar sexual offense (with murder added), lives on and emerges from suffering into happiness. A moral of some sort is at work, but it is operating in terms of distinctions which must be sought in Peele's deliberate presentation of two kinds of sexual attraction and offense, each distinctly characterized by its own rhetoric and its own symbolic actions.

The opening scene of the play is also the opening scene of the David plot, and it sets a distinctive tone of rich sensuality. First of all, the audience is invited to look on at a spectacle of deliberate erotic appeal: *"The Prologue-speaker, before going out, draws a curtain and discovers* BETHSABE, *with her Maid, bathing over a spring: She sings, and* DAVID *sits above viewing her"*[2] (following 23). This visual coup is supported and enriched by the lush and sensuous verse of Bethsabe's opening soliloquy. This verse is full of music (as well as nice dramatic irony):

> Let not my beauty's fire
> Inflame unstaid desire,
> Nor pierce any bright eye
> That wandereth lightly.   (30–33)

and it is full of the same kind of transforming erotic power that Dido's central speeches had:

2. George Peele, *The Love of King David and Fair Bethsabe*, in *Minor Elizabethan Drama*, ed. Ashley Thorndike, Everyman Library, Vol. I (London: J. M. Dent & Sons Ltd., 1910; rev. ed. 1958). All quotations from the play are from this text.

Come, gentle Zephyr, trick'd with those perfumes
That erst in Eden sweeten'd Adam's love,
And stroke my bosom with thy silken fan:
This shade, sun-proof, is yet no proof for thee;
Thy body, smoother than this wayeless spring,
And purer than the substance of the same,
Can creep through that his lances cannot pierce:
Thou, and thy sister, soft and sacred Air,
Goddess of life, and governess of health,
Keep every fountain fresh and arbour sweet;
No brazen gate her passage can repulse,
Nor bushy thicket bar thy subtle breath: . . .   (34–45)

There is no specific lover intended here, but this is a love song, a love invitation to a nearly bodiless, mythical paramour. It is also a lovely attempt to suggest a link between sensual erotic pleasure and the forces of love, life, fecundity, and natural beauty. The passage also helps to characterize Bethsabe, for it is essential to Peele's conception of her that she be a living manifestation of the potential and actual loveliness in female sexual attractiveness.

David's response to this lush imagery is in kind. Bethsabe is beautiful; David—musician, poet, "Israel's sweetest singer" (Prologue, 1)—has an artist's love of the beautiful, and it comes out in the closely complementary tone and imagery of his answering lines. Whereas Bethsabe spoke as the woman, the attracting force and receiver of attentions ("This shade, sun-proof, is yet no proof for thee"), David takes a stance of mild masculine jealousy: "What tree, what shade, what spring, what paradise,/Enjoys the beauty of so fair a dame?" (51–52). Throughout the speech, the emphasis is everywhere on pleasure in its widest sense—the prelapserian pleasure given by Eve to Adam:

Fair Eva, plac'd in perfect happiness,
Lending her praise-notes to the liberal heavens,
Struck with the accents of arch-angels' tunes,
Wrought not more pleasure to her husband's thoughts
Than this fair woman's words and notes to mine.
                                               (53–57)

and the more generalized sensuous pleasure of an erotically charged nature (note particularly the erotic verbs *pierce, play, embrac'd, sleeps, bear*):

                       . . . let the silver streams
That pierce earth's bowels to maintain the source,
Play upon rubies, sapphires, chrysolites;
The brims let be embrac'd with golden curls
Of moss that sleeps with sound the waters make

> For joy to feed the fount with their recourse;
> Let all the grass that beautifies her bower
> Bear manna every morn instead of dew, . . .   (61–68)

This is not to say, of course, that David's love is treated without irony, for such is not the case. The references to "fair Eva" are deliberately ambiguous, for they not only create an atmosphere of Edenic perfection, they also look forward by implication to the seduction and betrayal motif that becomes the theme of this play and the obsessive concern of the post-*Hamlet* dramatists.

The first unambiguous signs of moral disintegration appear the moment David begins to pass from pure contemplation to the messiness of action. Once this happens, emotion becomes adulterated by the exercise of political will, and the illegitimate confusion of political domination with sexual domination becomes one of the play's main themes.

This theme announces itself in a phrase used by David's servant Cusay: "What service doth my lord the king command?" (73). Service means "a service rendered," but it looks forward to, on a second level of meaning, sexual service. The same merging of meanings may be seen in David's way of pointing out Bethsabe:

> See, Cusay, see the flower of Israel,
> The fairest daughter that obeys the king
> In all the land the Lord subdu'd to me; . . .   (74–76)

The operative words are *obey, subdu'd*. Likewise, in Cusay's later warning to a resisting Bethsabe:

> David, thou know'st, fair dame, is wise and just,
> Elected to the heart of Israel's God;
> Then do not thou expostulate with him
> For any action that contents his soul.   (102–105)

Here the ambiguity is not in the language so much as in the overall concept. Political power has become the arbiter of right, wrong, even of love. It is here, of course, that the death motive intrudes into David's erotic affair. In these early love tragedies, to love and be loved is to live, but to enforce love by external means is to commit a kind of spiritual and emotional murder.

It is necessary to make such a distinction in order to show the good sense of Peele's attempt to make an amoral but beautiful and sensuous poetry lie down in the same bed with a scrupulous Biblical morality and to deal with all the moral complexities such a union must beget. For although, as Miss Ekeblad suggests, it may have been the Ovidian content of the David story that attracted Peele,[3] his critical and moral imagination was by no means lulled to sleep. Indeed, it could hardly be more lively than in a scene such as the following, in which the kingly David is forced to become a low trickster, acting as pander between his lover and her husband so as to hide the shame of her pregnancy. The sexual ironies are insistent, devastating, and a long fall from the Ovidian beauties of the opening scene:

> DAV: Well done, my good Urias! drink thy fill,
>   That in thy fulness David may rejoice.
> UR: I will, my lord.
> ABS: Now, Lord Urias, one carouse to me.
> UR: No sir, I'll drink to the king;
>   Your father is a better man than you.
> DAV: Do so, Urias; I will pledge thee straight.
> UR: I will indeed, my lord and sovereign;
>   I'll once in my days be so bold.
> DAV: Fill him his glass.
> UR: Fill me my glass.
> DAV: Quickly, I say.
> UR: Quickly, I say.—Here, my lord, by your favour now I
>   drink to you.
> DAV: I pledge thee, good Urias, presently.
> ABS: Here, then, Urias, once again for me,
>   And to the health of David's children.
> UR: David's children!   (517–34)

David hopes to rejoice in Urias' "fulness"; Urias speaks admiringly of David's manhood; and the final pledge is to David's children, a group which includes the one soon to be born to Bethsabe and the one who has just raped his half sister, Thamar. By showing everyone carousing while no one has, in fact, any reason for being happy, Peele is providing the bitter to balance out the opening sweet. His special and most important accomplishment is that he does not obliterate sweetness entirely.

2.

The entire Amnon-Thamar incident is compressed within one vivid, interesting—indeed prophetic—scene. This concentration gives the incident a certain force which a more diffuse handling might have robbed it of. In less than one hundred lines Peele turns Amnon from bemused and guilty lover to tyrant, and Thamar from solicitous sister to disgraced, discarded drab. The process is the same which entangled David: a movement from sexual desire through enforced satisfaction to disaster. But the difference in their

3. Ekeblad, *"David and Bethsabe,"* 61.

fates is so complete that the obvious thing is to ask why this should be so. The answer may be seen first in the imagery of the Thamar scene, for Peele has carefully worked his poetry of lust around one basic theme. The theme —love-sickness—is a common one, particularly in the medieval romances, but Peele pursues it with the same intensity that Shakespeare in *Othello* pursues the word *honest* and Middleton *service* to demonstrate the latent ambiguities and unhealthiness of the conception itself and the language which embodies it.[4]

The scene opens with Jonadab (a viler equivalent of David's Cusay) making the same kind of equation between political power and erotic dominance that David did. One notes immediately, however, that the imagery of love he uses makes love not a transforming and beautiful power but an illness, wearing and destructive:

> What means my lord, the king's beloved son,
> That wears upon his right triumphant arm
> The power of Israel for a royal favour,
>
> . . . .
>
> To suffer pale and grisly abstinence
> To sit and feed upon his fainting cheeks,
> And suck away the blood that cheers his looks?
> (245–47, 250–52)

Amnon answers in the same quasi-medical terminology:

> Ah, Jonadab, it is my sister's looks,
> On whose sweet beauty I bestow my blood,
> That make me look so amorously lean;
> Her beauty having seiz'd upon my heart,
> So merely consecrate to her content,
> Sets now such guard about his vital blood,
> And views the passage with such piercing eyes,
> That none can scape to cheer my pining cheeks,
> But all is thought too little for her love.   (253–61)

Faintness, bloodlessness, amorous leanness: all these represent a sharp and considerable falling off from the rich sensuousness of David's love. It is clear, I think, that Peele's intent is to make us see that Amnon's love is filled with ugliness, David's with beauty.

The motif of ugliness and sickness develops as Jonadab suggests "Then

---

4. For a full discussion of medical theories of love melancholy, see Lawrence Babb, *The Elizabethan Malady* (East Lansing: Michigan State College Press, 1951). One persistent strand in Elizabethan-Jacobean tragedy is the attempt to analyze, use, or shake off this dreary and conventional theory of love, along with its deadening conventional language.

from her heart thy looks shall be reliev'd,/And thou shalt joy her as thy soul desires" (262–63). Here again the terminology of medicine: sexual intercourse is seen as a kind of purge, lovemaking as a cure ("a relief") for love rather than a celebration of it. Still another level of meaning is added to the sickness motif when Amnon makes a (to Jonadab) naïve moral objection: "How can it be, my sweet friend Jonadab,/Since Thamar is a virgin and my sister?" (264–65). Jonadab immediately transforms the moral question ("How can it be?") into one of technique, and again we find the language of medicine, now become the very substance of the seduction stratagem:

> Thus it shall be: lie down upon thy bed,
> Feigning thee fever-sick and ill-at-ease;
> And when the king shall come to visit thee,
> Desire thy sister Thamar may be sent
> To dress some dainties for thy malady:
> Then when thou hast her solely with thyself,
> Enforce some favour to thy manly love.   (266–72)

We can see at this point how carefully Peele has made us feel the gulf between this love and David's. The early speeches of David and Bethsabe were full of images of joy and life. These are chilly, calculating, and diseased. Amnon's appearance is that of a sick man; his love is incestuous and thus sick in itself; Jonadab is morally ill, and the stratagem he suggests (having the betrayal of real sisterly love as its heart) is certainly no healthier. The actual mechanics of the plot—a feigned physical sickness—pulls together all the other meanings into one overriding symbolic action. And then one final touch to the motif is provided—the extraordinary semi-voyeuristic staging of the rape-seduction scene itself.

Reviewing the setting of erotic scenes thus far and considering how necessary such scenes are and, at the same time, how tricky they are to stage without outraging public morality, we must grant the Elizabethans credit for their inventiveness. The first, in the early Elizabethan *Gismond*, made no attempt at directly displaying the central erotic situation on stage, but the authors did nevertheless create an erotically charged atmosphere by having the sexual intercourse described after the fact and with great vividness by a man who was clearly extremely disturbed by his voyeuristic experience. Kyd exploited the voyeuristic impulse in a more explicit manner by having an outraged and jealous lover and an honor-conscious brother stirred into a state of murderous violence as they watched the two lovers go through the erotic preliminaries. Marlowe went a step further. He showed the lovers in a state of fierce but unrequited passion. Then they withdraw into their cave for the act itself, but audience attention is not allowed to slip away to another place or time; a brief conversation outside the cave by Anna and the jealous Iarbas bridges the time lapse and keeps us with fine dramatic irony staring at the cave imagining what we will until the lovers emerge clinging and satisfied.

Peele takes Marlowe's solution, keeps the immediacy of the withdrawal-return process and adds a perverse (as in *Gismond*) verbal commentary on the act taking place out of sight. Thamar goes in with Amnon to attend him and, in the interim before Amnon reenters *"thrusting out* THAMAR" (after 306), Jonadab holds the stage, smirking to himself as Thamar is deflowered. His monologue starts off applying machiavellian political principles to the affairs of the heart. Then he slips into his medical language again, making explicit the pseudo-rational turn of mind which connects the two attitudes:

> Now, Amnon, loose those loving knots of blood,
> That suck'd the courage from thy kingly heart.
> And give it passage to thy wither'd cheeks.   (286–88)

Peele is suggesting here that an idea of love which expresses itself in the utilitarian language of medicine violates the real meaning of love. Jonadab continues with a sadistic litany:

> Now, Thamar, ripen'd are the holy fruits
> That grew on plants of thy virginity;
> And rotten is thy name in Israel:
> Poor Thamar, little did thy lovely hands
> Foretell an action of such violence
> As to contend with Amnon's lusty arms
> Sinew'd with vigour of his kindless love:
> Fair Thamar, now dishonour hunts thy foot, . . .   (289–96)

This recital prepares us in several ways for the climactic moment. The obsessive repetition of her name, the relish he seems to feel in vicarious sexuality, in musing on her ripeness and on her disgrace (emphasized by the perversion of the nature imagery)—all suggest the sickness of an attitude which Amnon then confirms in action. Thrusting out Thamar after, as it were, relieving himself on her, Amnon moves the whole sickness motif inexorably towards its logical end as he displaces his own sickness onto the object of his lust: "Hence from my bed, whose sight offends my soul/As doth the parbreak of disgorgèd bears!" (307–308).

Thamar, for her part, takes what is, at first glance, a strange attitude—counting the rejection worse than the rape:

O, do not this dishonour to thy love,
Nor clog thy soul with such increasing sin!
This second evil far exceeds the first.   (313–15)

But although the brevity of her part makes it difficult to be certain, these lines seem to be Peele's attempt to make us understand that sexuality is neither moral nor immoral, beautiful nor ugly, except in terms of the emotional attitude which accompanies it. Attitudes in dramatic poetry are indicated by language and action. The language in this scene has been eloquent enough in communicating Amnon and Jonadab's attitude, particularly when taken in comparison with David and Bethsabe's language of beauty and joy. Even more eloquent is the like contrast in actions. Thamar is sent off with these words: "My lord hath done with you: I pray, depart" (319). David and Bethsabe, despite a period of mutual suffering and even recrimination, remain together. The difference between the two couples is the difference between the operation of a permanent love and a transient, chilly lust, between the operation of the love motive in sexual passion and the operation of the death motive.

3.

The news of the rape of Thamar serves as a symbolically appropriate reminder to David of his own sexual evil: "Sin, with his sevenfold crown and purple robe,/Begins his triumphs in my guilty throne" (384–85). The fate of his child by Bethsabe does the same thing. The child was the product of their lovemaking. But the betrayal and death of Urias was also the product of their love, and when the child grows ill this illness becomes an emblem of the corrupting element that has intruded into that love. In this way, again, love and death come together in close symbolic juxtaposition; that which was creative in the love of David and Bethsabe is negated by the destructive element.

But—as in Shakespeare's *Winter's Tale*—the death of the child also opens the way to the redemption and regeneration of what was good in the king's love for his mistress. For one thing, the child's sickness and death pull David into a consciousness of people outside of himself. It is a means of moving him into a state of maturity, of new insight. He thinks beyond his own moral misery to the personal misery of those whom he has involved with him:

The babe is sick, and sad is David's heart,
To see the guiltless bear the guilty's pain.
David, hang up thy harp; hang down thy head;

. . . .
The babe is sick, sweet babe, that Bethsabe
With woman's pain brought forth to Israel. (604–606, 612–13)

In these lines, the moral distinction between the two parallel sinners—
David and Amnon—is plain, and so also the logic of their differing fates. At
one moment in her anguish at the sickness of her child Bethsabe cries out,
"O, what is it to serve the lust of kings!" (600), but the rest of the play shows
that the term *lust* was the exaggeration of anger. If the kind of transient relief that Amnon displayed has claim to a word, it is the word *lust*; the whole
complex of sickness-ugliness-treachery-rejection-transience demands the
term. Peele, at first, had David move towards a similar realm but even
while doing so sowed the seeds of regeneration in him by giving him a
poet's sense of what it is to love. The sign of this sense is the rich appreciation of the beauty of woman and nature that pervades his language.

The death of the illegitimate child leads into a striking scene of rebirth
through love. Looking boldly to the future instead of morbidly to the past,
David orders feasting instead of mourning. And he transcends his own
earlier egotism by directing the celebration towards Bethsabe:

> Bring ye to me the mother of the babe,
> That I may wipe the tears from off her face,
> And give her comfort with this hand of mine,
> And deck fair Bethsabe with ornaments,
> That she may bear to me another son,
> That she may be lovèd of the Lord of Hosts;
> . . . .
> *They bring in water, wine, and oil. Music and a banquet;*
> *and enter* BETHSABE.
> Fair Bethsabe, sit thou, and sigh no more:—
> And sing and play, you servants of the king:
> Now sleepeth David's sorrow with the dead,
> And Bethsabe liveth to Israel.   (708–13, 716–19)

The ceremonial celebration of fidelity, love, and beauty reestablish David's
moral identity. It is a triumph of life set against the selfish, mechanical,
death-oriented transience of Amnon and Jonadab. It is even—if one adjusts one's expectations to the polygamous nature of the Hebrew royal
marriage—a statement of the triumph of the idea of romantic marriage, the
new union being again symbolized by a child—in this case a true heir to the
throne and a healer of social disunion.

We can best sum up Peele's accomplishment in *David and Bethsabe* by focusing on his ability to handle erotic themes in a way that looked—in the
treatment of both love and lust—distinctly towards the future. He seems to

have consciously made the attempt to take this great natural force, sexuality, and the erotic poetry that gives it literary expression and channel these back into a traditional moral context to see what would result. What does result is most interesting. First of all, eroticism linked with beauty and fidelity is found to lead to the truest moral actions, whereas eroticism treated as a sickness (as medieval and sixteenth-century physicians and moralists regarded it) is shown to be destructive, vicious, and death-oriented. We can see, therefore, in this rejection of the medieval love-malady idea and the deliberate directing of the music of sexuality away from adultery into a permanent union, the movement of the modern (postmedieval) world towards the idea of the love-marriage in which convention gives erotic energy form and erotic energy gives convention life. Ovid and eros are, therefore, brought into the service of social stability and the conventional institutions. Or perhaps it is the other way around. In any case, this is the distinctive sixteenth-century accomplishment in love tragedy, and the next play to be discussed is the crowning jewel of this movement towards the synthesis of love and beauty against death.

5 Romeo and Juliet

Romeo and Juliet brings virtually every theme we have been considering to its fullest amplification and complication thus far. It develops the interplay of love and death motifs beyond *The Spanish Tragedy* (nothing in that play is so explicit as Paris' "O love! O life! Not life, but love in death!" [IV. v. 58]), and it creates an ideal of romantic love that—as succeeding chapters will show—reverberated throughout the Elizabethan-Jacobean period, either as something to be developed, modified, imitated, or attacked. In this chapter I shall take up these concerns—the love-death opposition and the idea of love—in that order.

1.

The opposition of love and death is first struck in the Prologue sonnet, specifically in the lines: "From forth the fatal loins of these two foes/A pair of star-crossed lovers take their life" (Prologue, 5–6), and the reference to "The fearful passage of their death-marked love," (Prologue, 9). More important though—because it is an organic part of the dramatic argument itself—is the opening exchange between Samson and Gregory. This crude but amusing raillery quickly establishes the menacing atmosphere of social discord that centers on the Capulet-Montague feud. It also gives voice to a mode of thinking about sexual love that makes a very important contrast to that of Romeo and Juliet. Professor M. M. Mahood has said of the scene (without discussing specific lines): "Its purpose is to make explicit, at the beginning of this love tragedy, one possible relationship between man and woman: a brutal male dominance expressed in sadistic quibbles."[1] The im-

1. M. M. Mahood, *Shakespeare's Wordplay* (London: Methuen & Co. Ltd., 1968 reprint of 1957 edition), 60. This essay on *Romeo and Juliet* is so full of fine insights into the play that my references can only hint at what I have learned from it.

plications of the relationship between sadism and one prominent concept of masculinity are important to this study and need further exploration.

The relationship is developed in two ways: one, through a generalized flow of aggressive feelings; the other, by the ubiquitous analogy between the phallus and the sword. In Gregory and Sampson these are almost the same, so closely are they associated in their language. The phallic imagery ripples through the opening exchange,[2] both aspects of it being united by the aggressive motive and equal contempt for the victim of the assault:

> SAM: . . . women, being the weaker vessels, are ever thrust to the wall: therefore I will push Montague's men from the wall, and thrust his maids to the wall.
>
>   . . . .
>
> SAM: . . . when I have fought with the men, I will be cruel with the maids; I will cut off their heads.
> GRE: The heads of the maids?
> SAM: Ay, the heads of the maids, or their maidenheads;
>
>   . . . .
>
> GRE: Draw thy tool;
>
>   . . . .
>
> SAM: My naked weapon is out: . . .
>
> (I. i. 15–18, 22–26, 31, 33)

The whole dialogue is a testimony to the crude fertility of the vulgar language, but the attitudes expresssed here stretch out to include a wide range of characters. Obviously Tybalt is one. His ruling passion is the sword, so much so that the ordinary sexual element seems to have no place in his makeup. One never sees Tybalt except when he is reaching for his sword or using it, and his code of honor is as exaggerated as the one-sided militant quality of his masculinity. Old Capulet is almost as bad but is saved in the first scene by the frailty of old age.

Nor is Romeo wholly free from this kind of thinking since, in the process of speaking in traditional courtly love terms, he absorbs the motif in its more refined, socially acceptable form: "She will not stay the siege of loving terms,/Nor bide th'encounter of assailing eyes" (I. i. 211–12). Here the conquest metaphor has been robbed of its fullest force by being translated from swords into words and looks; yet the mode of thinking is the same: self-centered, self-seeking, transient and superficial. It is appropriate that such language should be associated with Romeo's pre-Juliet passion.

---

2. This exchange could be seen as a comic amplification of Lorenzo's "Ay, thus, and thus, these are the fruits of love" (*Spanish Tragedy*, II. iv. 55), as he thrusts the knife into Horatio.

Mercutio's place in this grouping is clear enough; he is infinitely wittier than Gregory and Sampson, but his wit often works with the same materials: "If love be rough with you, be rough with love;/Prick love for pricking, and you beat love down" (I. iv. 27–28). And Professor Mahood has hit happily on the word *lady-killer* to sum up his character and the significance of this character in the play's panorama of ideas about love: "'Mercutio appears in early versions of the tale as what is significantly known as a lady-killer, and his dramatic purpose at this moment of the play is to oppose a cynical and aggressive idea of sex to Romeo's love-idolatry and so sharpen the contrast already made in the opening scene."[3] This is not the whole of Mercutio the way the sword is the whole of Tybalt, but it represents a persistent bias, the aggressiveness of which is poetically consistent with his part in the precipitation of the duel.

If the character of Tybalt reminds us of Kyd's Lorenzo, it is not only because of their relationship with the sword. One is a vengeful brother, the other a vengeful cousin. Each has a fiery passion for the family honor. Each embodies within his individual dramatic construction the principle of hate and its concomitant, destruction. Each becomes an agent of death in a world that needs love. Two significant scenes are built around this idea. The first, the ballroom scene in which Romeo and Juliet meet, even bears distinct signs of the influence of Kyd.[4] The lovers of *The Spanish Tragedy* make their tentative explorations of each other's love under the menacing, undetected observation of the avenging brothers. A very similar device is used by Shakespeare. Romeo's first awestruck words about Juliet are followed by Tybalt's

> This, by his voice, should be a Montague.
> Fetch me my rapier, boy.
>
> . . . .
> Now, by the stock and honour of my kin,
> To strike him dead I hold it not a sin.   (I. v. 54–55, 58–59)

The preface to the lovers' very beautiful meeting is Tybalt's "I will withdraw, but this intrusion shall,/Now seeming sweet, convert to bitterest gall" (I. v. 91–92).

The context of these love-death oppositions also gives the duel scene much of its striking poetic validity. On one side there is Tybalt, preemi-

---

3. Mahood, *Shakespeare's Wordplay*, 62.
4. Philip W. Edwards, *Shakespeare and the Confines of Art* (London: Methuen & Co. Ltd., 1968), 71–72 and *Thomas Kyd*, 26–27, 33, notes other signs of influence between these superficially dissimilar plays.

nently the fighter and a man whom love never touches; on the other is Mercutio, a kaleidoscopic character, but still one for whom love, in the sense which Romeo has come to feel it, does not exist. Both firebrand duelists subscribe first to the sword and to the code of honor and masculinity that goes with it. Romeo, however, has moved on to another stage. According to John Vyvyan, he has even gone far in the direction of a mystical, platonic experience.[5] At the very least, I think we must say that the revelation of love for Juliet has driven home the need for a wider spread of concord. He attempts to achieve this in the encounter with Tybalt: "I do protest I never injured thee,/But love thee better than thou canst devise" (III. i. 67–68). When he fails, his failure is marked by a kind of psychological regression. From the spirit of Juliet, he falls for a few fatal seconds into the spirit of Mercutio:

> . . . fire-eyed fury by my conduct now!
>
> . . . .
>
> . . . for Mercutio's soul
> Is but a little way above our heads,
> Staying for thine to keep him company.   (III. i. 123, 125–27)

This is, of course, also the spirit of Tybalt, for Tybalt and Mercutio were much more like each other than either of them was to the new Romeo. The final love-death irony in this line of action is that Romeo in the heat of his anger temporarily comes to judge his own attempts at extending love in terms of the Tybalt-Mercutio idea of manhood:

> O sweet Juliet,
> Thy beauty hath made me effeminate,
> And in my temper softened valour's steel!   (III. i. 112–14)

The havoc caused by this sudden triumph of the death motive affects even Juliet's love, as her fevered oxymora show ("Beautiful tyrant, fiend angelical" [III. ii. 75]), but in her the love bond holds, bringing a temporary halt to the sequence of hatred and killing:

> Shall I speak ill of him that is my husband?
> Ah, poor my lord, what tongue shall smooth thy name
> When I, thy three-hours wife, have mangled it?
> (III. ii. 97–99)

At this point halfway through the play, there is nothing either in the

---

5. John Vyvyan, *Shakespeare and the Rose of Love* (London: Chatto & Windus, 1960), particularly 151ff.

prince's sentence of banishment or in the lovers' own relationship which would be an obstacle to a comic or happy ending. But Shakespeare maintains the tragic pressure of the play by the use of another motif drawing its force from the opposition of love and death: the Arranged Marriage.

In *The Spanish Tragedy* (and in the related Enforced non-Marriage of *Gismond*) this motif involves the attempt by the older generation to shape the emotional life of the new. The dominant force behind the Arranged Marriage is parental possessiveness, and the unrelenting prosecution of it leads to disaster. All these elements are present in *Romeo and Juliet*, but Shakespeare sharpens the effect of his version by making Capulet speak at first like the very model of a liberal father. After urging Paris to woo Juliet and "get her heart," he sets out his own humane position: that, in marriage, personal affection must have the central role in the pairing—

> My will to her consent is but a part:
> And, she agreed, within her scope of choice
> Lies my consent and fair according voice.   (I. ii. 17–19)

Yet, having now lost a nephew, he seems neurotically anxious to gain a son:

> Sir Paris, I will make a desperate tender
> Of my child's love: I think she will be ruled
> In all respects by me: nay more, I doubt it not.
> Wife, go you to her ere you go to bed;
> Acquaint her ear of my son Paris' love, . . .   (III. iv. 12–16)

His anxiety overrides his humanity; he substitutes his own desires for his daughter's and mistakenly identifies the two as one. They are, of course, quite different. Juliet stands for the personal, intuitive choice of lover—the essence of the romantic. Capulet's criteria for choosing a husband are external to her and thus of necessity peripheral. His insistence on second things first, the precedence of the outer over the inner, makes marriage emotionally null—and thus touched with death. This is one reason Capulet seems an archetypal character; the *good marriage* is a timeless phrase used by outsiders (which means everyone but the couple) to describe a marriage which adds either wealth or social status or both.[6] The marriage to Paris is a very *good marriage* and Capulet knows it.

But the actively sinister aspect of this attitude arises from its impersonality and from the father's will to exert his parental authority. A quick com-

---

6. For the strong elements of commercial imagery in Capulet's discussion of Juliet and of marriage, see Mahood, *Shakespeare's Wordplay*, 61.

parison between Capulet and Kyd's Castile brings this out. They share, for
instance, the same complacent sense of their own authority:

CAP: How now, wife?
Have you delivered to her our decree?

(III. v. 137–38)

There is the same covert egotism:

CAP: God's bread! it makes me mad. Day, night,
         work, play,
Alone, in company, still my care hath been
To have her matched; and having now provided
A gentlemen of noble parentage,
Of fair demesnes, youthful and nobly trained,
Stuffed, as they say, with honourable parts,
Proportioned as one's thought would wish a man—
And then to have a wretched puling fool,
A whining mammet, in her fortune's tender,
To answer "I'll not wed, I cannot love;" . . .

(III. v. 176–85)

and finally the same ultimate threat:

CAP: Graze where you will; you shall not house
         with me.
Look to't, think on't; I do not use to jest.

(III. v. 188–89)

The outcome of this fanatical determination to force an unwanted lover
on the bride is to push the Friar beyond his wits into suggesting that Juliet
feign death in order to remain true to her husband. It is in these last two acts
that Shakespeare really pulls out all the stops. He takes every implication
of the Kydian Deadly Nuptial dumb show and explodes it into giant size,
giving us not only a feigned Fatal Nuptial but a real one. The result is alter-
nately preposterous and devastating, but there can be no question but that
Shakespeare felt tremendous poetic and emotional force in the juxtaposition of love and death and was determined to exploit both to the fullest. The
nausea of bodily and psychological dissolution:

Alack, alack, is it not like that I,
So early waking—what with loathsome smells,
And shrieks like mandrakes' torn out of the earth,
That living mortals, hearing them, run mad—
O, if I wake, shall I not be distraught,
Environéd with all these hideous fears,
And madly play with my forefathers' joints,
And pluck the mangled Tybalt from his shroud,

And, in this rage, with some great kinsman's bone,
As with a club, dash out my desp'rate brains?
                                                (IV. iii. 45–54)

is set against the beauty and strength of love: "Romeo, I come! this do I
drink to thee" (IV. iii. 58). And the expected joy of the wedding day:

CAP: Nurse! Wife! What, ho! What, nurse, I say!
               '*Enter* NURSE'
       Go waken Juliet; go and trim her up.
       I'll go and chat with Paris. Hie, make haste,
       Make haste! The bridegroom he is come already:
       Make haste, I say.   (IV. iv. 24–28)

is set ironically against the actual misery of loss:

       O son, the night before thy wedding day
       Hath Death lain with thy wife. There she lies,
       Flower as she was, defloweréd by him.
       Death is my son-in-law, Death is my heir;
       My daughter he hath wedded! I will die
       And leave him all; life, living, all is Death's.
                                                (IV. v. 35–40)

   But these are mere preludes to the still more complex and profound dramatic poetry of the last act. The whole cloth of the catastrophe is a web of love-death ironies and interrelations. The death of Paris, for instance: it first seemed to me, and has to others, a singular piece of unwarranted savagery. But it has an interesting precedent: the murder of Castile in *The Spanish Tragedy*. There seems, at first, no pressing moral reason why death should swallow up either of the two, yet in each instance a kind of poetic logic is operating. Both men were involved in the Arranged Marriage process, for example. Paris seems consistently a decent person, but he is operating complacently within an established, customary institution, and he was no more assiduous than Capulet about requiring a personal, emotional relationship with Juliet.
   The real tour de force of love-death interplay, however, is Romeo's last long speech. The killing of Paris exhausts his fury, leaving him strangely contemplative. He comes to love the man he has killed well enough to put his body alongside Juliet's. Then he sees Juliet's beauty filling the tomb with light, without realizing that her beauty still holds life: "For here lies Juliet, and her beauty makes/This vault a feasting presence full of light" (V. iii. 85–86). The sight of Tybalt in his shroud pulls still more love from him:

> Tybalt, liest thou there in thy bloody sheet?
> O, what more favour can I do to thee
> Than with that hand that cut thy youth in twain
> To sunder his that was thine enemy?
> Forgive me, cousin!   (V. iii. 97–101)

Closer to the end he grows more passionate. Capulet's idea of Death personified as a son-in-law is given its final amplification as Romeo takes the role of protective, slightly jealous husband:

> Ah, dear Juliet,
> Why art thou yet so fair? Shall I believe
> That unsubstantial Death is amorous,
> And that the lean abhorréd monster keeps
> Thee here in dark to be his paramour?
> For fear of that I still will stay with thee, . . .
>   (V. iii. 101–106)

Finally Romeo ends as he began: "Thus with a kiss I die" (V. iii. 120). Juliet is much briefer:

> I will kiss thy lips.
> Haply some poison yet doth hang on them
> To make me die with a restorative.
> Thy lips are warm!   (V. iii. 164–67)

This kiss takes the compression of love, death, and joy as far as it will go. It is a baroque metaphor made flesh. Paradox and multiple meaning would appear to be the only forms of expression which can hold the terrible complexity involved in the verbal expression of ultimate things. The kind of love which Shakespeare is presenting and celebrating here (which Kyd before him had caught a hint of—that is, a love capable of inspiring self-sacrifice) is like religion in that it begins in mystery and ends in paradox.

The last stage, the final paradox, is that the death of the lovers turns social hatred into love, but I would prefer to defer comment on this until the end of this chapter.

2.

In this section I shall move from Shakespeare's more general use of patterns of love and death to certain specific aspects of the central love story and the ideal of love it represents.

The first element is the conscious rejection of courtly love. This is a motif which has been building slowly in previous plays. In *Romeo and Juliet* it is accomplished in the first act, but the bases of this rejection and particularly the part in it played by various kinds of death imagery are of the greatest importance, for they set a precedent which remains operative throughout Shakespeare's career.

We may approach this through one of Coleridge's typically acute notes: "Romeo running away from his Rosaline to woods and nature, in which she indeed alone existed, as the name for his yearning—contrast this with his rushing to Juliet." [7] The love for Rosaline is fruitless and one-sided. It contains a powerful element of repulsion, of the unnatural, that is an aspect of the courtly sonnet sequences such as Spenser's *Amoretti*. The male posture of supplication and highly embroidered misery may have its own obscure pleasures, but they are solitary ones founded in the failure of mutuality. Between Romeo and Juliet, however, there comes a love which draws the two inexorably towards each other, which both attracts and responds.

To the extent that the love of Romeo for Rosaline has elements of the failure of trust, communication, knowledge, or passion, it is linked to images of pain and misery, images in which the death motive cannot be separated from the love motive. For instance, to illustrate Coleridge's distinction, we have the testimony of Romeo's father:

> Away from light steals home my heavy son,
> And private in his chamber pens himself,
> Shuts up his windows, locks fair daylight out,
> And makes himself an artificial night: . . .   (I. i. 136–39)

The operative words are *heavy*, *pens*, *shuts*, *artificial night*. The whole motion is away from natural light towards an unnatural confusion of light and dark. Romeo's own speeches show the same awkward mingling:

> Ay me, sad hours seem long.
> . . . .
> O heavy lightness, serious vanity,
> Misshapen chaos of well-seeming forms,
> Feather of lead, bright smoke, cold fire,
>   sick health,
> Still-waking sleep, that is not what it is!
> This love feel I, that feel no love in this.
> . . . .
> Why, such is love's transgression.
> Griefs of mine own lie heavy in my breast,
> . . . .
> Love is a smoke made with the fume of sighs:
> . . . .
> A choking gall and a preserving sweet.
>   (I. i. 160, 177–81, 184–85, 189, 193)

7. Coleridge, *Shakespearean Criticism*, 6.

The oxymoron is an effective rhetorical device here because it is built precisely to answer this need to mingle opposites. Each term of each unit is negated by the one adjacent, just as love is negated by the failure of love from the other person. The images themselves are, of course, very much in the tradition of courtly complaint. Thus, when Benvolio would probe the matter, he takes the role of a doctor, and his language is the medical language of the treatises on the lover's malady: "Take thou some new infection to thy eye,/ And the rank poison of the old will die" (I. ii. 50–51). The emotional superficiality of the cure does in this case match the superficiality of the one-sided love. Other indications of this superficiality are apparent, notably Romeo's own statement of his seducer-like motive and techniques:

> . . . in strong proof of chastity well armed,
> From Love's weak childish bow she lives unharmed.
> She will not stay the siege of loving terms,
> Nor bide th'encounter of assailing eyes,
> Nor ope her lap to saint-seducing gold.   (I. i. 209–13)

and the oft-noticed "Where shall we dine?" (I. i. 172) that interrupts one seemingly heartfelt speech. This combination of hyperbole and incomplete emotion is by no means incompatible with the rhetoric of love-sickness as the Elizabethan dramatist was coming to see it. Romeo here has nothing of the cruelty of Peele's Amnon or Kyd's Balthazar, but Shakespeare is subtly placing and showing the limits of Romeo's love for Rosaline by showing in his language and actions the elements of deadness lodged at the heart of it. The urge to love is a good thing in Romeo, but this particular love is permanently grounded in courtly futility. This is a theme which becomes still more pronounced in the plays of John Marston and Shakespeare's own *Troilus and Cressida*.

The ballroom scene provides the shift which gives these images of the rejection of courtly love their meaning. Romeo goes to the ball not elevated or excited by love but rather made dreary and soul-dead:

> Being but heavy, I will bear the light.
> . . . .
>   I have a soul of lead
> So stakes me to the ground I cannot move.
> . . . .
> I cannot bound a pitch above dull woe:
> Under love's heavy burden do I sink. (I. iv. 12, 15–16, 21–22)

Then suddenly Romeo sees Juliet, sees "true beauty," and the images clarify and polarize. Instead of dark in light, we find light against dark:

> O she doth teach the torches to burn bright!
> It seems she hangs upon the cheek of night
> As a rich jewel in an Ethiop's ear—   (I. v. 44–46)

Instead of dullness and heaviness, the dominant atmosphere becomes one of joyous imaginative and emotional activity. The old is gone; the new tone—the new separation of love and death—remains constant except for one important wavering, the killing of Tybalt. Then love and death images again become intertwined temporarily in both Romeo and Juliet. The moment is the strongest test of the strength of their love.

As the love of Romeo and Juliet is developed, it takes on special qualities that make it the quintessential statement of the Elizabethan romantic ideal. The first of these is in the virtually unprecedented presentation of love as a phenomenon that is both very human and at the same time possessed of a powerful urge towards transcendence of the purely human. Romeo and Juliet always remain people—with real people's faults and charm—but in their very humanity they embody many elements of the religious impulse. The famous shared sonnet, for instance, holds both these tendencies in delicate balance:

> R: If I profane with my unworthiest hand
>   This holy shrine, the gentle sin[8] is this:
>   My lips, two blushing pilgrims, ready stand
>   To smooth that rough touch with a tender kiss.
> J: Good pilgrim, you do wrong your hand too much,
>   Which mannerly devotion shows in this:
>   For saints have hands that pilgrims' hands do touch,
>   And palm to palm is holy palmers' kiss.
> R: Have not saints lips, and holy palmers too?
> J: Ay, pilgrim, lips that they must use in prayer.
> R: O then, dear saint, let lips do what hands do;
>   They pray: grant thou, lest faith turn to despair.
> J: Saints do not move, though grant for prayers' sake.
> R: Then move not, while my prayer's effect I take.
>   (I. v. 93–106)

The deliberate formalism of the sonnet gives a special gravity to the meeting; it seems to isolate the lovers by means of a crystallized piece of lit-

8. Professor Wilson reads *pain* where Q1 has *sinne* and Q2 and F have *sin*. I have restored the latter.

erary form in a moment that is both timeless and highly charged with spiritual significance. This is further augmented by the imagery of the religion of love. Such items as "blushing pilgrims" and the tropes on religious and profane devotion may be conventional, but this does not rob them of their effect, particularly since here hackneyed expressions are given back their primal freshness by the infusion of true feeling.

The distinctively human aspects weigh equally with the religious ones. For one thing, this sonnet makes a radical break with those of the nondramatic tradition by allowing mutuality and exchange of emotion. If the orthodox sonnet was a testament to the separation of lovers, Shakespeare's dramatic technique here makes it a mode of uniting them all the more closely. As the two react to each other from line to line, so the mutuality of their love is built, and as they share the same system of images, so they share the same image of themselves. But the fineness of the passage goes beyond the purely verbal. It extends to the inclusion of touch, of physical contact, and sensuous pleasure. One sees here the beginnings of the Shakespearean attempt to fuse body with soul and to unite them in one union, one couple. The effort here and the success of it make this sonnet a radical contrast to those of Shakespeare's nondramatic sequence, where bodily desire and spiritual love are so completely separated that they must house themselves in totally different beloveds, of different sex.

The same balance may be seen in the vast number of images which lead out of the world and into the heavens. Typical are these from the balcony scene:

> But soft! What light through yonder window breaks?
> It is the east, and Juliet is the sun.
>
> . . . .
> Two of the fairest stars in all the heaven,
> Having some business, do entreat her eyes
> To twinkle in their spheres till they return.
>
> . . . .
> . . . her eyes in heaven
> Would through the airy region stream so bright
> That birds would sing and think it were not night.
>   (II. ii. 2–3, 15–17, 20–22)

Images like these recur throughout the play, and their effect is again an intense spiritualization of the love: "Romeo and Juliet stellify each other, the love which appears to be quenched as easily as a spark is extinguished is, in fact, made as permanent as the sun and stars when it is set out of the range of time."[9] But the stellifying is accomplished with no loss of human credibility, and timelessness is achieved with no diminution of that part of love which is of time. The result is again a full-bodied mixture of the spiritual and the sensual. The relevant text is Juliet's starlit speech of bridal anticipation:

> Spread thy close curtain, love-performing night,
> That runaways' eyes may wink, and Romeo
> Leap to these arms untalked of and unseen.
> Lovers can see to do their amorous rites
> By their own beauties;
> . . . .
> Come, gentle Night; come, loving, black-browed Night:
> Give me my Romeo; and, when he shall die,
> Take him and cut him out in little stars,
> And he will make the face of heaven so fine
> That all the world will be in love with night
> And pay no worship to the garish sun.
> O, I have bought the mansion of a love,
> But not possessed it; and though I am sold,
> Not yet enjoyed.   (III. ii. 5–9, 20–28)

Juliet's virginal but powerful sexuality has drawn the sideways glances of criticism, and by no means only from the Victorians. Thus, a comment like this from a modern critic with pretensions to psychoanalytic sophistication: "the consummation of her lust is an error, put in for the sake of the *aubade*."[10] This misses the point utterly. First of all, Juliet's innocence and her joy have the very important effect of giving new life to the language of sexuality so badly debased in different parts of the play by the male characters. Second, it is this merging of innocent love and sexual energy, of spirit and body which is the whole point of the depiction of love in *Romeo and Juliet*. Literary history had provided numerous images of sexual love as lust (the typical medieval image) and of the totally nonphysical love usually called platonic love. But the new idea of the Renaissance was that these two should be united. The means to this union is also the main object of Shakespeare's celebration in this play—the love-marriage, as opposed to both the courtly liaison and the marriage arranged by outsiders. These distinctions are important, for in Shakespeare neither of the latter two ever have the compelling imaginative and emotional force of the first.

The central passage celebrating the idea of love-marriage is that *aubade* to

---

9. Mahood, *Shakespeare's Wordplay*, 68.
10. J. B. Broadbent, *Poetic Love* (London: Chatto & Windus, 1964), 189.

which the critic referred. The tone of the scene seems absolutely perfect, touched as it is with sadness, joy, the knowledge of death and the knowledge of love. The experience of sexual love has transformed the lovers' poetry, bringing it out of its slightly frantic rush to the ether, down to a world where the sky is a distant wash of pale light and, right at hand, a lark sings. In this Edenic dawn the conversation wavers slowly through images of love and death with easy, gentle irony—as here in Romeo:

> Let me be ta'en, let me be put to death;
> I am content, so thou wilt have it so.
> I'll say yon gray is not the morning's eye,
> 'Tis but the pale reflex of Cynthia's brow; . . .
>
> (III. v. 17–20)

There are many quick, fine touches; light, so long a symbol for love and the lovers now becomes an enemy: "O now be gone! More light and light it grows" (III. v. 35). More important though is the way Romeo's answer to Juliet's fearful "O, think'st thou we shall ever meet again?" (III. v. 51) opens out a vision of the future that is foreign to the passion of the medieval romance tradition but central to the Shakespearean idea of the romantic marriage, whether here or in such a late play as *The Winter's Tale*: "I doubt it not; and all these woes shall serve/For sweet discourses in our times to come" (III. v. 52–53). This is the love motive. The fear of death is in the air, however, and is caught by Juliet's chilling final vision:

> O God, I have an ill-divining soul!
> Methinks I see thee, now thou art so low,
> As one dead in the bottom of a tomb.
> Either my eyesight fails or thou look'st pale.
>
> (III. v. 54–57)

Still, death remains an external force pressing in on them, or else it becomes something which they make use of and welcome—as at the end—when they bolt up accident and shackle change, thus preserving like an icon the value which they had created out of the flux of life.

There is one final extension of the idea of love in *Romeo and Juliet* that—because it is so well known and so distinctive—needs to be placed in the love tragedy context; this is the importance of love in society.

It is a commonplace to say of passionate love that it disrupts the fabric of society. Such, for instance, is the argument of Denis de Rougemont's influential book *Passion and Society* and of innumerable conservative critiques of romantic love through the centuries. The very commonplace nature of this wisdom makes it imperative to call attention to the fact that in the

Shakespearean vision it is hatred that disrupts society and the passion of Romeo and Juliet that heals it. Romeo and Juliet do rebel against the social order, casting off both name and history in the iconoclastic ecstasy of the balcony scene:

> j: What's in a name? That which we call a rose
> By any other name would smell as sweet.
> So Romeo would, were he not Romeo called,
> Retain that dear perfection which he owes,
> Without that title. Romeo, doff thy name;
> . . . .
> r: I take thee at thy word.
> Call me but love, and I'll be new baptized;
> Henceforth I never will be Romeo.[11]
>   (II. ii. 43–47, 49–51)

But they do not do it with purely destructive purposes. They do it to free themselves so as to re-create social forms on the basis of love.

The force of their example comes from the fact that—unlike the lovers of courtly romance or the *Liebestod* myths—they are not outside convention but very much in it, where the creative power of their love may operate effectively. The relationship between the lovers and society is therefore double. Because they are lovers creating their own world, the larger world isolates them. But because their own world has in it the seeds of a new society (the model of society being the family) their example has social efficacy. Romeo, in his last speech, unites the personal and the conventional in his epithets of address for Juliet—"O my love, my wife!" (V. iii. 91). The link between social concord and human love was therefore forged at the very base of the social organization. The beauty and love which the lovers affirmed in death fuses their small world to the larger one. It is a fusion that belongs finally not to something external to human life—like God's mercy or platonic essence—but to Shakespeare and to nature.

11. Harry Levin makes some important remarks on this subject and this scene in "Form and Formality in *Romeo and Juliet*," *Shakespeare Quarterly*, XI (Winter, 1960), 3–11.

6   Antonio and Mellida: I & II

The search for a unifying figure in the carpet of Marston's work has gone on at least since T. S. Eliot's famous intuition: "We are aware, in short, with this as with Marston's other plays, that we have to do with a positive, powerful, and unique personality. His is an original variation of that deep discontent and rebelliousness so frequent among the Elizabethan dramatists. He is, like some of the greatest of them, occupied in saying something else than appears in the literal actions and characters whom he manipulates."[1] The findings have varied. Some, such as Samuel Schoenbaum, have found nothing at all and, indeed, deny that Marston was capable of such subtlety of art: "There is too much of the turbulent and irrational in Marston's temperament for writing to have served as anything more than a means of expressing the disordered fancies and half-acknowledged impulses that rankled within him."[2] This is clearly too extreme, but it illustrates the passion which Marston's unique combination of violent melodrama and comical satire can produce. More moderate are the remarks made by G. K. Hunter in his recent introduction to *Antonio and Mellida*. Professor Hunter feels that the key to the play is the process by which stoical principles are first set up and then undercut.[3] But this also seems to me too negative, too insubstantial a basis even for the first play, to say nothing of the second. I would suggest that there is a coherent center to Marston's work and that the basis of it is the evolving love-death tradition. Certainly, Marston does strange things with the material given him by the tradition, but he is not quite the emotional anarchist (indeed, near-lunatic) that Professor Schoenbaum portrays.

1. T. S. Eliot, "John Marston" (1934), in *Selected Essays* (3rd enlarged ed.; London: Faber and Faber Ltd., 1951), 229.
2. Samuel Schoenbaum, "The Precarious Balance of John Marston," *PMLA*, LXVII (December, 1952), 1077.
3. G. K. Hunter (ed.), "Introduction to John Marston," *Antonio and Mellida*, Regents Renaissance Drama Series (London: Edward Arnold Ltd., 1965), xiv.

For instance, if we look at Marston in terms of Shakespearean influence, a recurring pattern appears: the determined idealization of the romantic marriage. It is the ideal of the romantic marriage that provides the moral foundation of the debate on love and lust which is a central theme in *The Dutch Courtesan*. And the climax of *The Malcontent* is a dance of husbands and wives, this marital concord being one of the chief symbols of the restoration of order and happiness to Malevole's dukedom. The seeds of both these plays may be seen in the Antonio plays, which themselves turn on the central love story of Antonio and Mellida. Even the satire comes from a primarily romantic basis.

1. *Antonio and Mellida*

Most authorities seem agreed that Marston had no one direct source for *Antonio and Mellida*. Professor Hunter lists Lyly, Sidney, and Seneca as indirect or partial sources or influences but gives the bulk of the play to the author's own invention.[4] My own feeling is that *Romeo and Juliet* should be added to this list,[5] for once past the bizarre opening of *Antonio and Mellida* one can see a basic human situation very much like that in *Romeo and Juliet*. The motive force of the play is the urge of two young lovers—Antonio and Mellida—to come together; the blocking force, a festering hatred that long predates the opening of the play's action. The agent of this hatred is Piero, one of those now-familiar domineering fathers in whom (though he is drawn in caricature) we can see the features of Capulet, Castile, and Tancred. True to type, he thinks of marriage entirely in political or social terms, ignoring love as an element in it:

> Look sprightly, girl. What! Though Antonio's
>   drown'd,
> That peevish dotard on thy excellence,
> That hated issue of Andrugio,
> Yet may'st thou triumph in my victories;
> Since, lo, the highborn bloods of Italy
> Sue for thy seat of love.[6]   (II. i. 156–61)

4. *Ibid.*, x–xi.
5. There are a few verbal reminiscences: in one place a suggestive conjunction of night imagery and jewel imagery (II. i. 298–99); in another, a Marston character makes what—in its total lack of a relevant context—sounds very like an in-joking side glance at Juliet's age (V. ii. 117–18). As the discussion advances, others will be noted, but it seems safe, in any case, to assume that an alert young literary man like Marston was not likely to have missed the birth of a promising and sympathetic new dramatic genre.
6. John Marston, *Antonio and Mellida*, ed. G. K. Hunter, Regents Renaissance Drama Series (London: Edward Arnold Ltd., 1965). All quotes from the play are taken from this text.

When Mellida attempts to balk him by escaping with her lover, he invokes the clichés of filial duty and family honor in order to browbeat her into giving up her emotional life:

> Light and unduteous! Kneel not, peevish elf;
> Speak not, entreat not, shame unto my house,
> Curse to my honor.   (IV. i. 248–50)

Still, like Romeo and Juliet in similar circumstances, Antonio and Mellida are true to their devotion, and Marston allows this passion to be virtually the only thing in the play to survive without sarcastic undercutting. The lovers are at times ludicrous by realistic standards, but the very fact that Antonio would go to such extremes of disguise and behavior for his love is seen by Marston to be a measure of its potency. The same is true of Antonio's terrific depressions. These seem to be inspired by the Friary scene in which Romeo raves, falls to the ground and threatens suicide. Romeo was plainly being absurb there, yet his very absurdity indicated the strength of his love. The same is true of Antonio, though in Marston's hands the absurdity is multiplied:

> —What was't I said?
> O, this is naught but speckling melancholy.
> I have been—
> That Morpheus tender skinp—Cousin german—
> Bear with me good—
> Mellida—Clod upon clod thus fall.
> *Hell is beneath; yet Heaven is over all.*   (IV. i. 23–29)

These lines are strangely effective; they have the haunting quality of a real poetry of lunacy. Moments of joy are governed by the same naïve but energetic tendency towards poetic extremism. When the two lovers meet unexpectedly and in great danger, their ecstasy is such that Marston must fly out of his own language into an operatic passage in Italian (IV. i.191–208). Extremes of emotion require linguistic extremes, and so conscious is Marston of the energies of language that linguistic images invade even his characters' love exchanges: "we'll point our speech/With amorous kissing, kissing commas" (IV. i. 213–14). This predilection for highly forced language does limit Marston somewhat. He shows little consciousness of the power of the quiet moment or that restraint in speech that suggests emotion so strong as to be inexpressible even by gibberish.

The progress of Marston's plot is often as erratic and ill-controlled as his language, but again we find identifiable motifs from the early love tragedies.[7] For instance, we have noted often a submotif based on the fury aroused when one lover must look on while a rival courts his beloved. The intermingling of the passions of love, hatred, and jealousy usually results in scenes of high psychological tension. Marston does not quite achieve high tension, but his attempt at an eccentric equivalent falls into the same pattern as that of previous writers. In Act II. i Antonio enters disguised as an Amazon and is forced in this status to observe as Mellida is wooed by amorous princes of her father's choosing:

> MEL: I pray thee intrude not on a dead man's right.
> GAL: No; but the living's just possession,
>   Thy lips and love are mine.
> MEL: You ne'er took seisin on them yet; forbear!
>   There's not a vacant corner of my heart,
>   But all is fill'd with dead Antonio's loss.
>   (II. i. 170–75)

Mellida's love holds firm while the frustrated and jealous Antonio lets forth a burst of violent death imagery:

> O how impatience cramps my cracked veins,
> And cruddles thick my blood with boiling rage.
> O eyes, why leap you not like thunderbolts
> Or cannon bullets in my rivals' face?   (II. i. 196–99)

Marston drives home the love-death ironies of the situation immediately after by having Antonio (now alone with Mellida) envision himself as a lovelorn ghost:

> Dost not behold a ghost?
> Look, look where he stalks, wrapp'd up in clouds
>   of grief,
> Darting his soul upon thy wondering eyes.
> Look, he comes towards thee; see, he stretcheth out
> His wretched arms to gird thy loved waist
> With a most wish'd embrace.   (II. i. 259–64)

As usual, elements of absurdity dominate the expression, but in these patterns of love and death one can perceive an organizing principle behind the absurdity.

The same is true of the larger movements of plot. As the conflict between the lovers and those who would keep them apart develops, we find key

---

7. Marston's use of them may indeed be one possible bridge between *Romeo and Juliet* and those dramatists who show Marstonian influence—Webster and, more notably, Tourneur.

scenes being shaped around the old motifs: first around the Arranged Marriage and then—at the last—the Deadly Nuptial. The former motif unfolds after Mellida is captured while attempting to elope with Antonio. Her attempts to placate Piero prod him into a Capulet-like (even to echoing Capulet's phrasing: "Thank me no thankings, proud me no prouds" [III. v. 152]) insistence on a hasty, undesired marriage:

MEL: Good father—
PIER: Good me no goods. Seest thou that sprightly
      youth?
      Ere thou canst term tomorrow morning old
      Thou shalt call him thy husband, lord and love.
MEL: Ay me!
PIER: Blirt on your ay me's! Guard her safely hence.
      Drag her away. I'll be your guard tonight.
      Young prince, mount up your spirits and prepare
      To solemnize your nuptial's eve with pomp.
                                        (IV. i. 253–61)

This movement is then capped by a comic version of the Deadly Nuptial. As the wedding festival begins, a coffin is rolled in with Antonio inside. Antonio's father Andrugio brings the love-death themes into explicit relationship:

Villain, 'tis thou hast murder'd my son.
Thy unrelenting spirit, thou black dog,
That took'st no passion of his fatal love,
Hath forc'd him give his life untimely end.
                                        (V. ii. 203–206)

Like Old Capulet, Piero is moved to repentance and gestures of peacemaking: "O that my life, her love, my dearest blood,/Would but redeem one minute of his breath!" (V. ii. 207–208). At which instant, Marston turns the death scene of *Romeo and Juliet* upside down to produce a most remarkable happy ending:

ANT: I seize that breath. Stand not amaz'd, great
      states;
      I rise from death that never liv'd till now.
                                        (V. ii. 209–10)

In *Romeo and Juliet* the death of the lovers brings social concord; in *Antonio and Mellida* a feigned death brings concord (though as the sequel reveals, it is also feigned concord). To enjoy this kind of nonsense requires more of a sense of humor than most critics will allow into their criticism, so I shall not argue the merits or demerits of this denouement. What I do want to insist on finally is the shaping pressure of the Shakespearean transformation of the materials of the early love tragedies: *i.e.*, in the love-death contrasts, the conventions of Arranged Marriage and Deadly Nuptial, and the idea of the love marriage.

It is these elements that give the plot its meaning, and if one does not take this meaning into account (and most recent critics do not[8]), the important satirical elements of the play are divorced from the very context that gives them their meaning. For the real object of Marston's satirical lash also has its roots in the attitudes and conventions of the early romantic tragedies. This real object is courtly love, a form of love which Peele and Shakespeare had already begun to suggest was outmoded and destructive. Thus, as Marston accepts the Shakespearean ideal of the romantic marriage, he vigorously rejects its leading rival, the courtly flirtation, and does so by displaying it in as gross and unflattering light as possible.

The satiric plot centers on several main characters: a sophisticated lady of the court named (significantly, it seems to me) Rossaline;[9] her "servants" Alberto, Calistio, and Balurdo; and Feliche, the plain-speaking truth-teller. The scenes are interestingly placed, normally coming in conjunction with some moment of high emotional stress in the action concerning Antonio and Mellida. In this way Marston gives to his overall action some sense of complication, though it is the complication of implication rather than of actual plot. The scenes fix in some way upon the exaggerations of courtly love, its trivialization of emotion, its elevation of hollowness, its implacable transience—these qualities being counterpointed by the struggles of the true lovers to marry.

In a typical scene Rossaline enters, followed by courtiers, and makes an odorous jest on socks which is taken up immediately by the idiot Castilio as a sign of her virtue. His request to be her servant is a parody of the masochism which lurks in the Petrarchan relationship and the idea of service and the servant which is at the heart of the courtly tradition: "Ha, her wit stings, blisters, galls off the skin with the tart acrimony of her sharp

---

8. For instance, Hunter, "Introduction to *Antonio and Mellida*," xiii; John Peter, *Complaint and Satire in Early English Literature* (Oxford: Clarendon Press, 1956), 221–26; and Anthony Caputi, *John Marston, Satirist* (Ithaca, N.Y.: Cornell University Press, 1961), 129–43.

9. It seems pretty certain that Marston is here building on Shakespeare's shadow-character. One of Rossaline's defeated lovers sounds very like the pre-Juliet Romeo:

I'll go and breathe my woes unto the rocks,
And spend my grief upon the deafest seas.
I'll weep my passion to the senseless trees
And load most solitary air with plaints.
For woods, trees, sea or rocky Appenine
Is not so ruthless as my Rossaline.   (V. i. 59–64)

quickness. By sweetness, she is the very Pallas that flew out of Jupiter's brainpan. Delicious creature, vouchsafe me your service; by the purity of bounty I shall be proud of such bondage" (II. i. 60–64). Rossaline takes this up and pursues the issue: "I vouchsafe it; be my slave" (II. i. 65). Feliche marvels at her wretched taste, but her answer is brisk and—given the perverse logic of a rotten system—impossible to argue with:

> FEL: 'Slud, sweet beauty, will you deign him your service?
> ROS: O, your fool is your only servant.   (II. i. 69–70)

Marston has Rossaline jolly them along a bit farther; then he pours on the gall in a singularly vicious bit of action:

> ROS: Poh! [she spits] Servant, rub out my rheum; it soils the presence.
> CAS: By my wealthiest thought, you grace my shoe with an unmeasured honor; I will preserve the sole of it as a most sacred relic, for this service.
> ROS: I'll spit in thy mouth, and thou wilt, to grace thee.
>   (II. i. 81–86)

As if this has not already demonstrated his contempt for courtly service, Marston lets Feliche's Tourneur-like rhetoric flow:

> O that the stomach of this queasy age
> Digests or brooks such raw unseasoned gobs
> And vomits not them forth! O slavish sots!
> "Servant," quoth you? Foh! If a dog should crave
> And beg her service, he should have it straight.
> She'd give him favors too, to lick her feet,
> Or fetch her fan, or some such drudgery—
> A good dog's office, which these amorists
> Triumph of. 'Tis rare.   (II. i. 87–95)

The indictment of courtly love continues unabated, though without quite such liquid disgust, throughout the play.

Another flaw in the courtly scheme of love, the tendency towards impermanence and transience in love, is satirized in this exchange, pertinently juxtaposed with scenes of Mellida's unshakable fidelity:

> ROS: What, servant, ne'er a word, and I here, man?
>   I would shoot some speech forth to strike the time
>   With pleasing touch of amorous compliment.
>   Say, sweet, what keeps thy mind? what think'st
>   thou on?
> ALB: Nothing.
> ROS: What's that nothing?
> ALB: A woman's constancy.
> ROS: Good, why, would'st thou have us sluts, and never
>   shift the vesture of our thoughts? Away for shame!
>   (II. i. 205–13)

The verbal texture of the scene is not without interest. The obsessive repetition (as it is becoming at this point in the play) of the word *servant* gives a foretaste of the way in which this same word comes to stick in the throat of Thomas Middleton. The same is true of the whole idea of "amorous compliment," which suggests even more than frivolous pleasantry the vices of hypocrisy, flattery, and such related evils as political double-dealing and the debasement of language by the divorce of word from thought, fact, and true emotion. To sum up then, just as Shakespeare and Romeo bade goodbye to courtly love in favor of Juliet and the love marriage, so Marston does the same—by means of his satire—in favor of the triumph of the love marriage in *Antonio and Mellida*.

It should be clear now why I disagree with those critics who believe Marston to have no center and see his plays as the product of ununified strains, whether they be of aesthetic or psychological origins. With the idea of truth and permanence in love as the organizing figure in the carpet, the main plot may be seen to reinforce the satire with a positive moral and emotional foundation. This does not, by any means, answer all one's objections to Marston's work, but it provides a better basis for understanding that work than theories based on despair of doing precisely that.

2. *Antonio's Revenge*

The morality, the thematic design, and the action of *Antonio's Revenge* follow directly from the situation of *Antonio and Mellida*. But this time the analogue is *The Spanish Tragedy*. A love affair sets into motion a plot of vengeance against the lovers. Then a final vengeance is wreaked by those who had loved upon the one who had violated the bonds of love—in this case, Mellida's father Piero.

These love-death oppositions are, of course, drawn in bold Marstonian strokes. The action of the play begins with the following stage direction: *"Enter* Piero *unbrac'd, his arms bare, smear'd in blood, a poniard in one hand, bloody, and a torch in the other,* Strotzo *following him with a cord"*[10] (I. i.). Having just murdered Feliche (the plain-speaking satirist of the previous play) as well as his ancient rival Andrugio (Antonio's father), Piero is in those high spirits which characterize all his moments of greatest ferocity:

> One. Two. Lord, in two hours what a topless mount
> Of unpeer'd mischief have these hands cast up!
> I can scarce coop triumphing vengeance up
> From bursting forth in braggart passion.   (I. i. 9–12)

10. John Marston, *Antonio's Revenge*, ed. G. K. Hunter, Regents Renaissance Drama Series (Lincoln: University of Nebraska Press, 1965). All quotes from the play are taken from this text.

We also learn for the first time that the source of the rivalry between Piero and Andrugio was itself a matter of love, and thus are reminded at the outset of the inexplicable ways in which love and hate are linked together:

> We both were rivals in our May of blood
> Unto Maria, fair Ferrara's heir.
> He won the lady, to my honor's death,
> And from her sweets cropp'd this Antonio;
> For which I burn'd in inward swelt'ring hate,
> And fester'd rankling malice in my breast,
> Till I might belk revenge upon his eyes.   (I. i. 23–29)

Marston shows us in Piero a man for whom violence has become pleasure and hatred a variety of love. These qualities are so interchangeable in him that when he is told that the murdered Andrugio's duchess is coming "in private state," having heard erroneously that the two dukes were reconciled, his language provides a textbook case of the imagery of sadism—particularly in its total perversion of the idea of the love marriage, a perversion far worse—because so active—than the motives of the courtly moths who were the threat to Antonio and Mellida in the first play:

> O, let me swoon for joy! By heaven, I think
> I ha' said my prayers within this month at least,
> I am so boundless happy. Doth she come?
> By this warm reeking gore, I'll marry her.
> Look I not now like an inamorate?
> Poison the father, butcher the son, and marry the
>   mother; ha!   (I. i. 100–105)

The power of the writing here comes from the merging of love motive and death motive in the same mind and in a highly aggressive form. This verse technique gave the Elizabethan playwrights great psychological range and flexibility—particularly in expressing strange and unusual states of mind. Thus Marston here makes advanced if erratic use of evolving poetic techniques to suggest certain complexities of the human will for which Freud three hundred years later developed a discursive prose vocabulary.[11]

---

11. "As regards active algolagnia, sadism, the roots are easy to detect in the normal. The sexuality of most male human beings contains an element of aggressiveness—a desire to subjugate; the biological significance of it seems to lie in the need for overcoming the resistance of the sexual object by means other than the process of wooing. Thus sadism would correspond to an aggressive component of the sexual instinct which has become independent and exaggerated and, by displacement, has usurped the leading position." Sigmund Freud, "The Sexual Aberrations," *Three Essays on the Theory of Sexuality* (1905), trans. and ed. James Strachey, International Psycho-Analytical Library, No. 57 (Rev. ed.; London: Hogarth Press, 1962), 23–24.

It would be a mistake, however, to think there is nothing in Marston but perversions and violations of nature. There is, in fact, a very considerable amount of positive morality and moralizing. The problem is that the extreme forms of expression that give the sadistic passages their somewhat monstrous impact also make the moralizing so blatant that it is painful to read and difficult to take seriously. Who but Marston would have a mother greet her son as "Fair honor of a chaste and loyal bed" (I. ii. 161)? It is ridiculous; yet, as happens so often in Marston, absurdity seems to carry the serious ideas. In this case the theme of married love and family unity is given full amplification so as to form an obvious and deliberate contrast to Piero's hatred and destruction. Antonio's mother, Maria, is characterized as the perfect wife; her first question on arrival interweaves ideas of love and concord:

> Art thou assur'd the dukes are reconcil'd?
> Shall my womb's honor wed fair Mellida?
> Will heaven at length grant harbor to my head?
> Shall I once more clip my Andrugio,
> And wreathe my arms about Antonio's neck?   (I. ii. 12–16)

And her anticipation of the embraces of son and husband links the idea of love to that of procreation and the bond between the generations. Her "womb's honor" is to repeat the process of love and marriage that she went through, and by this union and the link of love between the dukes, private love will bring civil peace. She adds to this a long disquisition on wifely virtues:

> No, Lucio; my dear lord's wise and knows
> That tinsel glitter or rich purfled robes,
> Curled hairs hung full of sparkling carcanets,
> Are not the true adornments of a wife.
> So long as wives are faithful, modest, chaste,
> Wise lords affect them.   (I. ii. 46–51)

This kind of moralizing seems like rather an imposition on the audience, but its relevance is clear enough in context. Having in *Antonio and Mellida* satirized the courtly vices of glossiness and superficiality, Marston now provides a positive example to set against them. This whole thematic development rises to its highest pitch when son and mother meet:

> MARIA: Sweet son!
> ANT: Dear mother!
> MARIA: Fair honor of a chaste and loyal bed,
>   Thy father's beauty, thy sad mother's love,
>   Were I as powerful as the voice of fate,

Felicity complete should sweet thy state;
But all the blessings that a poor banish'd wretch
Can pour upon thy head, take, gentle son;
Live, gracious youth, to close thy mother's eyes,
Lov'd of thy parents till their latest hour.
How cheers my lord, thy father? O, sweet boy,
Part of him thus I clip, my dear, dear joy.

ANT: Madam, last night I kiss'd his princely hand,
And took a treasur'd blessing from his lips.

(I. ii. 159–72)

Thus, the opposition is set in the first act: Piero mingling love and death motives in sadistic vengeance; Antonio, Mellida, and Antonio's family embodying love and concord. The rest of the play is organized completely around the conflict between them.

First, Marston sets Piero's murder of Feliche and Mellida's alleged unchastity against Antonio's vision of Mellida as the spirit of love:

ANT: The heart of beauty, Mellida, appears.
See, look, the curtain stirs; shine, nature's
        pride,
Love's vital spirit, dear Antonio's bride!
The curtain's drawn, and the body of Feliche, *stabb'd thick
with wounds, appears hung up.*

. . . .

PIER: Who gives these ill-befitting attributes
Of chaste, unspotted, bright, to Mellida?
He lies as loud as thunder; she's unchaste,
Tainted, impure, black as the soul of hell.

(I. ii. 191–93, 200–203)

After this, Mellida is tried for fornication; during this trial, in circumstances of extraordinary irrationality and eeriness, the guiltless Mellida dies—another victim of the long line of vindictive Elizabethan father figures.

This is one triumph of death over love. The next begins with the murder of Antonio's father and moves from there in a direction which in certain ways foreshadows the theme of the death of love in *Hamlet*.[12] Piero takes on the role of a Claudius, wooing—as he said at the beginning he would do—the widow of the man he had murdered while pretending to love. The dumb show which begins Act III tells the story: "Piero *passeth through his guard and talks with* Maria *with seeming amorousness; she seemeth to reject his*

12. Though precedence here is a disputed subject. See Donald J. McGinn, "A New Date for *Antonio's Revenge,*" *PMLA*, LIII (March, 1938), 129–37.

suit, flies to the tomb, kneels and kisseth it. Piero *bribes* Nutriche *and* Lucio; *they go to her, seeming to solicit his suit. She riseth, offers to go out;* Piero *stayeth her, tears open his breast, embraceth and kisseth her, and so they go all out in state"* (III. i). By literal murder, Piero triumphed the way death did in *Romeo and Juliet* —from the outside. But this remarriage theme shows death working against the memory of the beloved, causing the death of love by internal subversion. Marston's prescience here is again impressive, for he introduces another theme new (and inimical) to the romantic tragedy—the natural weakness of woman:

GHOST OF ANDRUGIO:
Disloyal to our hym'neal rites,
What raging heat reigns in thy strumpet blood?
Hast thou so soon forgot Andrugio?
Are our love-bands so quickly canceled?
Where lives thy plighted faith unto this breast?
O weak Maria! Go to, calm thy fears;
I pardon thee, poor soul. O, shed no tears;
Thy sex is weak.   (III. ii. 63–70)

The ghost of Andrugio is most Jacobean in his railing and his theory of woman. But Marston has not gone completely over to sexual pessimism. Even before the ghost's visitation Maria had shown strong signs that her love for her dead husband still had some life, as this speech indicates:

O thou cold widow-bed, sometime thrice blest
By the warm pressure of my sleeping lord,
Open thy leaves, and whilst on thee I tread
Groan out, "Alas, my dear Andrugio's dead!"   (III. ii. 58–61)

With the ghost's words her redemption is complete; womankind is reestablished as an object of reverence, and Antonio's mad, Hamlet-like query "Why lives that mother?" (III. ii. 85) is answered with gentleness. Gentleness, that is, between members of the regrouped family: for it is in Act III that the trend of the play shifts, with those people whose loves have been violated now turning—like new Bel-imperias and Hieronimos—on those who have caused their woe.

The final problem is that of Antonio's vengeance and the denouement itself, for these have been touchy spots in virtually all Marston criticism. I quote Samuel Schoenbaum's account at length because it is vividly written and states most of the relevant issues from an ethical point of view:

At the climax Piero is bound and his tongue plucked. A dish is opened, revealing the severed limbs of his son, a "prettie tender childe" sacrificed by Antonio for the purpose of tormenting Piero. The revengers taunt the duke, call him foul names, stab him one by one, and, finally, run all at once upon him with drawn rapiers. The scene owes much to Seneca, but exceeds even the Roman in violence. It is noteworthy that the author's sympathies lie entirely with the revengers; there is no suggestion that they have proceeded beyond the proper limits of retribution. After the bloody interlude has ended, the avengers clamor for recognition, until all finally agree that they are equally worthy of "the glorie of the deede." They are congratulated and offered generous rewards, but choose to

> live inclos'd
> In holy verge of some religious order,
> Most constant votaries.   (V. vi. p. 131)

This odd conclusion, so contrary to the conventional denouement, wherein the contaminated revenger must also perish, shows the playwright identifying himself with the forces of violence, enjoying vicariously the piling up of horrors.[13]

Without trying to excuse Marston, I would at least try to account for what he does in terms of a pattern which we have seen before in these tragedies of love and death: a theory of artistic symmetry based on the symmetry of powerful emotions, the same process which results in so many Deadly Nuptial endings in plays of love and death.

The key to this is that terrifying glimpse into the abyss of elemental human nature, Seneca's *Thyestes*. The opening dialogue of Seneca's play, between Atreus and the Attendant, opposes what are in essence two levels of civilization. Atreus represents the primeval and emotional one, the one in which a crime or a wrong which raises the emotion of hatred must be assuaged by a vengeance that relieves the emotion. Repression of this personal emotion is, of course, a necessary stage in the development of what we know as civilization and the rule of law, for justice by law is the depersonalization and de-emotionalization of the original impulse of vengeance. It is this point of view which the Attendant represents.

Atreus, however—being a king—considers himself above law and the ordinary pieties. Thus Seneca can focus almost totally on the unrestrained operation of the emotions. The pattern becomes clear quickly. Atreus has been the victim of a crime which destroyed the family bond, first because it was committed by his brother, and second because his wife assisted. The fact that his wife assisted adds a strong element of sexual violation and betrayal to the pattern. The subversion of virtually every bond that made Atreus a man and a king reduces him to wandering impotence: "Through-

---

13. Schoenbaum, "Precarious Balance," 1071–72.

out my kingdom have I wandered, a trembling exile; . . . my wife seduced, our pledge of empire broken, my house impaired, my offspring dubious —"[14] (237–40). So great and deep then are the offenses against Atreus—as he sees them—that they stir to life emotions that lie too deep for depersonalized justice to satisfy.

It was an insight of the old mythmakers and of Seneca to see that without the restraint of law, the emotion of hate—to find satisfaction—turns to vengeance in kind. In hate as in art, man loves symmetry. The motto is always an eye for an eye, never an eye for an ear. Thus, the voice of the law seeks to divert Atreus onto a clean, depersonalized punishment, but Atreus' emotions are in control, and these seek a punishment that is symbolically and emotionally appropriate to the original violation. This the worried Attendant quickly perceives: "What strange design does thy mad soul intend?" (254). Atreus' strange design demands that just as the original offense combined the sexual, familial, and social, so must the revenge. Thus, Atreus forces Thyestes to devour his own sons—the products of his loins—and thus negates his potency. This brutal triumph does, moreover, restore Atreus' own manhood: "Now do I believe my children are my own, now may I trust once more that my marriage-bed is pure" (1098–99). The point is that the play's structure and the incidents which make up its texture run parallel to the emotions involved. In the beginning of *Thyestes*, as in the third act of *Antonio's Revenge*, we have the brooding over a crime; the ends of both plays show that brooding finished. In both cases, the crime was one involving sexuality; consequently the vengeance does as well. The combination of cruelty and sexuality—of love motive and death motive—produces in both plays a conclusion of the grossest kind of sadism.

It is plain, I think, that Marston took not only the Thyestean banquet from Seneca but also the whole concept of extreme emotional symmetry on which it is based. Atreus, being violated in his bed, succeeds in a kind of crypto-rape, and this emotional and formal symmetry shocks because the design came out of and was aimed directly at the emotions. Antonio has been a victim of similar violations. His Thyestes, Piero, has violated, or tried to violate, with a great show of pleasure, virtually every sexual, love, or family bond with which Antonio is associated. He has murdered Antonio's father, wooed Antonio's mother, caused the disgrace and death of

14. Seneca, *Thyestes*, in *Tragedies*, trans. Frank Justus Miller, Vol. II, Loeb Classical Library (Rev. ed.; London: William Heinemann, 1929). Line numbers refer to the parallel Latin text.

Antonio's betrothed. Such a close student of the Roman tragedian as Marston would have seen in Piero a man for whom depersonalized justice was too good. Therefore he opts for emotional involvement, and the ironic, emotionally charged symmetry demanded by this involvement means not only that Piero must die but that he must suffer some sort of sexual-familial violation himself. Obviously the result is not justice, but Marston has shown how emotionally involved he himself was in the idea of the bond of love, and he has shown how much he had learned from Seneca on how to use extreme manifestations of the love-death motifs in an attempt to strike his audience at its deepest level of terror. The imbalance here, or the unease we feel in this conclusion, comes not so much from our pique at not seeing the tainted revengers get their own but from the horror of seeing the death motive given still one more triumph and given it by men in the name of love.

Summary

A few summary points will put these early plays in perspective and prepare the ground for the more complex variants on love-death themes to follow.

First of all: the basic theme is the attempt to establish love against various other contenders as a serious facet of adult life. The array of forces militating against it includes such things as family pride, economic or social interest, political Machiavellianism, jealousy, hatred, sexual cynicism, courtly superficiality, paternal domination and plain, unadorned, transient lust—the emotional emptiness of an Amnon.

Plots, therefore, tend to begin with the meeting of an attractive male and female. They proceed by showing the alchemy of love which binds the lovers and by tracing the progress of their attempts to form their own world and own union. In these early plots the forces against love tend to be external to the lovers themselves—whether they be the Capulet-Montague feud, the pressure of Spanish-Portuguese politics, or the rage of a maddened father. Thus, when death comes to the lovers, it comes in a way that leaves their love untarnished and vital. The archetypal example is *Romeo and Juliet*, but even in those plays in which love becomes involved with the death motive (as in *The Spanish Tragedy* and *Antonio's Revenge*) it happens in such a way—that is, the lovers must be victims before becoming revengers—as to keep a certain degree of sympathy on their side. In *The Spanish Tragedy* the attempt at this is obvious and successful; in *Antonio's Revenge* the attempt is even more obvious, but it is less successful. This foreshadows the blurring of the love and death motives which really begins with the psychological torment of Hamlet.

Organizing these various plots are certain repeated motifs: the Enforced Marriage and Deadly Nuptial being the central ones. These remain in use throughout the Jacobean period, despite the varied uses to which they are put. This is primarily because both bring love (Marriage . . . Nuptial) and death (Enforced . . . Deadly) into significant relationship.

Of the various character types which occur in these plays, five are of special importance and persist—with some variation of role—throughout Elizabethan-Jacobean love tragedy. On the side of love, the young man and the young woman: Gismond and Guishard, Bel-imperia and Horatio, Romeo and Juliet. They are characterized in terms of youth, beauty, and natural goodness. In them, sexual love is a force for fertility and life. Opposed to them are the old father, the rival lover, and the cynic. The rival lover and the father are interesting because in them animus and violence arise out of love for the girl. In this mixture of love and death motives are the seeds of many complex later plays. The sexual cynic is in these early plays usually a peripheral character. He may be—like Mercutio—on the side of the angels despite himself. More often, though, he foreshadows a type of character that becomes increasingly prominent with *Hamlet* and after; the central early example is Kyd's Lorenzo. He exemplifies the pure death motive, for he has no love for anyone but himself.

The language of love and the language of death are easily distinguished in these early plays. The language of love has tenderness,

> Bring ye to me the mother of the babe,
> That I may wipe the tears from off her face,
>
> (*D & B*, 708–709)

joy,

> O she doth teach the torches to burn bright!
>
> (*R & J*, I. v. 44)

generosity,

> I'll give thee tackling made of rivelled gold,
> Wound on the barks of odoriferous trees,
>
> (*Dido*, III. i. 115–16)

beauty,

> And when we whisper, then the stars fall down
> To be partakers of our honey talk.
>
> (*Dido*, IV. iv. 53–54)

The language of death is poisonously ironic,

> Ay, thus, and thus, these are the fruits of love.
>
> (*ST*, II. iv. 55)

shallow,

> Then from her heart thy looks shall be reliev'd,
> And thou shalt joy her as thy soul desires.
>
> (*D & B*, 262–63)

self-regarding,

> How now, wife?
> Have you delivered to her our decree?
>
> (*R & J*, III. v. 137–38)

violent,

> His slaughter and her teres, her sorrow and his blood
> shall to my rancorous rage supplie delitefull foode.
>
> (*Gismond*, IV. ii. 119–20)

Both tend towards images of nature: one of nature blooming and bearing fruit, the other of corruption and rot. For the lovers, the central mythic archetype is Eden, and in these early plays, at any rate, it is an Eden untouched by betrayal.

The moral weighting of the opposing forces of love and death in these early plays is clear: love equals good; the forces against it are all fallings off from the good. The Elizabethan love tragedian obviously felt not only that there should be no essential conflict between eros and society but that a society was corrupt to the extent that it obstructed its own regeneration through love.

Two final points: special attention is due the image of woman and the problem of time. For male writers concerning themselves with the nature and value of love the center obviously must be woman. To give high value to woman on the basis of her beauty and capacity for love is to make the distinctively romantic gesture, and it is a gesture which makes love a mode of spiritual elevation as well as physical pleasure. This was the typical response of these early dramatists, obviously including Shakespeare, whose Juliet is the central manifestation of this romantic faith. But—as succeeding chapters will show—a shift occurs after 1600; new images gain potency, those of Gertrude and Cressida.

Throughout Renaissance literature time is the enemy. In these early plays there are two stratagems with which love defeats it; both involve making love permanent. The first is to do as Gismond, Bel-imperia, Juliet, and Mellida do—end life when love is ended. Suicide becomes a paradoxical gesture of symbolic affirmation; it affirms the creation of a value in life which arises out of its natural conditions yet succeeds in freeing itself from the depredations of time.

The desire to defeat time is also, it seems to me, the heart of the symbolic attraction of the love marriage. It attempts to give coherent form to the union of pleasure and permanence. The private pleasures of love had been sung by poets for as long as poetry has existed, but the Renaissance attempted to pull the threads of life together—making duty, social organization, and private fulfillment all functions of the same bond. Without some appreciation of the large symbolic functions of love and the love marriage these early plays will always threaten to seem a bit lightweight and the great dramas of adultery and betrayal a bit extravagant. But it is not *merely* doting love, sexual intrigue, or domestic tribulations that these men write about; their true concerns are the very sources of good and ill in the natural life of human beings.

Part II

Shakespeare and the Death of Love

7   Hamlet

If the distinctive feature of the treatment of love in the Elizabethan plays of love and death was the fiery and passionate strength and goodness of love —its absolute incorruptibility—then the distinctive trait of those plays which follow in the seventeenth century is very much the opposite, a concentration on the problem of corruptibility. Instead of the death of the lovers, one has the decay and death of love. Instead of stories of the union of lovers, one has deeply pessimistic stories of lust, betrayal, and adultery. This is not to say that the older romantic materials are ignored, but they are used throughout the great tragedies of Shakespeare's middle period and in the works of many Jacobean writers with an acute sense of the fragility of human bonds and the romantic ideal of human love. Romantic and anti-romantic or disillusioned-romantic materials and attitudes come to coexist and complicate each other. This complication is one of the major sources of the distinctive greatness of seventeenth-century tragedy.

The pivotal play, it seems to me, is *Hamlet*, which I see as—not just a play about revenge—but a deliberate piece of negative analysis exercised on the same naïve romantic tradition which Shakespeare himself only five years before had brought to perfection.

1.

One of the oddities of *Hamlet* about which there has been little comment is the presence—in embryo—of another *Romeo and Juliet*. By the time the play opens the embryo is already very near abortion, but it does not die until the scene in which Ophelia describes Hamlet's coming to see her. Polonius asks "What said he?" But the point is that Hamlet had said nothing:

> He took me by the wrist, and held me hard,
> Then goes he to the length of all his arm,

And with his other hand thus o'er his brow,
He falls to such perusal of my face
As a' would draw it. Long stayed he so,
At last, a little shaking of mine arm,
And thrice his head thus waving up and down,
He raised a sigh so piteous and profound
As it did seem to shatter all his bulk,
And end his being; . . .   (II. i. 84–93)

Everywhere else Hamlet is full of wild and whirling words. Indeed, such words make up a large portion of his conscious disguise, his antic disposition. But here his silence itself speaks profoundly of a loss greater than words can express. The peculiar, urgent blankness of his withdrawal marks the end of what in a comedy or a romantic tragedy of love would have been a movement towards union in a powerful, protecting love between two young heroes.

There are fossil remains of this motif scattered all through the first two acts of *Hamlet*. At its center are the lovers themselves: Hamlet, a kind of older Romeo who has visited his Juliet often, written love notes and love poetry:

> 'Doubt thou the stars are fire,
>   Doubt that the sun doth move,
>   Doubt truth to be a liar,
>   But never doubt I love.
> O dear Ophelia, I am ill at these numbers, I have not art to reckon my
> groans, but that I love thee best, O most best, believe it. Adieu.
>   Thine evermore, most dear lady, whilst
>   this machine is to him, HAMLET.'
>   (II. ii. 116–24)

and who, according to Ophelia, "hath importuned [her] with love/In honourable fashion" (I. iii. 110–11). This is to say, he has wooed her with an eye to marriage, an event that much later in the play Gertrude remembers hoping for.

As usual, the lovers are set in opposition to the girl's male relations, father and brother. The father Polonius has often been discussed in terms ranging from typical court counselor to garrulous fool. He is all these things. But burrowing to the kernel we may see in him a kind of old Capulet. He is tetchy and impatient when crossed even mildly by his daughter:

OPH: My lord, he hath importuned me with love
        In honourable fashion.
POL: Ay, fashion you may call it, go to, go to.
                                          (I. iii. 110–12)

He distrusts the youthful flow of spirits, youth's passionate ideas of love:

> Ay, springes to catch woodcocks. I do know
> When the blood burns, how prodigal the soul
> Lends the tongue vows.   (I. iii. 115–17)

His meddling is touched with a strong tincture of self-regard: "You do not understand yourself so clearly/As it behooves my daughter and your honour" (I. iii. 96–97). He has no hesitation about enforcing his obstructive will on her.

> I would not in plain terms from this time forth
> Have you so slander any moment leisure
> As to give words or talk with the Lord Hamlet.
> Look to't I charge you, come your ways.   (I. iii. 132–35)

Laertes (again typically) is closely identified with the father's point of view:

> Then weigh what loss your honour may sustain
> If with too credent ear you list his songs,
> Or lose your heart, or your chaste treasure open
> To his unmast'red importunity.
> Fear it Ophelia, fear it my dear sister, . . .   (I. iii. 29–33)

Here, of course, Laertes is all good nature. But later, in his confrontation with his sister's lover in the grave and in his violent desire for vengeance, the Tybalt strain in him shows itself clearly.

There is a significant difference between the romantic pattern here and in *Romeo and Juliet*, however, and it is symptomatic of the play's whole outlook—the failure of the female lover to assert herself strongly in the cause of love. Ophelia, as she plays her version of Juliet, not only would fain dwell on form but does in fact do so. When her father orders her to refuse Hamlet's visits, she says "I will obey," most un-Juliet-like. This is before Hamlet's final descent into his manic role; afterwards it is too late to reverse the action, but in any case she goes along still further with the representatives of the older generation by surrendering love-letters and acting as the bait of falsehood to catch the carp of truth. Although she does this to try to save Hamlet from madness, the fact remains that she lets herself be used and thus shows a predilection for operating within repressive conventions that suits ill with the development of love.

I do not mean to reduce the more complex characters of *Hamlet* to the level of the simpler play and say they are nothing more. Nor am I trying to make value judgements by invidious comparisons between Juliet and Ophelia. My point is that although Shakespeare has in *Hamlet* made a new equation, he began with the same numbers: youth in love set against an older generation that makes fruition of that love impossible.

2.

Romeo and Juliet belongs to the Shakespeare of 1595; *Hamlet* to the Shakespeare of 1600–1602. In between come the great nondramatic sonnets. So deeply are these concerned with what woman is and what sexuality and love are that they provide an indispensable bridge between the two stages of Shakespeare's dramatic treatment of these subjects. We recall, for instance, the mutuality, the interchange of images and emotions which gave the sonnet that was the highlight of the banquet scene in *Romeo and Juliet* its great and distinctive life:

ROM: If I profane with my unworthiest hand
      This holy shrine, the gentle sin[1] is this:
      My lips, two blushing pilgrims, ready stand
      To smooth that rough touch with a tender kiss.
JUL: Good pilgrim, you do wrong your hand too much,
      Which mannerly devotion shows in this:
      For saints have hands that pilgrims' hands do
            touch,
      And palm to palm is holy palmers' kiss.
ROM: Have not saints lips, and holy palmers too?
JUL: Ay, pilgrim, lips that they must use in prayer.
ROM: O then, dear saint, let lips do what hands do,
      They pray: grant thou, lest faith turn to despair.
JUL: Saints do not move, though grant for prayers' sake.
ROM: Then move not,while my prayer's effect I take.
                                          (I. v. 93–106)

This was a shift in the sonnet form away from one-sidedness, from the loneliness of the love that the sonnet normally expressed.

In the later Shakespearean sonnet sequence this mutuality is again lost, and the loss goes far beyond just the change from dramatic to lyric forms. Not only has the speaker, the lover, been split away from the object of love but two objects of love—one male, one female—have replaced the more usual single beloved. More important, however, is the split in the idea of love which this implies. Where once there was one ideal—a union of spiritual and physical love—there are now two, the first asexual and intended for a fellow male:

Let me not to the marriage of true minds
Admit impediments: love is not love

1. See note 8, Chapter V.

Which alters when it alteration finds,
Or bends with the remover to remove.
Oh no! it is an ever-fixèd mark
That looks on tempests and is never shaken;
It is the star to every wandering bark,
Whose worth's unknown although his height be taken.
Love's not Time's fool, though rosy lips and cheeks
Within his bending sickle's compass come;
Love alters not with his brief hours and weeks,
But bears it out even to the edge of doom.
    If this be error and upon me prov'd,
    I never writ, nor no man ever lov'd.   (Sonnet 116)[2]

the second sexual, its object the woman:

Theexpense of spirit in a waste of shame
Is lust in action; and till action, lust
Is perjur'd, murderous, bloody, full of blame,
Savage, extreme, rude, cruel, not to trust;
Enjoy'd no sooner but despisèd straight;
Past reason hunted; and no sooner had,
Past reason hated, as a swallow'd bait
On purpose laid to make the taker mad,—
Mad in pursuit, and in possession so;
Had, having, and in quest to have, extreme;
A bliss in proof; and prov'd, a very woe;
Before, a joy propos'd; behind, a dream.
    All this the world well knows; yet none knows well
    To shun the heaven that leads men to this hell.
                                               (Sonnet 129)

Male friendship has thus gathered to itself all the angelic implications and spiritual beauties that once attended the love of Romeo and Juliet. Love for woman has become nothing more than a lust of the blood and permission of the will and woman herself a poisoning, maddening bait. The beautiful, healing, potentially fruitful synthesis of *Romeo and Juliet* is blown apart into morbid sexual disgust on one hand and a sexually chaste but still often morbid homoeroticism on the other.

    At the heart of this new antiromantic formulation are, it seems to me, three things: the idea of the impermanence of the sexual act, the idea that female love is no more permanent than sexual pleasure, and the idea that sexuality is itself not merely corrupt but corrupting. To these, in some of the

2. Quotations from Shakespeare's sonnets are from the following edition: *Shakespeare's Sonnets*, ed. W. G. Ingram and Theodore Redpath (London: University of London Press Ltd., 1964).

sonnets, one should add the presence of a certain mental climate that seems to be the inevitable consequence of such ideas—doubt, suspicion, jealousy, despair:

> Two loves I have, of comfort and despair,
> Which like two spirits do suggest me still:
> The better angel is a man right fair,
> The worser spirit a woman colour'd ill.
> To win me soon to hell, my female evil
> Tempteth my better angel from my side,
> And would corrupt my saint to be a devil,
> Wooing his purity with her foul pride.
> And whether that my angel be turn'd fiend
> Suspect I may, yet not directly tell;
> But being both from me, both to each friend,
> I guess one angel in another's hell:
>> Yet this shall I ne'er know, but live in doubt
>> Till my bad angel fire my good one out.   (Sonnet 144)

The emotional facts of the sonnets—disgust with woman, exaltation of the spiritual bond between man and man—and the moods attaching to these are also the facts and the moods of *Hamlet*. It is in large measure these complications that make it more than just another revenge play, though they are by no means to be separated from the revenge theme or revenge structure.

3.

Romeo and Juliet began with jesting on themes of love and death. In *Hamlet* the first emphasis is thrown on death, with the eerie appearance of the tormented ghost. But the jests come when we first meet Hamlet:

> A little more than kin, and less than kind.
> . . . .
> Not so, my lord, I am too much in the 'son.'
> . . . .
> Thrift, thrift, Horatio, the funeral baked meats
> Did coldly furnish forth the marriage tables.
>> (I. ii. 65, 67, 180–81)

Irony is Hamlet's public manner of dealing with a situation too oppressive to be borne quietly, a situation—the father dead, mother remarried to uncle within less than two months—that is itself a giant love-death irony. It is one so peculiar that even Claudius' serious state speech on the subject could be read almost as a joke:

> Therefore our sometime sister, now our queen,
> Th'imperial jointress to this warlike state,

> Have we as 'twere with a defeated joy,
> With an auspicious, and a dropping eye,
> With mirth in funeral, and with dirge in marriage,
> In equal scale weighing delight and dole,
> Taken to wife: . . .   (I. ii. 8–14)

The difference between the two young heroes' situation is that Romeo, once he had seen Juliet, could dissociate himself from the death motive psychologically and metaphorically. Love and death became isolated from each other, each compartmented in images of light against dark, white against black, stars against a dark sky. The death motive embodied in the feud was isolated against the young lovers, and their deaths paradoxically put their love out of death's reach.

For Hamlet no such dissociation is possible; he is the one who must do the ironical love-death jesting, and he cannot cut himself off from himself the way Romeo dissociates himself from the aggressive mingling of love and death images in the language of characters like Gregory and Sampson. It is as if Hamlet were permanently in a state like that of Romeo just before he kills Tybalt. The war of love against death is trapped within his own mind just the way the two are mingled symbolically in the new marriage. Claudius murders for love; Gertrude hastily marries in spite of her seeming love for her dead husband. In both their cases betrayal poisons the very emotional situation that it was intended to forward. The tangle of emotions in the older generation is projected into Hamlet, and in such a way that no dissociation from it is possible. How confused the situation is may be seen in Hamlet's anguished answer to the ghost's first revelation of murder:

> Haste me to know't, that I with wings as swift
> As meditation or the thoughts of love,
> May sweep to my revenge.   (I. v. 29–31)

Meditation and the thoughts of love are the very things that impede his sweep to revenge.

The source of Hamlet's confusion and therefore of many of the central tensions of the play may be sought first in his relation to his father, his idea of what his father was, and the idea of woman that the two of them come to share. The linking of names seems to suggest a strong link of character between the two Hamlets, and this is indeed what we find. Hamlet idealizes his father as a devoted husband:

> . . . so loving to my mother,
> That he might not beteem the winds of heaven
> Visit her face too roughly— . . .
>
>   (I. ii. 140–42)

Hamlet the father, we note, does the same for himself:

> O Hamlet, what a falling-off was there!
> From me whose love was of that dignity,
> That it went hand in hand even with the vow
> I made to her in marriage, and to decline
> Upon a wretch whose natural gifts were poor
> To those of mine; . . .   (I. v. 47–52)

Then he generalizes from the same premise, and his self-idealization becomes even more pronounced:

> But virtue, as it never will be moved,
> Though lewdness court it in a shape of heaven,
> So lust, though to a radiant angel linked,
> Will sate itself in a celestial bed
> And prey on garbage.   (I. v. 53–57)

The tendency in both men is to see the father as something out of the world, angelic, beautiful, perfect; the brother Claudius as very much a part of bestial nature—a satyr, an adulterate beast, a serpent, even garbage, something below the beasts.

More complicated and more important are the implications of the images for Gertrude. For Hamlet's melancholia, his disgust with the world, had begun well before the ghost's arrival. The true story of the murder was already anticipated in Hamlet's "prophetic soul" because the quick marriage of his mother was to him a symbolic murder (The Player Queen says as much: "A second time I kill my husband dead,/When second husband kisses me in bed" [III. ii. 183–84]). To think in terms of symbols and symbolic actions is, of course, typical of Shakespeare's characters. Gertrude's incest was, after all, more symbolic than physical as (it seems to me) was her adultery.[3] In any case, both the ghost and Hamlet see the unfaithful Gertrude in terms of the same symbolic story: the fall of Eve. In terms of this myth, Claudius becomes the deadly, phallic, seducing serpent in the orchard:

> 'Tis given out, that sleeping in my orchard,
> A serpent stung me, so the whole ear of Denmark
> Is by a forgéd process of my death
> Rankly abused: but know, thou noble youth,
> The serpent that did sting thy father's life
> Now wears his crown.   (I. v. 35–40)

The ghost plainly means us to take the cause of the seduction which followed hard on the murder to be Claudius' sexual appeal, his plain animal attractiveness:

3. For the case against Gertrude, see J. Dover Wilson, *What Happens in Hamlet* (3rd ed.; Cambridge: University Press, 1951), 292–94.

> Ay, that incestuous, that adulterate beast,
> With witchcraft of his wit, with traitorous gifts,
> O wicked wit and gifts, that have the power
> So to seduce; won to his shameful lust
> The will of my most seeming-virtuous queen;
> O Hamlet, what a falling-off was there!   (I. v. 42–47)

This kind of sexual interpretation of the fall is, of course, quite ancient. Henry Kraus has shown that a wide range of just such interpretations may be found in the art[4] of medieval Europe, noting particularly that often these representations swayed deeply towards a profound disgust for sexuality itself: "Surely it is not without meaning that the sculptured presentation of the Vice of Unchastity which one finds on so many church facades of the twelfth century should invariably be a woman, suffering eternally in Hell. She is usually shown in a revolting posture, her naked body entwined by serpents which feed on her breasts and sexual organs. Sometimes, too, she is accompanied by the Devil, who assumes an intimate relationship to her."[5] But the real significance of the mythologizing of Gertrude into Eve

---

4. For the prose foundations behind this art, see Roland M. Frye, "The Teachings of Classical Puritanism on Conjugal Love," in *On Milton's Poetry*, ed. Arnold Stein (Greenwich, Conn.: Fawcett Publications, Inc., 1970):

> Robert Briffault in his exhaustive study *The Mothers* points out that actual life in the middle ages was far from representative of the teachings of the church, but that in the official teachings "the sexual aspects of holiness came to eclipse all other issues, and morality came to mean, what it has ever since connoted in European tradition, sexual purity," while G. E. Howard writes that marriage was accepted "under protest," as it were, and "usually with a tone of apology or depreciation which is itself very suggestive of the pervading trend of the ascetic mind." This tradition was early established and grew in importance. Ambrose said that "married people ought to blush at the state in which they are living," and maintained that to alter the state of virginity in which man was created and into which he was born was to deface the work of the Creator, while according to Jerome it was the prostitution of the members of Christ. Origen castrated himself, while Clement of Alexandria said that "every woman ought to be filled with shame at the thought that she is a woman." Briffault summarizes the developments as follows:
>
>> Bishop Gregory of Nyssa held that Adam and Eve had at first been created sexless, and that the phrase "male and female created He them" referred to a subsequent act necessitated by Adam's disobedience; had not this taken place the human race would have been propagated by some harmless mode of vegetation. The view was endorsed by John of Damascus. The logical consequences of the advocacy of virginity were faced without hesitation; both Ambrose and Tertullian declared that the extinction of the human race was preferable to its propagation by sexual intercourse.
>
> The widespread medieval idealization of virginity is the continuation of these and similar views.   (pp. 100–101)

5. Henry Kraus, *The Living Theatre of Medieval Art* (London: Thames and Hudson, 1967), 42.

and Claudius into the seducer is that the emotions generated in these scenes spread away from the single case of Gertrude to taint all women and by extension—since we are all men of woman born—everyone. When Hamlet *pere* says

> So lust, though to a radiant angel linked,
> Will sate itself in a celestial bed
> And prey on garbage   (I. v. 55–57)

he is moving into the area of generalization, the area of iconography and symbol. It is woman who is Lust, man who is a "radiant angel." Preying on garbage is the metaphor for sexuality. Garbage, indeed, is the body itself, I should say. For to hate sexuality is to hate whatever is animal in humanity. When Hamlet says, "O, that this too too sullied flesh would melt" (I. ii. 129), he is expressing a transcendent urge not out of keeping with the idea of the body as garbage. And certainly the ghost's terrible description of the poison at work is an expression of nausea in the face of human corruption:

> And with a sudden vigour it doth posset
> And curd, like eager droppings into milk,
> The thin and wholesome blood; so did it mine,
> And a most instant tetter barked about
> Most lazar-like with vile and loathsome crust
> All my smooth body. . . .   (I. v. 68–73)

Sexuality and the human body are therefore linked with female duplicity and betrayal. The two Hamlets—betrayed by the woman—make a psychological regression which is itself a kind of death. From Renaissance humanism, they backstep together into a medieval monastic horror of woman. The following description from Kraus's fascinating chapter on "Eve and Mary: Conflicting Images of Medieval Woman" could just as easily apply to the viewpoint that the older Hamlet expresses and the younger one feels: "This viewpoint regarded woman as the Daughter of Eve and by that descent still primarily responsible for man's fall. As St. Bernard expressed it in sermons addressed to his 'sons' at Clairvaux, Eve was 'the original cause of all evil, whose disgrace has come down to all other women.'" [6]

But what are the practical implications of such generalizing? One is that Hamlet becomes—out of love for his father and against his own inclinations—literally and symbolically, an agent of death. [7] He is an agent of

6. *Ibid*. Kraus quotes Saint Bernard, *Textes choises et présentés par Étienne Gilson* (Paris: Plon, 1949), 65.
7. My analysis here is very similar to that in the first part of G. Wilson Knight's well-known essay, "The Embassy of Death: An Essay on *Hamlet*," in *The Wheel of Fire*, University Paperbacks (London: Methuen & Co. Ltd., 1965; reprint of 4th revised, enlarged edition, 1949), 17–30. We differ radically on what we make of this analysis, however.

death on the literal level quite simply because his personal intent is to kill, and the facts of the plot show him succeeding. On the symbolic level, however, the case is more subtle. Partly it comes from his fanatical self-identification with his father:

> Remember thee?
> Yea, from the table of my memory
> I'll wipe away all trivial fond records,
> All saws of books, all forms, all pressures past
> That youth and observation copied there,
> And thy commandment all alone shall live
> Within the book and volume of my brain,
> Unmixed with baser matter—yes by heaven!   (I. v. 97–104)

partly from his own patently obvious death wish: "Or that the Everlasting had not fixed/His canon 'gainst self-slaughter" (I. ii. 131–32), but mainly (and in a sense summing up all of these) it is because he has turned away from woman because she betrays; by this act, away from sexuality because it corrupts into bestiality; by this away from procreation itself and therefore physical life. He has turned from love which binds men together to vow himself to hatred—self-poisoning, claustrophobic to the spirit, in every way destructive.

In the progress of the play this syndrome finds expression with considerable frequency and with a wit and—at other times—despair and horror that is metaphysical in both a literary sense and a philosophical one. The scene with Ophelia usually referred to as the nunnery scene is one in which the wit of despair carries in it the fruit of bitter and gloomy speculations on the nature of man. In this scene Ophelia is both person and—for Hamlet—living symbol. It is in this latter aspect that I would treat her right now, saving the other aspect for the next section.

The proper introduction to Hamlet's remarks to Ophelia is his earlier exchange with Polonius. There he links procreation to death: "For if the sun breed maggots in a dead dog, being a good kissing carrion. . . . have you a daughter?" (II. ii. 181–82); and then to Ophelia herself as representative of virgin womanhood: "Let her not walk i'th'sun. Conception is a blessing, but as your daughter may conceive, friend look to't" (II. ii. 184–86). Nothing could more thoroughly signify the collapse of the humanist ideal of man than this rejection of birth itself, this metaphoric identification of man (once to Hamlet "the paragon of animals") with the product of corruption. Thus, what we have in Hamlet's constant refrain to Ophelia herself —"Get thee to a nunnery, why wouldst thou be a breeder of sinners? . . . go thy ways to a nunnery"(III. i. 121–22,130)—is not merely slang talk for brothel[8] but an image that idealizes the rejection of the physical, the rejection of the natural. The result is a polarization of images. On one extreme is the vision of the natural woman as corrupter and betrayer (whose symbolic figure is Eve) and on the other the perpetual virgin, the nun, whose model is the Virgin Mary, archetype of all sex-free, Platonic women. Thus we have a situation where the ordinary woman is damned with the stigma of the corrupt extreme and exhorted with the other (impossible) ideal. No center exists, for Hamlet has (I turn again to Kraus) in this way also taken a moral stance that is strongly medieval: "Examination will show that there is actually no contradiction between the monks' adoration of Mary and their very low view of ordinary woman. The relationship between the two stressed contrasts rather than similarities. In the glorification of the Virgin, it was the Woman-Without-Sin, the non-woman Woman, the Anti-Eve that was revered."[9] Having rejected fertility and natural womanhood, the next step is clear. Even the sanctified sexuality of marriage must go: "I say we will have no mo marriage—" (III. i. 150–51).

Hamlet's closet scene with his mother extends these same arguments and allows us to see even more clearly the implications of his ideas both for the nature of individual man and the possibility of social relationship. Both these elements are summed up in Hamlet's indictment of his mother:

> Such an act
> That blurs the grace and blush of modesty,
> Calls virtue hypocrite, takes off the rose
> From the fair forehead of an innocent love
> And sets a blister there, makes marriage vows
> As false as dicers' oaths, O such a deed
> As from the body of contraction plucks
> The very soul, and sweet religion makes
> A rhapsody of words; heaven's face does glow,
> And this solidity and compound mass
> With heated visage, as against the doom,
> Is thought-sick at the act.   (III. iv. 40–51)

This is a formidable statement, and it is an indication of the huge freight of meanings that the bond of man and woman may carry. In woman's betrayal, ethics are made uncertain; love is blighted; the institution of marriage is corrupted; the soul is made suspect, and the mind poisoned. The

---

8. See Wilson, *What Happens in Hamlet*, 134. Wilson puts second things first here. The pun is a nice piece of ironic bawdy, but the surface meaning must take precedence.
9. Kraus, *Living Theatre*, 46.

chief villain at this metaphysical level is man's animal nature itself. Hamlet is insisting that his mother's remarriage was motivated by pure bestial lust, which is, in the conventional sixteenth-century formulation Hamlet uses here, instinct uncontrolled by reason,[10] or "god-like" reason, as he calls it elsewhere:

> You cannot call it love, for at your age
> The hey-day in the blood is tame, it's humble,
> And waits upon the judgement, and what judgement
> Would step from this to this?   (III. iv. 68–71)

There is, of course, a damaging qualification in Hamlet's argument here: that is, the idea that middle age should be different in erotic constitution than youth. But this is just one of various inconsistencies of logic which are subsumed in the emotion of the scene and not clarified until later plays. The point here is that Hamlet is invoking *reason* or *judgement* as a barrier against sexuality, but how *unreasonable* this attitude is may be judged from the perversely excited tone his denunciations quickly fall into:

> Nay, but to live
> In the rank sweat of an enseaméd bed
> Stewed in corruption, honeying, and making love
> Over the nasty sty—   (III. iv. 91–94)

Again the aggressive hatred of sexuality links it—quite unreasonably— with pure bestiality. The aggression is obviously intended and obviously felt; as Gertrude says, the words are like daggers. Verbal weapons of death are used in the service of a death-haunted rejection of nature. All this is made explicit in Hamlet's major request of his mother:

> . . . go not to my uncle's bed,
>
> . . . .
> That monster custom, who all sense doth eat
> Of habits evil, is angel yet in this,
> That to the use of actions fair and good
> He likewise gives a frock or livery
> That aptly is put on. Refrain to-night,
> And that shall lend a kind of easiness
> To the next abstinence, the next more easy:
> For use almost can change the stamp of nature, . . .
>   (III. iv. 159, 161–68)

In other words, it is nature in its sexual and thus procreative aspect that has

10. Theodore Spencer, *Shakespeare and the Nature of Man* (New York: The Macmillan Company, 1942), 10–15.

aroused Hamlet's disgust and which he is fighting, that very aspect which Shakespeare was later to celebrate as "great creating nature" in *The Winter's Tale*. Nothing better shows how death-oriented Hamlet is than this move toward a general sterility. Nor could anything more eloquently show the futility of taking such a position as this.

4.

Of course, the fascinating thing about *Hamlet* is that love, though sick enough, is not quite dead in the play. Hamlet's mind is morbid and death haunted, but he can never quite go over to the kind of unimpeded hatred that marks the simpler minded Laertes in rebellion against Claudius. Laertes' lust for revenge is instinctive and immediate. Here, as I suggested earlier, we see the Tybalt in him. But is he, as some critics have suggested, acting in this situation in such a way that we must take him as a corrective or exemplar to shame Hamlet for his inactivity? With Helen Gardner I would suggest that it is neither good criticism nor good morals even to suggest that Hamlet would have been the better man had he stabbed the king in the back at his prayers.[11] It is worth reflecting that, had he done so, he would have been merely Laertes; no one would either have written, nor would still read, a play about Laertes.

It is the delay—it is his hesitation and his hatred of himself that his hesitation brings—that makes Hamlet as a character so fascinating. He tries to be a single-minded revenger and cannot succeed at it. His attempts at vengeance are misdirected or peripheral. At other times he is inevitably a near victim rather than a near slayer. This is as true at the end as at the beginning. But yet he wants to kill, knows (as the audience knows) that he must kill.

I would suggest that the dynamics of his disturbance show themselves most clearly when considered in terms of the tension between the love motive and the death motive. Hamlet, after all, would—if he could—be a lover. And I use the term to include his loving Ophelia, loving his parents, loving his country, loving his world. Indeed, these levels of love are plainly interconnected on a profound level. I wrote earlier of the fossil remains of his romantic love for Ophelia; similar fossils of the wider-spread attachment fill the great speech to Rosencrantz and Guildenstern:

> Indeed it goes so heavily with my disposition, that this goodly frame the earth, seems to me a sterile promontory, this most excellent canopy

11. Helen Gardner, *"Hamlet* and the Tragedy of Revenge," in *Shakespeare: Modern Essays in Criticism*, ed. Leonard F. Dean (Rev. ed.; New York: Oxford University Press, 1967), 222.

the air, look you, this brave o'erhanging firmament, this majestical roof fretted with golden fire, why it appeareth nothing to me but a foul and pestilent congregation of vapours. . . . What a piece of work is a man, how noble in reason, how infinite in faculties, in form and moving, how express and admirable in action, how like an angel in apprehension, how like a god: the beauty of the world; the paragon of animals; and yet to me, what is this quintessence of dust?

(II. ii. 301–12)

But out of love for one parent he must now hate the other. Out of love for his father, he must hate the king of his country. Out of love for his father, he must hate his own humanity. The problem is, however, that love does not die so easily. If hatred and death are in the ascendant, they have not become sole inhabitants of the Hamlet world. Some measure of how inextricable one is from the other may be seen in brief in this witty but tormenting formulation:

HAMLET: Farewell, dear mother.
   KING: Thy loving father, Hamlet.
HAMLET: My mother—father and mother is man and wife, man
   and wife is one flesh, and so my mother: . . .

(IV. iii. 48–51)

How, knowing what marriage is in terms of human union, is Hamlet to perform the full task the ghost has put on him—to revenge himself upon Claudius and yet "Taint not [his] mind, nor let [his] soul contrive/Against [his] mother aught" (I. v. 85–86)? After the long diatribe against woman, even the ghost is here hedging his bet. His own avenging spirit will not move in full measure against the woman he has loved. But the ghost can make the separation above because he is a ghost, a dead man, and does not have to try to fit vengeance into the world of the living. It is because Hamlet does have to do this that we get the confusions and passions which form a major part of the fabric of the play.

The nunnery scene with Ophelia is an important instance of the way in which hatred, pure aggression, is modified or given tension by the manner in which it is delivered. Previously I gave the scene a philosophical interpretation in terms of love and death, an interpretation which stressed the images and their content. In drama there is an added dimension—the sense of attraction and repulsion between characters expressed in terms of stage action and tone. In the nunnery scene these disturb rather than promote the free flow of what—if something in Hamlet were not working against it—would be total misogyny.

The chief facts of this scene in terms of tone and personal interaction are its terrible urgency and its quick reverses of mental direction. In his jesting philosophical paradoxes (such as the one on the power of beauty) and his own paradoxical behavior,

> I did love you once.
> . . . .
> . . . I loved you not.   (III. i. 115, 119)

we see Hamlet's mind racing between the opposing force fields of love and death. As morbidly aggressive as he is all through this scene, he never says he does not *love* Ophelia, as many critics have assumed. What he says above is not: in the past I loved you; now I do not. He says: in the past I loved you, then (in a true paradox) in the past I loved you not. He says nothing at all about the present; thus, I would hazard the following interpretation: that in the past he was drawn to her in love. The emotion still exists, but—no longer believing in love—he knows not what to call it other than lust. And lust is what he must loathe and reject. Therefore, some feeling, some unstated attraction still coexists with the stated repulsion—is, indeed, the cause of the repulsion and is most certainly the cause of the frantic emotionalism of his assault. He is trying to exorcize something which still exists most powerfully in him.

We can extend this interpretation to the staging of the scene. One would imagine that a truly symbolic staging of the expression of positive rejection and unqualified negation would consist of a long diatribe of images of dissociation, followed by a positive exit summing them up in an action. In this scene, however, diatribe is followed by exit which is in turn followed by a gesture of disappointed love in Ophelia. But this pattern is repeated; Hamlet makes two reappearances as if irresistibly drawn back by what he would fly from. And we need make no mistake about what this was, each time. The first sentences of the successive returns tell it: marriage and beauty—

> If thou dost marry, I'll give thee this plague for thy dowry—
> . . . .
> I have heard of your paintings too, well enough.
>   (III. i. 137–38, 145–46)

Both qualities he must associate in the most personal possible fashion with the girl he is now verbally assaulting and, indeed, with aspects of his own past which are too important to be easily whistled down the wind. The confrontation of Hamlet and Laertes over Ophelia's grave merely emphasizes the ironical reversal of normal romantic conventions. In the pure romantic convention, brother and lover would oppose each other across a living woman who is lover to one, sister to the other. Here they grapple over a kind of nothing, over a memory which neither did the best by. The whole theme of the death of love is summed up in the body of Ophelia, even in her death itself—passive and mad—and the maimed rites with which she enters the ground. Hamlet's windy posturing is also symbolic. His words are right, but the tone is wrong; it is hollow because it is built more on what should have been than what was.

Like the nunnery scene, the closet scene between Hamlet and Gertrude gets much of its dramatic life from the same kind of interaction between the said and the unsaid. As in the interview with Ophelia it is aggression, death, and negation that dominate. They run in a continuum from Hamlet's "I will speak daggers to her" (III. ii. 399) to the tone in his voice and actions that make her fear for her life, to the actual stabbing of Polonius. Indeed, Polonius' body lies on stage throughout the scene to heighten the effect, and when Hamlet leaves, he goes lugging the guts into a neighbor room.

But again, the scene is developed by means of violent fluctuations of emotion reinforced by repeated half-exits and returns. The effect is once again one of emotional complexity and confusion, and the confusing factor is once more the attraction that disturbs the intended aggression. Hamlet finds it impossible to speak only in daggers.

A few examples will demonstrate how this disturbance makes itself felt. One of the primary facts of the human mind is that nothing valued or known can ever during life be entirely lost. Thus, when Hamlet makes such a denunciation as this:

> Such an act
> That blurs the grace and blush of modesty,
> Calls virtue hypocrite, takes off the rose
> From the fair forehead of an innocent love
> And sets a blister there, makes marriage vows
> As false as dicers' oaths,   (III. iv. 40–45)

he recalls the positive even while stressing the negative, evokes love even while describing and acting in hatred. The effect of the past may also be seen in the shift in the scene's tone and Hamlet's intentions after the ghost's appearance in Gertrude's room. When Hamlet first enters he attacks relentlessly:

> Go, go, you question with a wicked tongue.
> . . . .

Come, come, and sit you down, you shall not budge,
. . . .
This was your husband—Look you now what follows.
Here is your husband, like a mildewed ear,
. . . .
                            Nay, but to live
In the rank sweat of an enseaméd bed. . . .
                            (III. iv. 12, 18, 63–64, 91–92)

But then the ghost interrupts, tries to ease the pressure in a manner that again recalls the tenderness that belongs to the past: "But look, amazement on thy mother sits,/O step between her and her fighting soul" (III. iv. 112–13). And though Hamlet does not let up very much, his next words to her show a modification of tone: "How is it with you, lady?" (III. iv. 115). His polemics take on less a destructive purpose than a redemptive one: "Mother, for love of grace,/Lay not that flattering unction to your soul" (III. iv. 144–45). The desire to redeem is itself a kind of love, or at least the product of some urge towards reunion. This is clear from these later lines:

                . . . once more, good night,
And when you are desirous to be blessed,
I'll blessing beg of you.   (III. iv. 170–72)

I referred earlier to the way in which Ophelia's death wrenches out of Hamlet a frenzied yet essentially true expression of the love he had always felt even when attacking the object of it. A similar pattern of reconciliation emerges at the end of the play with Gertrude's death. It is set up by two shifts in emphasis: first, Hamlet's more subdued manner after his return from England and discovery of Ophelia's death; second, the emergence of Gertrude as a peacemaker—which, of course she has tried to be throughout the play, though few critics have noted the fact. No one, I think, can miss the change in Hamlet as he approaches the duel. He seems deeply inclined towards peace and some kind of guarded truce. When his mother sends word that he should "use some gentle entertainment to Laertes before you fall to play" (V. ii. 204–205), he answers, "She well instructs me" (V. ii. 206). So fair an answer is itself a change in tone, as is his desire for Laertes' forgiveness. He is even prepared to admit frankly now what in his hatred he denied earlier, that his madness was not entirely feigned: "This presence knows, and you must needs have heard,/How I am punished with a sore distraction" (V. ii. 226–27). His intent here is plainly to defuse a dangerous confrontation. That it does not stay defused is not Hamlet's fault.

The turning point comes when Gertrude collapses by her husband's own hand. The instant she dies Hamlet is all activity: "O villainy! ho! let the door be locked—" (V. ii. 309). The last barrier—for that, it is clear, is what Gertrude was—between Hamlet and his victim is down. Man and wife are no longer one. Hamlet's father is no longer his mother. In the case of Ophelia, death released the dammed flow of love into empty, frenzied rhetoric. With Gertrude's death, it is the dammed up course of hatred that can flow. Revenge can move without impediment to an end which embodies the two chief tensions of the tragedy:

> Here, thou incestuous, murderous, damnéd Dane,
> Drink off this potion. Is thy union here?
> Follow my mother.   (V. ii. 323–25)[12]

5.

A few words should be said about Horatio, Hamlet's own "better angel," and even to evoke the male friend of the sonnets helps place him. Masculine love has this advantage over the love of man and woman: being free from sexual passion it cannot—so goes the convention—be subject to the transience that necessarily limits the sex act and cheapens sexual love. Of course, one feels at times in the depiction of masculine love in the sonnets the intrusion of intimations of sexuality or something very like it; some sort of strong passion, even repressed, disturbs the surface. But between Hamlet and Horatio there is nothing of this. Horatio has nothing in him of the exotic, the feminine, or the erotic. He is solid conventionality; to think in metaphysical conceits about death is to "consider too curiously" (V. i. 200); his response to Hamlet's exhausted lapse into simple faith in a divinity that shapes our ends is "That is most certain" (V. ii. 11). Hamlet places him perfectly when calling him a man who is not passion's slave. To Hamlet, wracked by contrary passions, conventionality (the same pressure shapes his admiration of Laertes and Fortinbras) must seem an ideal much to be longed for. And Horatio—far more than those relatively hollow men Laertes and Fortinbras—is the best that conventionality can offer. He is the perfect friend for the man treading the razor edge of despair.

But is he the perfect Friend? A question to be asked, for if there is anything clear about the end of the play, it is that almost nothing, certainly

---

12. This, it seems to me, is Hamlet's final punning reference to the love-death theme. The "union," we know, is the poisoned pearl in the cup. But it may also be read, coming as it does just before "Follow my mother," as an ironic reference to a marriage union which no longer exists on earth.

none of the major emotional or intellectual issues of the play, is resolved. Hamlet's personal resolution is the most negative kind possible: death. Whatever Shakespeare may have felt about life—if we take into consideration the whole of his production—it is not what Hamlet felt. Nor, since the character Hamlet so dominates the play, does *Hamlet* represent Shakespeare's maturest vision. The play may well have been, however, a necessary transition. It is a critical cliché to say of Romeo and Juliet that they gain maturity in love through suffering and the consciousness of death. Speaking metaphorically, *Hamlet* as a play seems to me the great play of suffering and death that enables Shakespeare in later plays to deal with love in the fullest, most mature fashion.

As one step to making this position good, I would quote here a part of what I think is the finest formulation of the rationale of the drive behind Shakespeare's searching art:

> Shakespeare was not a system-builder: he was an artist, a dealer in dramatic fictions. But I do not see this 'negative capability' which is supposed to accompany his not being a metaphysician. He appears to me to thirst, quite irritably sometimes, after fact and reason. But his only way of 'explaining the universe' was to draw a map, using the conventions of play-making. By adjusting the patterns of art, he would seem to be looking for that fictional ordering which could act as a powerful interpretive formula not only for the experience of his audience, but for his own.[13]

Bringing this to my own subject I would point out that, as fine and ideal a male friend as Horatio is to Hamlet, the love between the two cannot of itself carry the full metaphysical weight required by a love that must create and hold together marriages, families, and ultimately whole societies. Thus, love of man and man, though it is more efficacious in *Hamlet* than sexual love of woman and man, is still found wanting. To pose an interpretive fiction of my own, I would suggest that Shakespeare found *Hamlet* unsatisfactory as an interpretive pattern for a view of the world because he found a world without love between man and woman unsatisfactory. His next plays—*Troilus and Cressida* and *Othello*—are therefore severe reexaminations of the conventional formulations of love between man and woman best known to his own time: courtly romance and the romantic marriage. They are, in other words, a return to the early naïve material of the tragedy of love and death, but with a chastened heart, a knowing eye.

13. Edwards, *Shakespeare and the Confines of Art*, 14.

8 Troilus and Cressida

In *Troilus and Cressida* Shakespeare again takes up the problem of betrayal in love, and again the treatment is—as indeed it inevitably must be—touched with bleak disillusion. One important way in which this play differs from *Hamlet*, however, is in its breadth of scope. This wide focus allows Shakespeare to detach the play from the dominating consciousness of a single, uniquely attractive figure like Hamlet and to externalize his themes, symbols, and psychological patterns onto what is really an epic scale. Not content with reinterpreting for Renaissance sensibilities the great medieval Romance of courtly love and betrayal, he reaches wider still—to embrace the background struggle of the two nations over Helen and use it to make some unconventional but important explorations into the role of love in the maintenance of social concord.

I shall take up each of these issues in turn and then make a few final remarks on the growth of Shakespeare's thinking on love. In each case the approach will be made in terms of the same love-death conventions and configurations found in previous tragedies in this tradition. One result will be to remove the problem of Cressida's character from the realm of emotional denunciation and put her betrayal into the perspective of Elizabethan ideas on Romance love. Another will be to undermine a few commonplaces about the allegedly necessary separation of love and reason in politics. This is a constant issue in the background plot of the Trojan War itself and Shakespeare's dramatic thinking on the matter is subtle in the extreme. Also, certain of the more puzzling features (such as why Hector switches sides so suddenly in the council scene and why the Greeks are in such a continual state of political bitchiness) will be illuminated by recourse to previous treatments of the relationship between emotion and politics.

123

Troilus and Cressida is a bleak and disillusioned play, but one distinction should be made at the outset. The disillusion is no longer with love (as it was in *Hamlet*) but with the failure of love, and it is coupled with a very powerful attempt to understand that failure and organize it in terms of the dramatic conventions which Shakespeare knew so well.

1.

Pressed to formulate briefly the story of the love and the death of love between Troilus and Cressida, I would call it a *Romeo and Juliet* written in the *Hamlet* mood, *i. e.*, a love story filled with the mood and imagery of death. The central characters are, once more, a young woman and young man of exceptional beauty and talents. They are powerfully attracted to each other, and this attraction serves as the motive force in the plot in which they are the major characters. As in *Romeo and Juliet* they also have the aid and comfort of a member of the older generation (Pandarus is a priest of the religion of courtly love), and they are eventually separated by a feud which is not of their making. Of course, in the end the story is no tale of deathless love; it is a retelling of a classic betrayal myth, to some a classic antifeminist myth.

The central element of the *Hamlet* mood in *Troilus and Cressida* is a disturbing and pervasive distrust of love which is active even when the lovers want most to give themselves over to love. The result in Troilus is a rhetoric of love[1] which has the heroic aspirations of Romeo's but is shackled firmly to the ground by the infusion of images of pain and death. An instance is this well-known speech:

> O Pandarus! I tell thee, Pandarus—
> When I do tell thee there my hopes lie drowned,
> Reply not in how many fathoms deep
> They lie indrenched. I tell thee I am mad
> In Cressid's love. Thou answer'st she is fair;
> Pour'st in the open ulcer of my heart
> Her eyes, her hair, her cheek, her gait, her voice;
> . . . .
> But saying thus, instead of oil and balm,
> Thou lay'st in every gash that love hath given me
> The knife that made it.   (I. i. 50–56, 63–65)

---

1. D. A. Traversi makes a number of acute comments on the language of *Troilus and Cressida*. They do not approach the question from precisely this point of view, but they seem to support it. Certainly he is right to locate the source of the troubling aspects of the lovers' language in a pervasive "uncertainty about the value of experience." For "experience," in this study at least, we may read "love." *An Approach to Shakespeare* (3rd ed. rev.; Garden City, N.Y.: Doubleday & Company Ltd., 1969), II, 6.

The emotion is powerful, but where there should be images of life there are instead such things as the open ulcer (an obvious refugee from the *Hamlet* mood), death by drowning, the knife in the wound. The death motifs continue throughout the courtship. Even as Troilus waits to be admitted to Cressida's presence, he conceives of himself—not just as a lover—but a dead man:

> No, Pandarus; I stalk about her door,
> Like a strange soul upon the Stygian banks
> Staying for waftage.   (III. ii. 8–10)

Thinking about the act of love, Troilus shows the same ambiguity. Inasmuch as he thinks of lovemaking as love, he relishes it; inasmuch as he thinks of it as a kind of death, he fears it:

> I am giddy: expectation whirls me round.
> Th'imaginary relish is so sweet
> That it enchants my sense. What will it be
> When that the watery palate tastes indeed
> Love's thrice repuréd nectar?—death, I fear me,
> Swooning distraction, or some joy too fine,
> Too subtle-potent, tuned too sharp in sweetness.
> For the capacity of my ruder powers;
> I fear it much, . . .   (III. ii. 18–26)

This mingling of uncertainty and longing results in a confusion of love and death motives of a kind foreign to the Romeo who loved Juliet, though appropriate to the Romeo who loved Rosaline.

There are various hints throughout the play concerning the sources of Troilus' uncertainty. For one thing, he closely indentifies "love" with the act of love and therefore with the common metaphoric link between orgasm and death. The passage quoted above is evidence of this, and it gains special relevance because as Troilus looks forward into the future of his love for Cressida he sees it mainly in terms of sexuality:

> Tell me, Apollo, for thy Daphne's love,
> What Cressid is, what Pandar, and what we?
> Her bed is India; there she lies, a pearl;
> Between our Ilium and where she resides
> Let it be called the wild and wandering flood;
> Ourself the merchant, and this sailing Pandar,
> Our doubtful hope, our convoy and our bark.   (I. i. 100–106)

The first lines show that Troilus can sense that awesome questions of self-knowledge and individual fate are involved in love, but the rest of the passage comes to focus relentlessly on the bed and on the necessity for a well-meaning but essentially obtrusive third party to lead them there. This third party—for all his good will—serves to sharpen and narrow their scope by ringing them in with his own emphasis on the joys of the bed:

> Whereupon I will show you a chamber with a bed; which bed, because it shall not speak of your pretty encounters, press it to death. Away!
> And Cupid grant all tongue-tied maidens here
> Bed, chamber, pandar, to provide this gear!
> (III. ii. 206–10)

The result of such a complete merger of death and love motives is a terrible fear of time and of human limitation. This takes several forms. One is the feeling that no human action can ever fully satisfy the emotion of love:

> Nothing but our undertakings, when we vow to weep seas, live in fire, eat rocks, tame tigers; thinking it harder for our mistress to devise imposition enough than for us to undergo any difficulty imposed. This is the monstruosity in love, lady—that the will is infinite and the execution confined; that the desire is boundless and the act a slave to limit.
> (III. ii. 76–82)

When Troilus refers to the "execution" and the "act" of love, he is not referring merely to coitus; but it is plain that the shortness of that act is the metaphoric basis for the other tests and activities out of which the courtly lover tries to build some kind of spiritual superstructure over and around the primal act.

Indeed, what gives all the scenes between the lovers their great poignancy is the realization that this is what all romantic love must do: make body and spirit lie down together and produce something which has the attributes of both but is fuller than either. Certainly this is what Troilus wants—sensual pleasure united with the permanence of mutual faith. He wants it because something in his very nature seems to demand it:

> CRES: My lord, will you be true?
> TROI: Who, I? alas, it is my vice, my fault!
>
> . . . .
>
> CRES: Fear not my truth: the moral of my wit
>   Is 'plain and true'; there's all the reach of it.
> (IV. iv. 101–102, 107–108)

But despite this, we see the qualifications and fears at work undermining the foundations of this principle of faith. There is still one of these to be mentioned: the image of woman in the male mind.

When, for instance, we think of Romeo's vision of woman, of Juliet, we think of a single, unified, brilliant image. For Troilus, the *Hamlet* vision of

woman intrudes, dividing the mind, breaking down his image of Cressida
into a double one composed of an uncertain combination of hope and fear:

> O that I thought it could be in a woman—
> As, if it can, I will presume in you—
> To feed for aye her lamp and flame of love;
> To keep her constancy in plight and youth,
> Outliving beauties outward, with a mind
> That doth renew swifter than blood decays!   (III. ii. 157–62)

The hope is embodied in the idea of a woman who could love forever; the
fear is in the "O that I thought" and the debilitating "if" clause.

The battle of love motive and death motive becomes particularly sharp
the next day when the lovers must part. It is this struggle, in fact, which is
the real focus of the scene. The harder Troilus tries to shore up his one
night's lovemaking into a lasting union, the more the union seems to slip
away from him. Both his hope and his fear speak out when he says "Hear
me, my love: be thou but true of heart—" (IV. iv. 58). Cressida hears only
the suspicion and fear: "I true! how true! what wicked deem is this?" (IV. iv.
59). He tries to retrieve, rather desperately, and only sounds pompous,
avuncular: "Nay, we must use expostulation kindly" (IV. iv. 60). Then, in a
more direct expression of feeling, we see this morbid fear of the death of
love called by one of its right names—jealousy:

> Alas, a kind of godly jealousy,
> Which, I beseech you, call a virtuous sin—
> Makes me afeard.   (IV. iv. 80–82)

The epithet "godly" for jealousy is, of course, a politic though deeply felt
masculine equivocation that is explored in greater depth in *Othello*. Here it
serves mainly to point out that the end of this love was at least partly implicit in its beginning: that the strumpet Cressida the world now knows has
her image in her lover's doubting mind even before the fact of her betrayal.

The question now arises, if Troilus' image of Cressida is so unsure, what
of Cressida herself? One strong tradition in Elizabethan criticism is exemplified by the comments of E. C. Pettet: "She is a shallow, sensuous, theatrical, utterly selfish creature, whose every other word or gesture is a pose
sultry with suggestiveness—the instinctive whore in fact."[2] But this, I
think, oversimplifies her considerably, makes her one-sided in a way that a
Shakespearean character almost never is. To me she seems a very complex

---

2. E. C. Pettet, *Shakespeare and the Romance Tradition* (London: Staples Press Ltd., 1949),
142. F. M. Dickey and H. B. Charlton are also extremely harsh critics of Cressida.

creation indeed, and an approach to her complexities may be made by means of her ideas on love and the relation of these to her behavior. The primary fact is that she does feel a powerful attraction to Troilus which is not mere lust. It comes out first after Pandarus has finished his attempt to puff up Troilus' qualities as man and lover: "But more in Troilus thousandfold I see/Than in the glass of Pandar's praise may be" (I. ii. 285–86). The same kind of confession occurs during her first conversation with Troilus:

> Boldness comes to me now and brings me heart:
> Prince Troilus, I have loved you night and day
> For many weary months.   (III. ii. 112–14)

But some inkling of her own problem in the conduct of the love affair emerges when Troilus asks with typically masculine logic: "Why was my Cressid then so hard to win?" (III. ii. 115). Again, she appears to answer honestly, but—and here again we see Shakespeare's mastery of the techniques of indicating a tumultuous inner life—her answer is indirect, residing mainly in her fears:

> Hard to seem won; but I was won, my lord,
> With the first glance that ever—pardon me;
> If I confess much, you will play the tyrant.
> I love you now; but not, till now, so much
> But I might master it. In faith, I lie!
> My thoughts were like unbridled children, grown
> Too headstrong for their mother. See, we fools!
> Why have I blabbed?   (III. ii. 116–23)

Behind the shifting thoughts here—the desire to confess love and the fear of being weakened by the confession—lie the permanent psychology of the sex war and those feminine insecurities that are the counterpart of the masculine urge to seduction and temporary relationships, the same fears given mythic status in the story of Dido. Cressida, therefore, has her own worries about the transience of lovers and of love. Coming as they do into direct conflict with her desire to love, they give her a complexity of motive hardly less acute than Troilus'.

It is in such a context that we must read Cressida's earlier, much more confident statement of principle:

> But more in Troilus thousandfold I see
> Than in the glass of Pandar's praise may be.
> Yet hold I off: women are angels, wooing;
> Things won are done—joy's soul lies in the doing.
> That she beloved knows nought that knows not this:

> Men prize the thing ungained more than it is.
> That she was never yet that ever knew
> Love got so sweet as when desire did sue.
> Therefore this maxim out of love I teach:
> 'Achievement is command; ungained, beseech.'
> Then though my heart's content firm love doth bear,
> Nothing of that shall from mine eyes appear.   (I. ii. 285–96)

Mr. Pettet calls this "whorish calculation,"[3] but it is obviously much more than that. Again it is a logical though dispiriting and deadening reaction to the male syndrome of conquest and abandonment, a timeless piece of female uncertainty and canniness concerning the motives behind fine words.

The significant comparison here is Juliet. She too felt for a moment that she had given away too much in the dark: "Fain would I dwell on form; fain, fain deny/ What I have spoke" (*R & J*, II. ii. 88–89). But she is confident enough that Romeo's love is going to be "honorable" and permanent that she immediately arranges to send an emissary the next day to learn the time and place of the wedding. The difference lies in the fact that Juliet lives in the modern world where—given the right conditions—sexual love and the desire to marry go hand in hand. Cressida's world is one in which love naturally leads not to marriage but to the clandestine affair, the code of service and secrecy. One is the world of the romantic marriage, the other of the Romance. In this context, Cressida's speech on the need to hold back from loving to make love more desirable is one answer before the fact of Troilus' great council scene question: "What's aught but as 'tis valued?" (II. ii. 52). All Cressida's delays, her witty sparring, her whole carefully cultivated image of the distant, unattainable courtly ideal compose a system by which she tries to give extrasexual value to sexual love. By demanding a long, arduous courtship she both tests and—as she sees it—increases her value. The problem is that the method used—evading love while seeking it—wars with itself and, once the courtship is over and the lovers have united in bed, provides no further security.

The texture of their relationship, therefore, is a web of insecurity and fear as well as love. At times the pure love motive in them seems to triumph, but it is almost always immediately undercut:

> TROI: O Cressida, how often have I wished me thus!
> CRES: Wished, my lord?—The gods grant—O, my lord!
> TROI: What should they grant? What makes this pretty abruption? What too
>   curious dreg espies my sweet lady in the fountain of our love?
> CRES: More dregs than water, if my fears have eyes.
>   (III. ii. 60–67)

3. Pettet, *Romance Tradition*, 142.

This conflict is even worst at the scene of parting. There they find out how little they really know each other. Crippled by doubts, they never make the imaginative leap that took Romeo from calflike courtly lover to a man with a powerful imaginative vision of the future. The difference between the two couples is summed up in this. It is the difference between Romeo and Juliet's

> JUL: O, think'st thou we shall ever meet again?
> ROM: I doubt it not; and all these woes shall serve
>   For sweet discourses in our times to come.
>   (*R & J*, III. v. 51–53)

and Troilus and Cressida's

> TROI: . . . I cannot sing,
>   Nor heel the high lavolt, nor sweeten talk,
>   Nor play at subtle games—fair virtues all,
>   To which the Grecians are most prompt and pregnant;
>   But I can tell that in each grace of these
>   There lurks a still and dumb-discoursive devil
>   That tempts most cunningly. But be not tempted.
> CRES: Do you think I will?   (IV. iv. 85 –92)

These references to *Romeo and Juliet* are important because they recall the imaginative force of the earlier Elizabethans' ideal of the romantic marriage and, consequently, the Elizabethan view of courtly love conventions.[4] Shakespeare's special perception, it seems to me, concerns the shapes that the Romance conventions give to love and the failure of these shapes to do justice to the emotion. The courtly love convention of the clandestine affair is, of course, the centerpiece and the most tyrannical and destructive one of all, for it fixes the emotional focus on only the night games of love and excludes the complementary bonds of the day; it fails to give these lovers the public status that would keep Cressida in Troy, and, more important, it fails to give them the psychological substance that would allow the love to endure. To Shakespeare, therefore, the code is as much a dead hand as the Arranged Marriage.

The restrictive, emotionally deadening pressure of convention also helps make sense of Cressida's facile transition from one lover to the next. Troilus is a courtly lover in whose desire to transcend time we may see the seeds of

---

4. Shakespeare's treatment of courtly love here is, of course, also part of a long Elizabethan tradition of denigration of it on the grounds of superficiality and triviality. See particularly Peele's *David and Bethsabe* and Marston's *Antonio and Mellida*. The experience of writing *Hamlet* seems to have given Shakespeare the poetic tools to do the job with unprecedented thoroughness.

some stillborn revolt against courtly transience. But Cressida is completely a child of the code; and, for all her uncertainties, she always adapts to it rather than seeking to go beyond it. Thus, in private moments she is either a sober analyst of her position in life or a tongue-tied, confused, teenaged girl, while in public she confidently bandies bawdry with Pandarus and with the Greeks. One Cressida is the essential, mainly unformed young girl; the other is a deliberate mask, a role assumed as part of the Trojan cultural convention of courtly love. The model for the mask is, of course, that archetype Romance lover Helen of Troy. Helen in her typical public face speaks this kind of banter:

> HEL: My Lord Pandarus; honey-sweet lord—
> PAND: Go to, sweet queen, go to—commends himself most affectionately to
> you—
> HEL: You shall not bob us out of our melody. If you do, our melancholy upon
> your head!
> PAND: Sweet queen, sweet queen; that's a sweet queen, i'faith.
> HEL: And to make a sweet lady sad is a sour offence.
>   (III. i. 66–73)

Cressida—in a courtly situation in Troy—puts on the same style of speech with Pandarus. In this style she is confident, witty, playing and enjoying the role of mistress of a prince. Likewise, when faced with her new Greek audience, she leaves off her private uncertainties and again plays the role that served her so well in Troy:

> CRES: In kissing, do you render or receive?
> MENE: Both take and give.
> CRES: I'll make my match to live,
> The kiss you take is better than you give;
> Therefore no kiss.   (IV. v. 36–39)

But the mind boggles at the insensitivity to audience that leads her to play Helen of Troy to an audience of Greeks.

This is the point of one of the important minor ironies of the play: that the liaison of Diomedes and Cressida is from the start couched in the terminology of courtly love. Diomedes sees that Cressida is Troilus' beloved and immediately begins to speak the language of courtliness she understands so well:

> Fair Lady Cressid,
> So please you, save the thanks this prince expects.
> The lustre in your eye, heaven in your cheek,
> Pleads your fair usage; and to Diomed
> You shall be mistress, and command him wholly.
>   (IV. iv. 116–20)

The important line is the last one, for he pretends to place her upon a pedestal in typical Petrarchan fashion; the lines thus look forward directly to the scene in which Troilus observes Diomedes' conquest of Cressida. Leaving Troilus aside, we can see that throughout the seduction scene she is still trying to play her game of delaying the sexual act in hopes of gaining value thereby. But with the Greeks she is out of her element, and Diomedes plays the game by different rules:

DIOM: Why then, farewell;
        Thou never shalt mock Diomed again.
CRES: You shall not go; one cannot speak a word,
        But it straight starts you.
DIOM: I do not like this fooling.

DIOM: What, shall I come? the hour?
CRES: Ay, come.   (V. ii. 99–102, 104–105)

The courtly mistress becomes with a change of location and emotional context the "commodious drab" (V. ii. 194), and Diomedes' total lack of sympathy shows up every weakness in the code. By emptying it of all emotional content, he makes it less a struggling ground of love and death than a simple brutal form for the death of love.

2.

To place the role of love in a large perspective, a few preconceptions will have to be cleared away. The main one of these is that love and the order of the state are mutually inimical. I quote here a modern version taken from a discussion of *Troilus and Cressida*:

> Broadly speaking, the government of public life seems to be most effectively conducted by adopting schemes devised by thought—the wisdom of Ulysses, for example, or the plain common sense of Agamemnon, or the summary principles arrived at by the observation of such long experience as Nestor has enjoyed. On the other hand, in the major moments of individual life, the more decisive and the more irresistible impulses appear to proceed from instinct, intuition and emotion: love, for instance, sexual love, surges up and makes havoc of reason—for, it seems, "to be wise and love exceeds man's might."[5]

Behind this is the belief that reason is the only proper foundation of a happy state and that love of necessity must drive out reason. But (*Romeo and Juliet* provides the evidence) Shakespeare's thinking was much more

5. H. B. Charlton, *Shakespearian Comedy* (London: Methuen & Co. Ltd., 1966 reprint of 1938 edition), 242.

original than this. Undoubtedly he was familiar with this ancient theory, but, almost alone in his time, he realized that powerful irrational forces were at work in the bonding of the social order. In the Verona of the Capulets and Montagues a rational prince imposing order from outside could effect no peace. It required the irrationality of love. It is this insight which Shakespeare now carries over into the portrayal of not one but two social orders.

Consideration of two texts will illustrate what I mean. Both are well known, but they are not often juxtaposed, despite their similarities of idea, language, and point of view. The first is a section from Ulysses' speech on order:

> Take but degree away, untune that string,
> And hark what discord follows! each thing meets
> In mere oppugnancy: the bounded waters
> Should lift their bosoms higher than the shores,
> And make a sop of all this solid globe;
> Strength should be lord of imbecility,
> And the rude son should strike his father dead;
> Force should be right; or rather, right and wrong,
> Between whose endless jar justice resides,
> Should lose their names, and so should justice too.
> Then everything includes itself in power,
> Power into will, will into appetite;
> And appetite, an universal wolf,
> So doubly seconded with will and power,
> Must make perforce an universal prey,
> And last eat up himself.   (I. iii. 109–24)

The second is a central passage from Hector's very rationalistic argument in favor of handing Helen back over to the Greeks:

> What nearer debt in all humanity
> Than wife is to the husband? If this law
> Of nature be corrupted through affection,
> And that great minds, of partial indulgence
> To their benumbéd wills, resist the same,
> There is a law in each well-ordered nation
> To curb those raging appetites that are
> Most disobedient and refractory.   (II. ii. 175–82)

Where both are alike is in their common sense of the necessity of a fixed order, united with a fear and distrust of the "appetites." Furthermore, they both refer back to situations in life, as it were, where, for one reason or another, the order and degree taken to be the primary values have disappeared. The Greeks are squabbling among themselves, and Helen has long since left her husband for a man she loves. What I would suggest in this section is that neither speaker perceives what Shakespeare himself perceives about these situations: that—desirable as it unquestionably is—lasting order is not imposed by force or by Machiavellian politics, but rather grows of its own accord from within a social union. In the context of this play, the central paradox is why the Greeks should be painted as a group of wrangling egoists when the Trojans—a nation of lovers—should enjoy as if by gift of nature a free, easy, perfectly functioning social order. The answer, it seems to me, depends a great deal on the way in which the two sides regard Helen and their relationship to her. The starting point for discussion of this problem is the great Trojan council scene, where it is first taken up explicitly.

To properly appreciate the full complexity of this debate it is necessary to see it as both abstract and yet highly personal and dramatic (that is, completely embedded in the local emotion and personal circumstances of the play's specific action). In this light, it becomes apparent that Hector's arguments are deliberately abstract, indeed academically so, and that the counterarguments by Troilus and Paris are pointedly personal, situational, and dramatic. Hector is disengaged; Troilus is engaged. The object of both these points of view is Helen, and the nature of the two ways of thinking about her tells a great deal about the overall organization of the play. The problem from the critic's point of view is that almost all previous critics discussing this scene have supported the disengaged, philosophical arguments of Hector as if the scene had no roots in a dramatic, personal situation. I would suggest an alternate reading, one which gives more weight to the existence among the characters of human bonds of affection.

The very starting point of Hector's argument—that is, that Helen should forthwith be returned as the Greeks demand—is itself a formidable feat of abstraction. In talking about Helen he is talking about someone who for all practical purposes is a member of the family, his own brother's beloved. To argue that they should forcibly deprive Paris of her and abandon her to a society that she loathes and that loathes her is a gesture of withdrawal from the personal; appropriately enough it is propounded in the language of mathematics:

> Since the first sword was drawn about this question,
> Every tithe-soul 'mongst many thousand dismes
> Hath been as dear as Helen—I mean, of ours.
> If we have lost so many tenths of ours

> To guard a thing not ours, nor worth to us—
> Had it our name—the value of one ten,
> What merit's in that reason which denies
> The yielding of her up?   (II. ii. 18–25)

and economics and commerce: "Brother, she is not worth what she doth cost/The keeping" (II. ii. 51–52). Furthermore, it is not merely economics, but a very bookish and—it seems to me—rather naïve economics:

> But value dwells not in particular will:
> It holds his estimate and dignity
> As well wherein 'tis precious of itself
> As in the prizer.   (II. ii. 53–56)

This statement of Hector's is often taken as an unanswerable rebuke to Troilus' arguments, but it is at very best a half-truth. In the human mind, nothing is really "precious of itself"; it must be precious to some "particular will" or group of wills. The best one can say is that some things are more precious than others, to some people. Such is the case even with things; how much more relative must the situation be when applied to people, to the woman loved by one's brother.

In any case, Hector is determined to be theoretical and to talk in terms of a lofty and judicial ideal of human relationships. To quote again Hector's statement on marriage and enforcement of the marriage law:

> What nearer debt in all humanity
> Than wife is to the husband? If this law
> Of nature be corrupted through affection,
> And that great minds, of partial indulgence
> To their benumbéd wills, resist the same,
> There is a law in each well-ordered nation
> To curb those raging appetites that are
> Most disobedient and refractory.   (II. ii. 175–82)

Marriage here is not an emotional bond, a bond of "raging appetite" between man and woman; it is instead a contract, specifically a debt owed from woman to man. This is, of course, the conventional medieval conception of marriage that existed side by side with courtly love. There is no question but that Shakespeare believed in marital fidelity and that Hector is here trying to provide a theoretical foundation to enforce that fidelity. But what makes it such an un-Shakespearean defense is the legalism of its language and the violence of its remedies.

The main result of Hector's detached and impersonal mode of argument is that he leaves open and uncovered large areas of personal reasons for the keeping of Helen. Philosophy flourishes best in abstract situations, but the substance of drama is human contingency. It is these areas of human feeling which Troilus exploits with very considerable polemic vigor.

Troilus never forgets the personal and the immediate, and at his best he combines this attention to the human background with a sense of the mythic greatness of the large action in which he is participating:

> . . . why, she is a pearl
> Whose price hath launched above a thousand ships
> And turned crowned kings to merchants.
> If you'll avouch 'twas wisdom Paris went—
> As you must needs, for you all cried 'Go, go';
> If you'll confess he brought home worthy prize—
> As you must needs, for you all clapped your hands
> And cried 'Inestimable!'; why do you now
> The issue of your proper wisdoms rate,
> And do a deed that Fortune never did,
> Beggar the estimation which you prized
> Richer than sea and land?   (II. ii. 81–92)

Here, he starts on the level of mythic exaltation, with a Marlovian phrase to boost the high feeling. But he quickly builds up a foundation of fact under his fireworks. Nothing could be less abstract than to remind them all that they had "clapped [their] hands" and cried "Inestimable!"—that, in other words, they all share in the responsibility of the deed. This kind of argument is the reverse of Hector's, but in its dramatic situation it is no less relevant.

Paris' best points have this same quality. He—as Priam at one point reminds him—is speaking from self-interest, but his words must strike home very forcibly to them all for, although in one sense he is talking about Helen, his main point concerns the Trojan warriors' own self-respect:

> What treason were it to the ransacked queen,
> Disgrace to your great worths, and shame to me.
> Now to deliver her possession up
> On terms of base compulsion! Can it be
> That so degenerate a strain as this
> Should once set footing in your generous bosoms?
> There's not the meanest spirit on our party
> Without a heart to dare or sword to draw
> When Helen is defended; . . .   (II. ii. 150–58)

It is in this kind of crux that Shakespeare's dramatic problem becomes acute. Certainly the law of well-ordered nations demands that Helen be returned. But it is men who "On terms of base compulsion" would have to do it. To do this the Trojans would have to violate their own bonds of faith and trust, their own natures even, and become a nation of Enobarbuses—men who betray something they value and find when it is done that they have betrayed themselves in the process. There is no question throughout this debate of whitewashing Helen, Paris, or the fact of war. Yet—and in Shakespeare it is no small "yet"—the bonds of human affection must hold somewhere, even in the face of extreme danger and moral ambiguity or else man is really as miserable a beast as Thersites so pungently maintains.

This seems to me the complicated context in which the great debate must be studied. It also seems to me the only one which makes Hector's capitulation explicable without making him into a fool. Few occasions in Shakespeare have roused more puzzled comment than this, and the comment is usually most adverse to Hector. I quote Theodore Spencer, whose sentiments are representative. After outlining Hector's early arguments, he begins:

> This is the traditional view, and all rational opinion would support it; to do otherwise is to go against Nature. But what happens? Hector immediately switches to the opposite, irrational side, and supports the argument of passion:
>
>   Hector's opinion
> Is this, in way of truth; yet, ne'ertheless,
> My spritely brethren, I propend to you
> In resolution to keep Helen still;
> For 'tis a cause that hath no mean dependence
> Upon our joint and several dignities.

Spencer says it would be "hard to find a more lame and impotent conclusion than this."[6] But one need not really be so hard on Hector, for in coming around to Troilus' opinion he is really coming back to his own truest nature. In a sense, during the period he argued for the expulsion of Helen, he was taking the role and personality of the Greek side, just as he was using Greek arguments for Greek ends. One might even surmise from the academic quality of his language that the arguments were indeed academic to him. His purpose in taking them may be—he suggests this himself—less persuasive than exploratory:

>   The wound of peace is surety,
> Surety secure; but modest doubt is called
> The beacon of the wise, the tent that searches
> To th'bottom of the worst.   (II. ii. 14–17)

---

6. Spencer, *Shakespeare and the Nature of Man*, 113.

This concept of "modest doubt" would explain his deliberate abstraction, his conscious use of impersonal language to judge very personal matters. In reversing he is coming back to himself and back to his actual, temporal situation. As he himself points out:

> I am yours,
> You valiant offspring of great Priamus.
> I have a roisting challenge sent amongst
> The dull and factious nobles of the Greeks
> Will strike amazement to their drowsy spirits.
>
> (II. ii. 206–10)

This kind of panache does not belong to a man who would give up his own brother's lover. This spirit, and this admiration for what is bold and colorful in the human spirit, is what makes the Trojans what they are and, as such, puts the question of personal valuation in a rather different light. To quote Troilus again:

> Why, there you touched the life of our design:
> Were it not glory that we more affected
> Than the performance of our heaving spleens,
> I would not wish a drop of Trojan blood
> Spent more in her defence. But, worthy Hector,
> She is a theme of honour and renown,
> A spur to valiant and magnanimous deeds, . . .
>
> (II. ii. 194–200)

Helen has her value in what the Trojans make of themselves. It is no use for moralists to point out the triviality of her courtly chat any more than it is for Diomedes to vent his spleen on her in conversation (or symbolically, through Cressida). As long as the Trojans do valiant and magnanimous deeds, honor their human ties, and commit themselves with honor and renown, then to the Trojans Helen has the value which Troilus places on her. The object of Paris' "particular will" becomes by symbolic identification the object of a whole communal will; and this communal will and communal valuation is a much more considerable matter.

To put it plainly: the Trojans have no factions or severe internal dissensions because they love each other, and they are all united in a kind of symbolic love for Helen. The Greeks, on the other hand, have no love for their cause, no love certainly for Helen, no love even for one another; indeed they have for the most part a general and undisguised contempt for each other. For instance, although Trojan wit is bawdy and often trivial, it is the bawdiness of affection—objectionable only to those outside the circle. But Thersites' wit is something else again:

PATR: Male varlet, you rogue! what's that?
THER: Why, his masculine whore. Now, the rotten diseases of the south, the guts-griping, ruptures, catarrhs, loads o' gravel i'th'back, lethargies, cold palsies, raw eyes, dirt-rotten livers, wheezing lungs, bladders full of impostume, sciaticas, limekilns i'th'palm, incurable bone-ache, and the rivelled fee-simple of the tetter, take and take again such preposterous discoveries!   (V. i. 16–23)

This is the wit of alienation: corrosive, destructive, lonely, unhealthy in a way that even Pandarus never is—at least until the Epilogue when he sounds more like Thersites than himself.

Likewise, when Achilles withdraws from battle it is done out of pettishness, embellished with destructive satire, and has the effect of releasing all the worst in the other highly egoistic characters. But Troilus and Paris can use the excuse of love to drop out whenever they wish, and there is no dissension, no jealousy, no embarrassment. Here, for instance, are Paris and Helen after a day of dalliance:

PARIS: They're come from th'field: let us to Priam's hall,
        To greet the warriors. Sweet Helen, I must woo you
        To help unarm our Hector.
              . . . .
HEL: 'Twill make us proud to be his servant, Paris;
        Yea, what he shall receive of us in duty
        Gives us more palm in beauty than we have,
        Yea, overshines ourself.
PARIS: Sweet, above thought I love thee.
                                                (III. i. 149–51, 156–60)

This is not so much triviality as the kind of freedom that exists within a truly unified community. One feels in these exchanges that the Trojans are in spirit a large and closely knit family. But the Greeks can only put together —for all their *policy*—parodies of this kind of family unity, as in the hilarious climax to the politic elevation of Ajax. Throughout the scene Ulysses has been cutting at Ajax from behind:

AJAX: An all men were o' my mind—
ULYS: Wit would be out of fashion.   (II. iii. 213–14)

But, to Ajax's face, he is all feigned love and respect:

ULYS: But pardon, father Nestor, were your days
        As green as Ajax', and your brain so tempered,
        You should not have the eminence of him,
        But be as Ajax.
AJAX: Shall I call you father?
NESTOR: Ay, my good son.   (II. iii. 250–54)

With the Greeks "love" has become an instrument of policy; the father-son relationship a form without feeling, which is indeed the case with most of the Greek relationships. We have arrived at the heart of one of the major "problems" of this problem play when we accept this. Thinking back to Ulysses' great speech on order one recalls that he treats his ideal of degree as something to be imposed from without or from above, whereas in Troy the observance of degree is free, natural, organic, a function of mutual love.

But an important part of the puzzle remains: why could not or did not Shakespeare also give the bond of affection to those who also had conventional morality on their side? The answer is to be sought, I think, in the typical configurations of the romantic versions of love-death tragedy and in a latent romanticism that persists in Shakespeare even in the face of his abhorrence of adultery and betrayal and thus provides the large formal grouping of his characters and his own sympathies.

Helen may serve as an image of beauty and aspiration for the Trojans, but the Greeks have only Menelaus to identify with, only Menelaus' cause to bind them emotionally. He is not an inspiring figure; even Cressida could twit him:

> CRES: You're an odd man; give even, or give none.
> MENE: An odd man, lady! every man is odd.
> CRES: No, Paris is not; for you know 'tis true
>   That you are odd, and he is even with you.
> MENE: You fillip me o'th' head.   (IV. v. 41–45)

Diomedes despises him; Ulysses does also; Thersites goes almost beyond language: "To what form but that he is, should wit larded with malice and malice forced with wit turn him to? To an ass, were nothing: he is both ass and ox; to an ox, were nothing: he is both ox and ass. To be a dog, a mule, a cat, a fitchew, a toad, a lizard, an owl, a puttock, or a herring without a roe, I would not care; but to be Menelaus, I would conspire against destiny!" (V. i. 55–62). The Greeks despise Helen, whom they seek; they despise the man whose cause they die in; and they despise themselves and each other for being there. Thersites' jest about their being multiples of the word *fool* sums them up well: "Agamemnon is a fool to offer to command Achilles; Achilles is a fool to be commanded of Agamemnon; Thersites is a fool to serve such a fool; and Patroclus is a fool positive" (II. iii. 61–64). But it does even better to think of them as an army of cuckolds, a whole corps of men who have been victims to one degree or another in the kind of symbolic betrayal by woman that Hamlet goes through. Some such alignment does, it seems to me, help account for the way in which the sexual cynicism and loathing of the body that is so distinctive of Hamlet's melancholia is diverted like a river into the Greek point of view, finding its most powerful expression in Thersites, but present (particularly the sexual cynicism) in successively lesser degrees in Diomedes and Ulysses.

It also makes the question of "What's aught, but as 'tis valued?" a little clearer. For just as the kind of humanity which Nestor eulogizes in Hector here:

> I have, thou gallant Trojan, seen thee oft,
> Labouring for destiny, make cruel way
> Through ranks of Greekish youth; and I have seen
>   thee,
> As hot as Perseus, spur thy Phrygian steed,
> And seen thee scorning forfeits and subduements
> When thou hast hung thy advancéd sword i'th'air,
> Not letting it decline on the declined,
> That I have said to some my standers-by
> 'Lo, Jupiter is yonder, dealing life!'   (IV. v. 183–91)

belongs only to those who love and therefore give high value to woman and to man, so the kind of inhumanity shown by Achilles to Hector is linked to the low value the Greeks hold for men in general, including each other. To value men down (as the whole history of the Machiavel in Elizabethan-Jacobean drama shows) may aid one in local victories, but to overvalue them would appear to be one way to a kind of goodness that has nothing to do with success.

To think in this manner about *Troilus and Cressida* also makes the moral and dramatic structure of the play seem a little less peculiar. Basically the framework plot of *Troilus and Cressida* is a vast story of revenge, just as much of one as *The Spanish Tragedy*, for instance. The reason it does not seem like one is that the whole Trojan nation is the lover who wins the girl and refuses to betray her, and the entire Greek army is the jealous, bitter, cynical, Machiavellian revenger. In embryo in the Trojan ethos are heroic young lovers like Don Horatio or Don Andrea; in Helen, Bel-imperia; in the Greeks (except Ulysses) such types as Balthazar (not unlike Menelaus) and Lorenzo (not unlike Diomedes). This is the reason finally that for all their having the "law of nations" on their side the Greeks seem so unhealthy: because they are trying to impose law (the marriage law) where there is no feeling (Was there ever more of an Enforced Marriage than that which was eventually effected by the return of Helen?), because they are on the side of death against the side of love. Shakespeare, as I have said, has no starry-eyed illusions about the Trojans or the code of courtly love they practice, but set against a cuckold's rage, any kind of genuine love has a moral life that hollow legalism and triumphant revenge can never attain.

3.

There are two further passages which require special notice, for they appear to confirm the idea that Shakespeare is holding a continuing debate with himself on the nature of love and they point the direction it is taking.

The first is a brief segment of the scene in which Troilus watches Cressida betray him. The setting of the scene is obviously very much a part of the love-death tradition, the most obvious analogue being Kyd's voyeuristic bower scene. The disappointed lover watches a sexual encounter between his beloved and his rival and flies from love into hatred and the desire for revenge. This is one of the staple scenes of the tradition.

But more important is the way the scene answers one of the major ideas in *Hamlet*. Hamlet—on the basis of his mother's hasty marriage—had accepted in principle the idea of the natural moral turpitude of woman and had done so very readily by generalizing out of his own experience. Shakespeare has Troilus—after seeing his own betrayal—explicitly take off in the same direction:

> Was Cressid here?
>
> . . . .
> Let it not be believed for womanhood!
> Think we had mothers. Do not give advantage
> To stubborn critics, apt without a theme
> For depravation, to square the general sex
> By Cressid's rule; . . .   (V. ii. 125, 129–33)

But he is taken up sharply by Ulysses, who gives him—and by implication all "stubborn critics" so "apt without a theme"—a lesson in the improper use of vast generalization: "What hath she done, prince, that can soil our mothers?" (V. ii. 134). It is not important that Troilus goes on untouched by the remark into a murderous misanthropy; it was meant mainly for those outside the play, and it marks Shakespeare's own detachment from the Hamlet point of view.

The second passage is the peculiar and evocative exchange between Ulysses and Achilles (III. iii). In its dramatic situation it is a discussion of the impermanence of fame and arises specifically out of one of Ulysses' stratagems to bring Achilles into the battle; along the way, however, some conceptions are expressed which point to wider relevance. Ulysses begins the discussion by noting some tantalizingly obscure book and paraphrasing from it what could very well be a theory of love:

> A strange fellow here
> Writes me that man, how dearly ever parted,
> How much in having, or without or in,
> Cannot make boast to have that which he hath,
> Nor feels not what he owes, but by reflection;
> As when his virtues, shining upon others,
> Heat them and they retort that heat again
> To the first giver.   (III. iii. 95–102)

Basically this is an affirmation of the social nature of man, and it makes the point very clearly that man has neither a sense of his own identity nor a sense of his own worth except inasmuch as he feels the admiration or love of others confirming this and giving it form. Particularly striking in Ulysses' expression is the image of heat though, for it suggests irrationality, even to the edge of passion, and gives an unorthodox resonance to what is—as Achilles points out—a not unfamiliar position. Achilles then attempts to restate it—but in very different images:

> This is not strange, Ulysses.
> The beauty that is borne here in the face
> The bearer knows not, but commends itself
> To others' eyes; nor doth the eye itself,
> That most pure spirit of sense, behold itself,
> Not going from itself; but eye to eye opposed
> Salutes each other with each other's form:
> For speculation turns not to itself
> Till it hath travelled and is mirrored there
> Where it may see itself. This is not strange at all.
>   (III. iii. 102–11)

But the reason Ulysses' idea does not seem strange to Achilles is that in re-stating it he thins it out into something conventional and superficial by making the beauty merely facial beauty and the reflection merely the mirror quality of the eye. For this kind of reflection a pool of water would serve as well—as Narcissus found.

Ulysses will not settle for this, and he develops the idea more powerfully, with a driving insistence on the quality of heat that sets it in a deeper realm of psychological interaction than Achilles' *bellettrist* delicacy:

> I do not strain at the position—
> It is familiar—but at the author's drift;
> Who in his circumstance expressly proves

That no man is the lord of anything,
Though in and of him there be much consisting,
Till he communicate his parts to others;
Nor doth he of himself know them for aught
Till he behold them forméd in th' applause
Where they're extended; who, like an arch, reverberate
The voice again; or, like a gate of steel
Fronting the sun, receives and renders back
His figure and his heat. I was much rapt in this, . . .
                                                                (III. iii. 112–23)

There is obviously a strong touch of the political in this, and Ulysses goes on to call up the new fame of Ajax and shame Achilles into fighting. But the real profundity of Ulysses' position is in the way it combines a powerful sense of the potency of the attraction from person to person with—and this is why it is so potent—a sense of how deeply and actively the whole ego, the whole self, is bound up in this attraction. Ulysses is, in other words, giving voice and image to a theory of love which shows love to be more, certainly, than animal lust—for the context is not sexual—but not merely rational alliance. It is a theory which can include sexual love and yet does very obviously apply to the political relationship of leader and followers, with its complicated two-way process of identification. Certainly it helps us understand why Shakespeare sees love playing so important a part in human life, for knowledge of the self and formation of bonds between man and man are two of the major imperatives of life. It also opens the way to understanding the violence with which both good and evil flow from love, for to destroy one's love is to destroy something in the lover's very core of being—a profound act and one of the central subjects of *Othello*.

9   Othello

Hamlet can be seen as Shakespeare's fullest expression of the antiromantic point of view: woman is evil; love but a glossy, deceptive cover name for animal lust. *Troilus and Cressida* was still largely antiromantic, but this was tempered by intimations that love did indeed have some value and, furthermore, might well be one of the primal conditions of life itself. *Othello* by this scale is a return to romanticism, but it is a romanticism which incorporates into itself all the disturbing insights of the antiromantic mind and places them definitively within a larger romantic context. One could go farther; the special Shakespearean insight of this play could very well be that the snarling, bitter, life-denying vein of the antiromantic convention is itself both source and symptom of the evil it fears in sexual love.

1.

Drama thrives on conflict, and the conflict in *Othello* is quickly established and has a long Elizabethan tradition: a daring, romantic elopement set against the entrenched inertia of the bride's irascible, ranting father. The basic structure of character and action go, in other words, back to *Romeo and Juliet*, but in this play, coming about ten years later, the individual conventions are treated with much greater amplitude and penetration.

For instance, old Capulet had expressed a civilized liberality of attitude towards his daughter in saying he would not force her affections. Brabantio was equally liberal; as Othello says, "Her father loved me, oft invited me" (I. iii. 128), and then allowed him hours in private conversation with Desdemona. But his liberalism, like Capulet's, is short-lived, lasting only until the daughter attempts to exercise her own will and judgment in a sexual matter. Juliet had only to try to postpone a forced marriage to draw her father's

145

curses. Desdemona's insistence on choosing her husband without consult-
ing her father brings out the tyrant in him, but in even stronger modes of
expression, the chiefest immediate ones being recourse to the sword (I. ii.
80–81) and the fervent wish that he had given her to Roderigo, a man
whom he had previously despised (I. i. 176). For Roderigo—no matter how
pitiful a personal specimen of manhood he may be—is still a Venetian citi-
zen and a white man. Here then is one way in which an old convention of
romantic tragedy is used to touch deeper levels of alienation of man from
man.

In *Romeo and Juliet* Shakespeare had based his destructive antipathies on
a family feud which, although its roots were obscure, still had temporal origins and was indeed largely on the wane except among hot bloods. The re-
sentments which well up in *Othello* are more subtle and more profound.
Othello's race had never before been a barrier to his acceptance into the
houses of society, but as soon as sex intrudes so do a new set of attitudes
and words. The obvious racial slurs in Roderigo's term "the thick-lips" or
Iago's "Barbary horse" are prompted specifically by Othello's marriage to a
white woman, and they find a ready acceptance in Brabantio, with his frantic, credulous idea of the unnatural:

> For nature so preposterously to err,
> Being not deficient, blind, or lame of sense,
> Sans witchcraft could not.   (I. iii. 62–64)

and his obscure, overinflated fear of social dislocation:

> Mine's not an idle cause: the duke himself,
> Or any of my brothers of the state,
> Cannot but feel this wrong as 'twere their own;
> For if such actions may have passage free,
> Bond-slaves and pagans shall our statesmen be.
>   (I. ii. 95–99)

Like Bottom's dream, racial hatred "hath no bottom"; it seems to exist with
no discernible origins, causeless yet potent. But its link with sexual consciousness and paternal possessiveness is obvious and intentional.

In any case, the very depth of the antipathy stirred up by Othello's marriage to Desdemona provides a measure of love's positive value in its role as
a beneficial kind of unreason that unites people instead of dividing them.
For the dominant mood of the first half of the play—despite the counterpointed antiromantic scenes with Iago—is that of triumph, the triumph of
love and life itself against all sorts of deadness: the deadness of convention-

ality, unthinking negation, cynicism, prejudice, repression. Love in this play is—as it was in *Romeo and Juliet*—an imaginative leap, and its most natural mode of expression is poetry of great confidence and power and beauty. I think of a formal and yet subtly intimate passage like this of Othello's:

> I did consent,
> And often did beguile her of her tears
> When I did speak of some distressful stroke
> That my youth suffered. My story being done,
> She gave me for my pains a world of sighs:
> She swore, in faith 'twas strange, 'twas passing strange;
> 'Twas pitiful, 'twas wondrous pitiful;
> She wished she had not heard it, yet she wished
> That heaven had made her such a man; she thanked me,
> And bade me, if I had a friend that loved her,
> I should but teach him how to tell my story,
> And that would woo her.   (I. iii. 155–66)

with its hidden history of two people exchanging, as one of the senators very pleasantly puts it: "such fair question/As soul to soul affordeth" (I. iii. 113–14) and coming to an unspoken union that precedes actual words of love. It is not, after all, merely a collection of fantastic adventure stories that Othello tells Desdemona and Desdemona is won by. The story of a man's life told in his own voice embodies and expresses the man himself; there is nothing trivial in Othello's winning her this way.

Shakespeare's depth of apprehension is particularly evident in passages concerning the relation of love to the passing of time. This may be seen in Desdemona's very important answer to her father's question on the proper location of her loyalty:

> My noble father,
> I do perceive here a divided duty.
> To you I am bound for life and education;
> My life and education both do learn me
> How to respect you. You are the lord of duty;
> I am hitherto your daughter. But here's my
>   husband;
> And so much duty as my mother showed
> To you, preferring you before her father,
> So much I challenge that I may profess
> Due to the Moor my lord.   (I. iii. 180–89)

For Romeo and Juliet, love was the product of a timeless moment caught in the shared sonnet, and only at their final parting were they allowed any vision of the long stretch of time. But in Othello's storytelling there is a sense of roominess, a sense of temporal expansiveness that marks what one might call the adult consciousness of romantic love. Desdemona's statement shows the same largeness of vision, placing love in the context of the ever-renewing cycles of life itself.

The most important point in these passages between the lovers is that in their transformed state the best joy they have is their sense of union. Joy and union thus become inseparable, as do their converse qualities—misery and disunion. The first important expression of this is Desdemona's request to accompany Othello to the wars. It sums up a whole Elizabethan tradition of romantic poetry and drama:

> That I did love the Moor to live with him,
> My downright violence and scorn of fortunes
> May trumpet to the world. My heart's subdued
> Even to the very quality of my lord.
> I saw Othello's visage in his mind,
> And to his honours and his valiant parts
> Did I my soul and fortunes consecrate.
> So that, dear lords, if I be left behind,
> A moth of peace, and he go to the war,
> The rights for why I love him are bereft me,
> And I a heavy interim shall support
> By his dear absence. Let me go with him.   (I. iii. 248–59)

The movement of lovers towards each other may well be the most important single motive force in Elizabethan literature, particularly since the obverse state, the desire to annihilate instead of unite, is so closely related to it. Throughout the first part of *Othello* the motion towards union dominates, even to the point of putting the lovers on separate ships to Cyprus so that—on arrival, complete with cannon salutes and trumpet fanfares—the lovers can reenact their union, this time in conditions of triumph (over the enemy, over the great storm) that seem designed especially to enshrine this archetypal lovers' moment in a purity and brilliance of expression that allows no doubts about the fineness of the relationship which is to be destroyed:

> CAS: Lo where he comes!
>   *Enter* OTHELLO *and attendants*
> OTH: O my fair warrior!
> DES: My dear Othello!
> OTH: It gives me wonder great as my content
>   To see you here before me. O my soul's joy!
>   If after every tempest come such calms,

May the winds blow till they have wakened death!
And let the labouring bark climb hills of seas
Olympus-high and duck again as low
As hell's from heaven! If it were now to die,
'Twere now to be most happy; for I fear,
My soul hath her content so absolute
That not another comfort like to this
Succeeds in unknown fate.
DES: The heavens forbid
But that our loves and comforts should increase,
Even as our days do grow!
OTH: Amen to that, sweet powers!
I cannot speak enough of this content:
It stops me here; it is too much of joy.
And this, and this, the greatest discords be [*they kiss*]
That e'er our hearts shall make!

                                              (II. i. 178–96)

Othello starts in his heroic vein, but he feels a joy so great it cannot be completely expressed in the spoken language, so great indeed it threatens for a moment to obliterate any future joy in its completeness. But Desdemona's more domestic consciousness of the passing of time as growth and fruition corrects and complements this so that the accompanying music imagery, with all its Elizabethan connotations of universal harmony, beauty, order, and peace, is a legitimate expression of what they feel.

                                         2.

What I have called the antiromantic convention can be seen as a mode of knowing or a certain emotional configuration of knowledge. Basically the configuration shows a drop from happiness to unhappiness, from a sense of life to a sense of death. The word used to sum it up—*disillusionment*—refers specifically to knowledge. The other great word—the *fall*—is a physical-spatial metaphor for the emotional reaction involved. As I suggested in the section on *Hamlet*, Shakespeare knew that the greatest myth of the antiromantic convention, the source of its configuration, was that of the betrayal of man by woman. Therefore it is not surprising to find this antiromantic configuration at work in *Othello* with both these major elements given prominence—the idea of female betrayal and that of disillusioning knowledge; there is, of course, this extremely important proviso—that in *Othello*, unlike the previous plays—these things are seen as figments of the masculine imagination.

The idea of knowledge is the obsessive concern of the crucial third scene of Act III:

OTH: Was not that Cassio parted from my wife?

. . . .

IAGO: Did Michael Cassio,
When you wooed my lady, know of your love?

. . . .

OTH: Indeed? ay, indeed. Discern'st thou aught in that?

. . . .

IAGO: My lord, for aught I know.
OTH: What dost thou think?
IAGO: Think my lord?

. . . .

IAGO: My lord, you know I love you.

. . . .

IAGO: Why then, I think Cassio's an honest man.

. . . .

OTH: I'll see before I doubt; when I doubt, prove;

. . . .

IAGO: . . . their best conscience
Is not to leav't undone, but keep't unknown.
(III. iii. 38, 94–95, 102, 106–108, 120, 132, 192, 205–206)

What is less often noticed, however, is that the fall motif is enacted on two occasions preceding the fall of Othello. These are the respective disillusionments of Brabantio and Roderigo, both instances engineered by Iago and both involving some breakdown of previously held conceptions of Desdemona.

The fall of Brabantio is important because of its explicit structural connection with Othello's: the parallel thrown up by Iago in III, iii—

> She did deceive her father, marrying you;
> And when she seemed to shake and fear your looks,
> She loved them most.   (III. iii. 208–10)

This first deception is the structural basis for all those that follow, and it displays in abbreviated form most of the qualities that we associate with such occasions. Behind it in turn is the first of these great Shakespearean disillusionments, that of Hamlet. The continuity becomes clear, I think, when we recall that the ghost spoke to Hamlet in the language of the fall from Eden, heavily charged with bestial metaphors. In *Othello*, Brabantio's *ghost* is

Iago, and Iago's imagery is very much akin to the ghost's, as is his intention, which is to destroy contentment:

> . . . though he in a fertile climate dwell,
> Plague him with flies; though that his joy be joy,
> Yet throw such changes of vexation on't
> As it may lose some colour.   (I. i. 71–74)

The dominant imagery is sexual, primarily bestial and satanic:

> Even now, now, very now, an old black ram
> Is tupping your white ewe.
> . . . .
> I am one, sir, that comes to tell you your daughter and
> the Moor are now making the beast with two backs.
>   (I. i. 89–90, 116–18)

The main effect of this kind of vivid language is to break down complacency and force a gulf between the victim's idealizations and the intransigent fact of human sexuality. In the service of a wit as freewheeling as Iago's, these facts seem to spread out, embracing and undermining the whole range of family relationships which weigh so heavily with a settled, conventional character like Brabantio: "Because we come to do you service and you think we are ruffians, you'll have your daughter covered with a Barbary horse; you'll have your nephews neigh to you; you'll have coursers for cousins, and jennets for germans" (I. i. 110–14). The next stage is, of course, the seeking of "ocular proof," which in this case is easily forthcoming. Then comes the plunge into resentment, despair, and rage. Brabantio's quick recourse to violence and his wild accusations of witchcraft against Othello are manifestations of this. But a more significant and permanent manifestation is sexual cynicism; it begins early and is the product of a habit of thought also seen in *Hamlet*: making generalizations about woman on the basis of personal disappointment:

> With the Moor, say'st thou? Who would be a father!
> . . . .
> O heaven! How got she out? O treason of the blood!
> Fathers, from hence trust not your daughters' minds
> By what you see them act!   (I. i. 165, 170–72)

Then, after hearing Othello tell how Desdemona had very plainly dropped hints concerning her desire to marry him, he throws up his hands in the face of female waywardness and gives expression to a peculiar feeling of masculine solidarity:

> If she confess that she was half the wooer,
> Destruction on my head, if my bad blame
> Light on the man!   (I. iii. 176–78)

This is a considerable change from his initial reaction, which was to blame Othello and regain his daughter. Now his behavior to a daughter would be far different, all liberality gone:

> I am glad at soul I have no other child;
> For thy escape would teach me tyranny,
> To hang clogs on them.   (I. iii. 196–98)

And his final parting shot at Othello himself has more than just simple malice in it; it is the distilled wisdom of post-Adamic man: "Look to her, Moor, if thou hast eyes to see:/She has deceived her father, and may thee" (I. iii. 292–93).

The thinking behind all this is shallow, but the emotions are not. The following piece of dialogue at the Senate is a piece of literal emotional truth; in a sense it is a restatement in miniature of one great principle of human behavior that became visible to the dramatist of love and death:

> DUKE: Why, what's the matter?
> BRAB: My daughter! O, my daughter!
> ALL: Dead?
> BRAB: Ay, to me:
>   She is abused, stolen from me and corrupted. . . .
>   (I. iii. 58–60)

This is first of all an expression of loss, but it is also an expression of despair and jealousy: not sexual jealousy but a lover's jealousy all the same. Iago himself had the key to the link between these emotions when he shouted:

> Your heart is burst; you have lost half your soul;
> Even now, now, very now, an old black ram
> Is tupping your white ewe.   (I. i. 88–90)

Brabantio's heart is burst, and Shakespeare in showing us this is probing deeply into that important but little-explored conventional figure, the enraged father. The exact mystery at the heart of this character can only be guessed at, but it clearly has to do with the relationship between possessiveness and love and the subtle way a lover makes the beloved part of himself so that any honor done the beloved honors the lover and anything disgusting in the beloved creates a core of disgust (self-disgust as well as disgust with the other) that is destructive in proportion to the love felt. If these seem excessively portentous terms in which to discuss a relatively minor figure like Brabantio, we should remember Brabantio's death, the end of a process which converted powerful love into alienation (psychological death) and finally physical death:

> Poor Desdemon! I am glad thy father's dead.
> Thy match was mortal to him, and pure grief
> Shore his old thread in twain.   (V. ii. 207–209)

We should also recall that Shakespeare went on in *King Lear* to explore the profundities of the love of father and daughter in his most ambitious and far-ranging study of the sources of good and evil and of life itself.

Roderigo's fall is of a different nature; it is concerned with love for Desdemona but nevertheless remains much more a cerebral experience. Roderigo never stops desiring Desdemona, but the modes of his desire shift even as his vision of Desdemona changes before the corrosive acid of Iago's *knowledge*. Even Iago is more cerebral—that is, theoretical—when he is talking to Roderigo. Taking advantage of his dullness, Iago bemuses him with reductive theories of love and of human nature that Roderigo can only at first gasp at ("It cannot be," he says, upon hearing Iago's definition of love) but which he finally ends by accepting. Thus, although Roderigo began as a romantic suitor (no matter how bumbling) hoping for marriage, haunting Desdemona's door in Petrarchan disappointment, helping to lead her rescue party, and finally—with the failure of all else—readying himself to make the great romantic gesture of defeat ("I will incontinently drown myself" [I. iii. 305]), he ends—after Iago's relevations—as a would-be seducer and hopeful roué, working through a pander: "The jewels you have had from me to deliver to Desdemona would half have corrupted a votarist" (IV. ii. 187-89). But Roderigo in himself is unimportant; what is important is that his decline shows still another victim to the Iago vision and increases our sense of its effectiveness, particularly since Roderigo's naïve romanticism is a poor man's version of Othello's.

In any case, as a foil to Iago Roderigo is perfect; being unsure of himself, he is always ready to be educated; being weak-minded, he cannot answer Iago's tough-minded arguments. And Iago's arguments really are difficult to answer; they are extremely conventional and traditional and have the status of commonplaces in conservative antiromantic thought of both the classical and the Christian eras. Would, for instance, a follower of either Seneca or St. Augustine have found anything to quarrel with in this pronouncement of Iago's on love?

> If the beam of our lives had not one scale of reason to poise another of
> sensuality, the blood and baseness of our natures would conduct us to
> most preposterous conclusions. But we have reason to cool our raging
> motions, our carnal stings, our unbitted lusts; whereof I take this, that
> you call love, to be a sect or scion.
> . . . .
> It is merely a lust of the blood and a permission of the will.
> (I. iii. 326–32, 334–35)

This is a standard rationalist ethical position.[1]

The interesting question therefore is not only why Iago's argument is so effective, but why Shakespeare allows such respected commonplaces to become the philosophy of his most thorough and impenitent evildoer. Suffice it now to suggest that Shakespeare regarded the automatic equation of reason with good and blood with evil as—at the least—suspect, and that the thing that made it suspect was that it does away with love of other humans as a source of good. It could even be argued that the whole idea of the rational man, the Senecal man, the politic man, was rendered suspect by the very detachment of such a character from those "unbitted lusts" that move men to women and, in transmuted forms, to their fellow men. Iago's love is *rational* love: "O villanous! I have looked upon the world for four times seven years; and since I could distinguish betwixt a benefit and an injury, I never found a man that knew how to love himself. Ere I would say I would drown myself for the love of a guinea-hen, I would change my humanity with a baboon" (I. iii. 311–16). To love anyone other than oneself is irrational; it hinders policy.

Once Iago has placed love among the purely animal attributes in a philosophy which (like the Christian one) makes a sharp moral separation between spirit and body, he is then able to break down the social manifestations of love to reveal their basis in physical contact. From this he may draw a steady supply of pejorative inferences. A powerful instance of the process is Iago's treatment of the ideal of woman, a masterpiece of diction in which preciosity ("required conveniencies," "delicate tenderness") and a sharp consciousness of the animal functions merge with tremendous effect: "When the blood is made dull with the act of sport, there should be—again to inflame it and to give satiety a fresh appetite—loveliness in favour, sympathy in years, manners, and beauties; all which the Moor is defective in."

---

1. For a useful outline of some of the ramifications of attitude concerning the "scale of reason" in men, see Theodore Spencer's two chapters "Man in Nature: the Optimistic Theory" and "Man in Nature: the Renaissance Conflict." *Shakespeare and the Nature of Man*, 1–50.

Now, for want of these required conveniencies, her delicate tenderness will find itself abused, begin to heave the gorge, disrelish and abhor the Moor. Very nature will instruct her in it and compel her to some second choice" (II. i. 223–32). Iago's power here is not unlike that commanded by reductionist Darwinians and Freudians in our own day, and it is founded on the same idea: that if one shows low origins to a complicated state of being, one has revealed that condition's essence. The small part, the presumed essence, becomes the whole in the mind of the hearer.

Iago's explanation of courtesy is another excellent example of how this process works:

> IAGO: Didst thou not see her paddle with the palm of his hand? Didst not mark that?
> ROD: Yes, that I did; but that was but courtesy.
> IAGO: Lechery, by this hand; an index and obscure prologue to the history of lust and foul thoughts. They met so near with their lips that their breaths embraced together—villanous thoughts, Roderigo! When these mutualities so marshal the way, hard at hand comes the master and main exercise, th'incorporate conclusion.   (II. i. 249–57)

The power of this passage comes from two related things. One is the brilliant handling of language that carries the "hand" image from observed fact (the touching of hands) into the very sinews of the argument and insists so completely on the physical nature of the spirit of love that we find that even "breaths embraced together." The other is the element of half-truth in Iago's argument that gives the linguistic subtlety a hold in reality. The heart of the Elizabethan romantic idea was that love between man and woman was a spiritual endeavor as well as a physical one and all the better for the union of the two things. The worst enemy of this romantic vision is that which takes either the physical or the spiritual end of the spectrum and gives it a disproportionate weight. The traditional medieval or Renaissance thinker who makes love purely an attribute of the spirit and gives it to the angelic part of man, thus separating it from human sexuality, diminishes the full romantic idea of love as much as an Iago, who does the opposite—defines love purely in terms of the physical. They both work at making temporal, physical life seem one-sided and mechanical. Set against this tendency to diminish human life, Shakespeare gives us human love. When Desdemona says,

> That I did love the Moor to live with him,
> My downright violence and scorn of fortunes
> May trumpet to the world.   (I. iii. 248–50)

and Othello:

> Amen to that, sweet powers!
> I cannot speak enough of this content:
> It stops me here; it is too much of joy.
> And this, and this, the greatest discords be [*they kiss*]
> That e'er our hearts shall make!   (II. i. 192–96)

they have come to each other with a sense of value in themselves and in life itself that leaves them open to love, and it is plain that the reward for their openness to life is a new Edenic stage of secular revelation, a new knowledge of joy, one that partakes mutually of spiritual and earthly beauty. This then is how the lines of the conflict in this play are drawn—between love, which gives life value, and those perverse ideas, powerful from both an imaginative and a traditional moral standpoint, that militate against love. The battleground in this case is Othello's mind, and the central issue is the crucial one in Elizabethan-Jacobean love literature: the idea of woman.

All this has relevance to the fact that there has always been in Shakespearean criticism a nagging sense of unease over Othello's actual fall into jealousy. In its simplest form it crystallizes in the debate over Othello's character—whether or not he is the "noble Moor" of A. C. Bradley[2] or Helen Gardner,[3] or the depraved egotist of F. R. Leavis.[4] The answer, it seems to me, lies partially with both sides, and this doubleness—Othello's nobility in most things set against his ready fall into ignobility concerning his wife—is in fact one of Shakespeare's most significant touches. The suggestion would appear to be that even a man of great nobility may have this blind spot concerning erotic matters.

It is for this reason that, although F. R. Leavis is correct to say that "Iago's power, in fact, in the temptation-scene is that he represents something that is in Othello—in Othello the husband of Desdemona: the essential traitor is within the gates"[5] and further that "Iago . . . points out that Othello didn't really know Desdemona, and Othello acquiesces in considering her as a type—a type outside his experience—the Venetian wife,"[6] he is di-

---

2. A. C. Bradley, *Shakespearean Tragedy* (2nd ed.; London: Macmillan & Co. Ltd., 1905), 186–98.
3. Helen Gardner, "The Noble Moor," British Academy Shakespeare lecture (1955): reprinted in *Shakespeare Criticism, 1935–1960*, selected by Anne Ridler (London: Oxford University Press, 1963), 348–70.
4. F. R. Leavis, "Diabolic Intellect and the Noble Hero" (1937), in *The Common Pursuit* (London: Chatto & Windus, 1952), 136–59.
5. *Ibid.*, 140–41.
6. *Ibid.*, 145.

minishing the extent of Shakespeare's insight by turning it merely into the grist for an anti-Othello, anti-Bradley mill. The whole point, it seems to me, of having Iago exercise his magic successfully on two other men—men who whatever their faults were not essentially bad—is to bring into question the whole matter of the male ego and male sexual imagination and the ability of men in general to believe in the union of sexual and spiritual love. There is, after all, not a single male character in the play with a generosity of love equal to that which their women show to them. One need not mention Desdemona yet. Even Emilia—though there is obviously little love left between Iago and her—is faithful to him until the final revelations, and the prostitute Bianca has a tenderness and concern for Cassio that belies any charge of her being motivated purely by appetite. But in succession, Iago (recall how he suspects both Othello and Cassio with his nightcap), Brabantio, Roderigo, and then Othello turn on the women of the play as soon as the traditional vision of female evil begins to weigh heavily on their minds. Even Cassio, who is nothing if not a gentleman and a good man, has a double standard, with two widely separated ideas of love and two very different women as their objects. Desdemona is the idealized woman, the object of chaste, Petrarchan reverence. But nature demands also some sexual satisfaction; for this Cassio has a whore with whom he may lie at one minute and mock for it the next, using the same kind of animal imagery that comes so easily to Iago's lips:

> This is the monkey's own giving out: she is persuaded I will marry her, out of her own love and flattery, not out of my promise.
>
> . . . .
> 'Tis such another fitchew!   (IV. i. 128–30, 145)

It is one of the play's nicer ironies that Cassio convicts himself most grossly in Othello's eyes while leering about a woman whom he is treating badly.

The point is that Othello's fall in what Leavis calls the "temptation-scene" is completely of a piece with the other male attitudes in the play. Iago's technique was to first plant doubts which stimulated the imagination and then to weigh in with his stereotype of woman, his Venetian wife:

> I know our country disposition well;
> In Venice they do let heaven see the pranks
> They dare not show their husbands; their best
>   conscience
> Is not to leave't undone, but keep't unknown.
>   (III. iii. 203–206)

Behind this stereotype though are many women: in Shakespeare, Gertrude, Cressida, and the Dark Lady of the sonnets; in *Genesis*, Eve; in Shakespeare's predecessors, the whole legion of minor erring females in history plays and narrative verse that Hallett Smith refers to in his important article on Heywood.[7] Professor Smith's point is that because of conventional Elizabethan psychology and such conventional stories as that of Jane Shore, the average Elizabethan theatergoer would unblinkingly accept the proposition that woman was morally inferior. Hamlet, before learning the ghost's story, was moved by his mother's conduct to generalize—"Frailty thy name is woman." The generalization was for many audiences and writers an accepted psychological fact. It is this commonplace—with all of its traditional moral weight—that Iago brings forth for Othello's contemplation, garnished with the same conception of the animal nature (and its necessary transience) that he had expounded to Roderigo:

> Ay, there's the point: as—to be bold with you—
> Not to affect many proposéd matches
> Of her own clime, complexion, and degree,
> Whereto we see in all things nature tends—
> Foh! one may smell, in such, a will most rank,
> Foul disproportion, thoughts unnatural.
> But pardon me: I do not in position
> Distinctly speak of her; though I may fear
> Her will, recoiling to her better judgement,
> May fall to match you with her country forms,
> And happily repent.   (III. iii. 230–40)

It is not merely personal perversity on Othello's part that he should have introduced the subject of "nature erring from itself" (III. iii. 229); it is the same kind of almost automatic theoretical (the *theoretical* is important, for Shakespeare persistently sets destructive theory against living intuition) distrust of woman that Brabantio, for instance, showed in his emotional warnings to fathers: "Fathers, from hence trust not your daughters' minds" (I. i. 171). Thus, there is great irony and considerable psychological validity in Othello's ready acceptance of Iago's devastating point: "She did deceive her father, marrying you" (III. iii. 208); and in the way Othello then goes on to restate Brabantio's complaint in his own terms:

> O curse of marriage,
> That we can call these delicate creatures ours,
> And not their appetites!   (III. iii. 270–72)

---

7. Hallett D. Smith, *"A Woman Killed with Kindness,"* PMLA, LIII (March, 1938), 138–47.

Indeed, here perhaps is the source of one of the play's dominating structural ironies: the way Shakespeare has this phantasmagoric questioning, raving, mocking debate go on among the men about their stereotype women, while at the center of it Desdemona sits, an uncomprehending denial of a whole tradition of masculine invention and myth.

The key words, therefore, for a discussion of Othello's jealousy are myth, invention, and aggression. The invention aspect is, of course, self-evident. Othello demands verifiable "ocular proof" and gets instead conventional theory and certain small provocative, imaginative events that one is tempted to call little plays. I mean, for instance, Iago's vivid retelling of Cassio's alleged dream:

> And then, sir, would he gripe and wring my hand,
> Cry 'O sweet creature!' and then kiss me hard,
> As if he plucked up kisses by the roots,
> That grew upon my lips; then laid his leg
> Over my thigh, and sighed, and kissed, and then
> Cried 'Curséd fate that gave thee to the Moor!'
>
> (III. iii. 423–28)

or his imaginative use of Cassio's mockery of Bianca. These are inventions that spur Othello's invention. He takes the hints and spins on, envisioning whole episodes of which only the surfaces show in dialogues like this:

OTH: You have see nothing, then?
EMILIA: Nor ever heard, nor ever did suspect.
OTH: Yes, you have seen Cassio and she together.
EMILIA: But then I saw no harm, and then I heard
Each syllable that breath made up between
them.
OTH: What, did they never whisper?
EMILIA: Never, my lord.
OTH: Nor send you out o'th'way?
EMILIA: Never.
OTH: To fetch her fan, her gloves, her mask,
nor nothing?
EMILIA: Never, my lord.
OTH: That's strange. (IV. ii. 1–11)

or in the brutal and terrifying brilliance of his transformation of Desdemona's room into a house of prostitution, Desdemona into the "cunning whore of Venice" (IV. ii. 90), and Emilia into a bawd. There are few more devastating demonstrations of the potential destructiveness of the imagination than these scenes, but Othello is hardly unique in this, for his delusion is not more than an extreme version of a time-sanctioned mythology.

This leads back to what I said earlier about love and the question of knowledge. L. C. Knights has made several perceptive remarks on this question, and one of them is this: "To know it is necessary to love—to love with that outgoing generosity of spirit for which this play constantly finds the word 'free.'" [8] What Othello does, therefore, in accepting the stereotype of woman is to allow a preset configuration to be placed on his perception of a living woman and on his reaction to her. Thus, in the love relationship[9]—which demands knowledge of self and knowledge of the beloved—Othello has taken on not merely blinders but a peep show in a dark room. In showing this Shakespeare is throwing overboard the conventional forms of antiromantic cynicism and rationalism because they put a barrier of distrust and mockery where people most need trust and the kind of living personal contact that animated Romeo and Juliet and in this play Desdemona. When Othello looks at Desdemona in Act III and says:

> Look where she comes:
> If she be false, O, then heaven mocks itself!
> I'll not believe't.   (III. iii. 279–81)

he is reacting to a human being. When, in Act V, he mutters those strange words:

> It is the cause, it is the cause, my soul.
> Let me not name it to you, you chaste stars!
> It is the cause.   (V. ii. 1–3)

he is acting a part in a discredited and discreditable myth and dignifying his murder of Desdemona into a purifying ritual, a godly vengeance on fair Eve and her sex.

3.

In the chapter on *Hamlet* I suggested that much of the distinctive character of the play came from the manner in which the impulse to love and the impulse to hate operated simultaneously in Hamlet's own soul. His hatred of infidelity and of woman warred against his very natural, indeed necessary, emotion for his mother and Ophelia. The result was a peculiarly clotted, manic state of mind, full of reversals and turmoil. That this suffering

---

8. L. C. Knights, *An Approach to 'Hamlet'* (London: Chatto & Windus, 1960), 21–22.

9. I take this opportunity to call attention to the extremely perceptive chapter "Love and Identity: *Othello*," in John Bayley's important book *The Characters of Love* (London: Constable & Co. Ltd., 1960). This is the only chapter that touches directly on a play taken up in this study, but Bayley's general principles and his critical point of view have been of the greatest interest and aid.

has reminded some critics of jealousy is hardly surprising. We can see from *Othello* that the emotional torments of Othello were built on and illuminated by those of Hamlet, as well as the parallel experience of Brabantio and other tragic fathers.

Brabantio, for instance, was moved by his loss to violence and to rejection, but he did not die of hatred. The description indicates something more like what is known ordinarily as a broken heart; he loved Desdemona but had also to reject her. In the end the violence of his conflicting emotions turned inward upon himself. In Hamlet's case, the full revelation of the ghost moves him to attempt a gesture of pure, single-direction hatred:

> Haste me to know't, that I with wings as swift
> As meditation or the thoughts of love,
> May sweep to my revenge.   (*H*, I. v. 29–31)

But, as I suggested earlier, the seeds of the conflict of love and hate are already there in the wording. Hamlet's much-discussed delay is a product of the conflict and a sign, one might add, of his humanity. One cannot, for instance, imagine an Iago—unencumbered as he is by love of others—exhibiting such symptoms of uncertainty. With Othello, Shakespeare goes still further into this phenomenon of mixed love and hate and isolates two main aspects of it: one, the relation between the person who loves and hates and the object of the emotions; the other, the relation of a man and his own soul.

The first of these is easily demonstrated; Hamlet's wild fluctuations in Ophelia's presence are the direct predecessors of such obvious turmoil as Othello shows here:

OTH: I would have him nine years a-killing. A fine woman! a fair woman! a sweet woman!

IAGO: Nay, you must forget that.

OTH: Ay, let her rot, and perish, and be damned tonight; for she shall not live. No, my heart is turned to stone: I strike it, and it hurts my hand. O, the world hath not a sweeter creature: she might lie by an emperor's side and command him tasks.

IAGO: Nay, that's not your way.

OTH: Hang her! I do but say what she is: so delicate with her needle, an admirable musician—O, she will sing the savageness out of a bear—of so high and plenteous wit and invention—

IAGO: She's the worse for all this.

OTH: O, a thousand, thousand times—and, then, of so gentle a condition!

IAGO: Ay, too gentle.

OTH: Nay, that's certain; but yet the pity of it, Iago!
O Iago, the pity of it, Iago!   (IV. i. 177-95)

He flies from blood-thirsty rhetoric to remembrances so melting in tone and subject that they make Iago nervous. At the heart of this turmoil are the two images of Desdemona, the romantic one that dominated the first two acts and the antiromantic one that obscures, but cannot completely supplant, the other.

But Shakespeare's thinking on the nature of love has gone farther than this. In the midst of what is possibly Othello's deepest suffering, that is his verbal attack on Desdemona in what is often called the "brothel scene," Shakespeare gives Othello a speech that seems—in its relentless stripping away of the layers of the self—to go as far into the human soul as language can take one:

> Had it pleased heaven
> To try me with affliction; had they rained
> All kind of sores and shames on my bare head,
> Steeped me in poverty to the very lips,
> Given to captivity me and my utmost hopes,
> I should have found in some place of my soul
> A drop of patience; but, alas, to make me
> A fixéd figure for the time of scorn
> To point his slow unmoving finger at!
> Yet could I bear that too; well, very well;
> But there, where I have garnered up my heart,
> Where either I must live or bear no life,
> The fountain from the which my current runs,
> Or else dries up—to be discarded thence!
> Or keep it as a cistern for foul toads
> To knot and gender in!   (IV. ii. 48–63)

I think this speech is best taken as a complement to the conversation between Achilles and Ulysses in *Troilus and Cressida* (III. iii). There the main point was that a man can have full understanding of his own value and own nature only as it is reflected in the love of another. That is to say, the individual soul is confirmed only as it strikes an answering reverberation. Othello's speech takes this farther, for it locates love in the very center of the self so that the conflict of love and hate towards the beloved becomes a question of accepting or rejecting one's own essence. The key lines are these:

> But there, where I have garnered up my heart,
> Where either I must live or bear no life,
> The fountain from the which my current runs,
> Or else dries up— . . .   (IV. ii. 58–61)

Thus, in the midst of loss, Othello is able to express the now lost joy that in

Act II blocked his tongue. Also, he can define why love has a special value and why that value is also the source of its danger. In *Othello* the joys of love seem to lie in the combination of a transfigured sense of one's own value and the complementing joy of being drawn out of oneself—as Othello is at the meeting in Cyprus. The fear is that in love, in that identification of one-self with another that is central to the word *union* one has put one's own soul at the mercy of another's behavior. Othello's cry—

> O curse of marriage,
> That we can call these delicate creatures ours,
> And not their appetites!   (III. iii. 270–72)

is the cry of a self-sufficient man whose horizons have been widened by the experience of love, but who is just beginning to fear the measure of exposure his commitment has put at the mercy of another. This conflict lies at the heart of any intimate relationship and has importance in plays to come. Lear, we remember, finding relationship breaking up around him, prayed first and mainly not to be mad. The terrible agonies of Hamlet, Troilus, and Othello prepare for that fear and for the great scene on the heath.

Complex emotions require a complex form. A play built on the internal conflicts of love and death requires a form which will externalize these. For this, Shakespeare still has the formal logic of the past tradition of love-death tragedies upon which to draw. Thus, the symmetry, the organizing pattern, of the Deadly Nuptial appears in what is perhaps its most terrible and subtle form. The very full elaboration of it in this play, coming after the truncated version in *Hamlet*, suggests that Shakespeare has now got a more confident mastery—emotionally and intellectually—over the shaping of the total structure of his material. The fineness of the details go beyond anything else which he had done with these themes yet, particularly in the varied tones he gives the scenes leading up to the murder and the structure and tone of the death scene itself.

The key to the Deadly Nuptial is again the analogy between the marriage bed and the death bed. Iago is the first to propose it:

IAGO: Do it not with poison: strangle her in her bed, even the bed she hath contaminated.
OTH: Good, good: the justice of it pleases; very good.
                                                    (IV. i. 206–209)

The justice here is, of course, poetic justice masquerading under the pressure of rage as legal justice. But the poetry of the analogy can develop in different ways depending on the circumstances. In Othello's hands in the "brothel" scene it converts the marriage bed into a whore's bed, thus indicating another kind of death, the death of love by sexual infidelity. But when the scene switches to Desdemona and Emilia, the whole emotional tone changes and one begins to feel—in ways difficult to express in critical prose—the real range and depth of this stage convention. In Desdemona's requests to Emilia: "Prithee, tonight/Lay on my bed my wedding sheets—" (IV. ii. 105–106) and later, "If I do die before thee, prithee, shroud me/In one of those same sheets" (IV. iii. 24–25), the convention takes on a terrible poignancy, partly because Desdemona seems to feel her own death in the air, but more in that her request to be buried in her wedding sheet seems to symbolically link love and death, union and final dissolution, as the central experiences—the south and north poles—of adult life.

The death scene brings both points of view—that of the killer and the victim—together, and almost every detail of it seems to turn in one way or another about this meeting of love and death. Othello's initial speech, with its profound and beautiful meditation on life and light, death and darkness, the rose alive and the rose plucked, pushes the love-death imagery to its widest possible application:

> Put out the light, and then put out the light:
> If I quench thee, thou flaming minister,
> I can again thy former light restore
> Should I repent me; but once put out thy light,
> Thou cunning'st pattern of excelling nature,
> I know not where is that Promethean heat
> That can thy light relume. When I have plucked
>   the rose,
> I cannot give it vital growth again,
> It needs must wither: . . .   (V. ii. 15)

As soon as he says "I'll smell it on the tree" (V. ii. 15) and kisses her, the focus narrows to the personal:

> Be thus when thou art dead, and I will kill thee,
> And love thee after. One more, and that's the last.
> So sweet was ne'er so fatal. I must weep,
> But they are cruel tears; this sorrow's heavenly:
> It strikes where it doth love.   (V. ii. 18–22)

But the images are no less important for that; they show again how love and death fight in Othello's heart even on the point of the murder and how narrow—when the strange logic of the passage is analyzed—the line is that separates Othello from full-blown lunacy. The only thing that keeps him in control is his conviction that he is performing an exalted sacrifice (he uses

the term himself—V. ii. 68). This, in part at any rate, accounts for his peculiar, stilted religiosity in the final moments, as he—like a medieval preacher
—exhorts Desdemona to think upon her sins, to remember she is on her
deathbed, to confess.

The final turn is the movement from the terrible irony of his immediate
sense of loss—"If she come in, she'll sure speak to my wife—/My wife! my
wife! what wife? I have no wife" (V. ii. 99–100)—through the new pieces of
knowledge that come to him from Emilia and Cassio to his final recovery
and full consciousness of himself. His final speech and his suicide should
be seen as all of one piece with the recovery of his vision of Desdemona. All
of these were necessary components in the act of taking his life, the act that
puts the final touch to the Deadly Nuptial design, crystallizing into a sentence the play's formal and emotional tension: "I kissed thee ere I killed
thee: no way but this,/Killing myself, to die upon a kiss" (V. ii. 360–61).

Summary

The great theme of Shakespeare's middle tragedies is the death of love: the betrayal of one person by another who is very close. In the early plays death encroached from the outside; in these it works from within—within the couple or indeed within a single mind and heart. Of necessity the stories chosen for such tragedies are less inclined to demonstrate the beauties of love (a romantic theme) than to show the potential in it for evil and destruction (an antiromantic theme). The great problem, therefore, in these plays and in numerous others to follow is sexual evil—its causes, results, its relationship to love.

As one would expect, the tone and imagery of the plays shift radically. In the simpler, more innocent tragedies of the earlier romantic period, sexual love could be frankly and confidently equated with life and therefore with good. The language was alive with images of nature and beauty. The result was the creation of a kind of paradise on earth. In *Hamlet*, however, character and language are expelled from the garden together:

> O God, God,
> How weary, stale, flat, and unprofitable
> Seem to me all the uses of this world!
> Fie on't, ah fie, 'tis an unweeded garden
> That grows to seed, things rank and gross in nature
> Possess it merely.   (I. ii. 132–37)

Troilus and Cressida is swamped with images of disease and death: "Now, the rotten diseases of the south, the guts-griping, ruptures, catarrhs . . . take and take again such preposterous discoveries!" (V. i. 17–23), and in the diseased, death-haunted mind of Othello sexual nature is reduced to the status of a horror which makes the soul a "cistern for foul toads/To knot and gender in!" (IV. ii. 62–63).

166

In the early tragedies of love the romantic ideal tended to bring man and woman together with the same object in mind: mutual love, mutual self-surrender, mutual creation. Shakespeare's middle tragedies split this union apart and fire the first shots of the sex war which becomes a prominent motif in later plays. In terms of plot, of course, the betrayal motif carries this theme. In *Hamlet*, Gertrude's betrayal is an act of war which sets Hamlet against all women and thus against the sources of his own creation and nature. In *Troilus and Cressida* the sex-war motif puts a permanent edge of distrust between the young lovers and serves as a source of some of the larger structural groupings, such as the division of those who want Helen to love her from those who want her to despise her:

> DIOM: For every false drop in her bawdy veins
> A Grecian's life hath sunk; for every scruple
> Of her contaminated carrion weight
> A Trojan hath been slain;
>
> . . . .
>
> PARIS: Fair Diomed, you do as chapmen do,
> Dispraise the thing that you desire to buy; . . .
> (IV. i. 71–74, 77–78)

In *Othello* the idea of it acts as the acid that undercuts masculine contentment:

> O curse of marriage,
> That we can call these delicate creatures ours,
> And not their appetites! (III. iii. 270–72)

One result of this war in terms of characterization and therefore general tone is the rise to prominence of the sexual cynic. In early plays he had been a minor figure; with Hamlet, Thersites, Diomedes, and Iago he gains tremendous dramatic force and a very considerable antiromantic, even anti-humanist, metaphysical weight. In Shakespeare, to hate woman is to hate beauty and to hate life. Despite (or possibly because of) the fact that Shakespeare seemed to recover from the antiromanticism of *Hamlet* and *Troilus and Cressida*, he continued to put on the stage antierotic voices of tremendous power. After Iago, Hamlet, and Othello comes Lear on the heath:

> Behold yond simp'ring dame
> Whose face between her forks presages snow,
> That minces virtue and does shake the head
> To hear of pleasure's name;
> The fitchew nor the soiléd horse goes to 't
> With a more riotous appetite.
> Down from the waist they are centaurs,
> Though women all above.
> But to the girdle do the gods inherit,
> Beneath is all the fiend's. (IV. vi. 118–27)

and Timon at his cave:

> Down with the nose,
> Down with it flat, take the bridge quite away
> Of him that his particular to foresee
> Smells from the general weal. Make curled-pate
> ⸱ ruffians bald;
> And let the unscarred braggarts of the war
> Derive some pain from you. Plague all,
> That your activity may defeat and quell
> The source of all erection.   (*T of A*, IV. iii. 158–65)

The important point here, however, is that Shakespeare had come to see this kind of rhetoric as a symptom of mental and moral turpitude, usually the product of the shock of betrayal. Nevertheless, the voices are powerful, and a number of later playwrights echoed their antiromanticism as if what Shakespeare saw as a partial view was to them the whole truth. Tourneur's moral stance and Middleton's female psychology owe more to Hamlet's punitive mood and the philosophy of Iago than Jacobean criticism has yet pointed out. Thus, the treatment of woman remains a fascinating subject and an excellent moral touchstone. The Jacobeans have got the women of both Shakespeare's romantic stage and his antiromantic stage before them. They have Juliet and Cressida, Desdemona and Gertrude. What they make of these images (and that of Cleopatra, whom I discuss later) and the relationship of their male characters to their women is as interesting a subject in the later writers as it is in *Hamlet* or in *Othello*.

One final point: Shakespeare's middle love tragedies severely modified the early romantic conventions but by no means did away with them. The relationship of love and death remained the central organizing focus. This same is true in the playwrights to come—indeed, perhaps it holds with even greater force since the lesser writers have a narrower scope. The problem, however, is that for Shakespeare love and death motives had definite moral valuations. Kept free from the death motive (that is, jealousy, murder, hatred, self-love), eros had positive values of creativeness, beauty, and goodness. Many of the conservative moralists who followed him, however, took up his categories but tended to reinterpret them in light of their own tradition-sanctioned distrust of erotic love. The result is often a sharply antiromantic moral rectitude combined with a rather narrow, slanted reading of life. I approach these coming plays with not only the themes and conventions so far discussed in mind but also the following precepts:

> The ethics of most of the greater Elizabethan dramatists is only intelligible as leading up to, or deriving from, that of Shakespeare: it has its significance, we mean, only in the light of Shakespeare's fuller revelation.[1]
>
> (T. S. Eliot)
>
> That author . . . is best on love who best loves his own creations.[2]
>
> (John Bayley)

1. Eliot, "Thomas Heywood" (1931), in *Selected Essays*, 180.
2. Bayley, *Characters of Love*, 7.

Part III

Jacobean Reverberations

10   Thomas Heywood

The frequently repeated epithet for Thomas Heywood—*prose Shakespeare*—suggests that he was strongly under Shakespearean influence, an influence which has, of course, been formulated in various ways. My own interest is in showing how Heywood took up and used the imagery and conventions of the tragedies of love and death and in noting the conflict in him between the essentially pre-*Hamlet* romantic idealism which he never entirely lost and his very post-*Hamlet* concern with the theme of adultery. It is through these shared concerns, I think, that Heywood's place in the evolving Jacobean tragedy is best determined.

First, a few words on what appears to be direct borrowing from Shakespeare: one interesting scene in *The English Traveller* is definite evidence that Heywood found the relationship between the Machiavellian intriguer, male images of woman, and the idea of marital infidelity a subject of great interest—even some twenty-two years after the first production of *Othello*. In the scene, the Iago-like Delavil tries to inspire his friend's old father with suspicions concerning the friend and Mrs.Wincott. He begins with the kind of semantic double-talk which Iago was so good at:[1]

> O. GER: A mistress, said you?
> DEL: Yes, sir, or a friend,
>   Whether you please to style her.[2]   (III. i. p. 195)

1. For instance:
   OTH: What? what?
   IAGO: Lie—
   OTH: With her?
   IAGO: With her, on her; what you will." (*O*. IV. i. 33–34)
2. Thomas Heywood, *The English Traveller*, in *Thomas Heywood*, ed. A. Wilson Verity, The Mermaid Series (London: Vizetelly & Co., 1888). All quotations from the play are from this text.

173

The next step is to play on conventional fears of woman. Who can blame her, he says,

> Hugging so weak an old man in her arms,
> To make a new choice of an equal youth,
> Being in him so perfect? Yet, in troth,
> I think they both are honest.   (III. i. p. 195)

The last line is a giveaway, and indeed it echoes like a refrain through the scene:

>   . . . yet in my conscience
> I think them truly honest.
> .   .   .   .
>   . . . for, as I live,
> I think they both are honest.   (III. i. p. 196)

Old Geraldine responds like a prose Othello:

>   You have, sir,
> Possessed me with such strange fancies—
> .   .   .   .
> 'Tis suspicious.
> .   .   .   .
>   I much thank you,
> For you have clearly given me light of that
> Till now I never dreamt on.   (III. i. pp. 195–96)

There is a similar instance of relationship in *A Woman Killed With Kindness*. This passage from a speech of Frankford's has definite verbal likenesses to certain of Othello's meditations. The passion is slighter but the subject and the thoughts are similar—even down to the reference to Nick (in this case a genuinely honest Iago) as honest:

> 'Tis probable; though blunt, yet he is honest.
> Though I durst pawn my life, and on their faith
> Hazard the dear salvation of my soul,
> Yet in my trust I may be too secure.
> May this be true? O may it? Can it be?[3]   (viii. 72–76)

It is, however, impossible to say for certain which was written first, *A Woman Killed* or *Othello*, so what is notable is not that Shakespeare was Heywood's model in this instance, but the possibility of a kind of creative interchange of artists both working a dramatic vein due to burgeon in coming years—the theme of sexual betrayal.

3. Thomas Heywood, *A Woman Killed with Kindness*, ed. R. W. Van Fossen, the Revels Plays (London: Methuen & Co. Ltd., 1961). All quotations from the play are from this text.

It is important, however, to note the differing attitudes the two writers bring to their stories of adultery. For Shakespeare, *Othello* marked the recovery from the misogynous mood and mythology of *Hamlet*. For Heywood, the mythology of Hamlet's ghostly father was still the authentic one. In *A Woman Killed* this myth is sketched out more in sorrow than in anger; in *The English Traveller* more in anger than in wisdom. But in both it provides the basis for Heywood's homiletic intentions, artistic structures, and dramatic psychology.

1. *A Woman Killed with Kindness*

A Woman Killed opens with a scene that looks for its meaning and symbolic importance back to the romantic love tragedy ideal of the love marriage. T. S. Eliot has suggested that to save Anne Frankford's fall from accusations of overquickness, the play might better have opened at some point after she had been wed for some length of time.[4] This is certainly true, but Heywood was clearly more interested in the force of his symbols than in plausibility. To stage a wedding complete with song and festivity brings home—the way the Cyprus reunion of Othello and Desdemona does—all the joyous connotations of union and concord in the most direct way possible. The kind of comic festivity[5] that usually ends a comedy in this case begins the tragedy; it also establishes the marriage as the high point of happiness from which all goes downhill.

Heywood's treatment of the romantic marriage has the traditional associations. The festive celebration and affirmation of sexual pleasure:

SIR FRA: Some music there! None lead the bride a
          dance?
SIR CHA: Yes, would she dance 'The Shaking of the
          Sheets':
          But that's the dance her husband means to
          lead her.   (i. 1–3)

is balanced against a sense of the gravity and seriousness of personal relationships and bonds that defy time:

        You both adorn each other, and your hands
        Methinks are matches. There's equality
        In this fair combination; you are both scholars,

---

4. Eliot, "Thomas Heywood," 176.
5. See C. L. Barber, *Shakespeare's Festive Comedy*, for the importance of festival motifs in Shakespeare and other Elizabethans. Meridian Books (Cleveland, Ohio: The World Publishing Company, 1966 reprint of 1959 edition).

Both young, both being descended nobly.
There's music in this sympathy, it carries
Consort and expectation of much joy,
Which God bestow on you, from this first day,
Until your dissolution—that's for aye.   (i. 65–72)

The scene—with its pastoral setting, its dancing and music reinforcing the verbal metaphors for concord—moves out of the particular occasion into a celebration of marriage itself as the reachievement of Eden. The perfect woman—"She's beauty and perfection's eldest daughter,/Only found by yours, though many a heart hath sought her" (i. 23–24)—completes the happiness of the ideal gentleman:

How happy am I amongst other men
That in my mean estate embrace content.
I am a gentleman, and by my birth
Companion with a king; a king's no more.
I am possess'd of many fair revenues,
Sufficient to maintain a gentleman.
Touching my mind, I am study'd in all arts,
The riches of my thoughts, and of my time
Have been a good proficient. But the chief
Of all the sweet felicities on earth,
I have a fair, a chaste, and loving wife,
Perfection all, all truth, all ornament.
If man on earth may truly happy be,
Of these at once possess'd, sure I am he.   (iv. 1–14)

Frankford becomes a complacent new Adam, innocently delighted with his Eve.

Just as Heywood mythologizes his idea of human happiness in romantic terms, so he turns to the antiromantic mythologies to portray the disintegration of this happiness. The death motif is embodied in a story of adultery and betrayal, death working as a sickness from within the relationship itself, with the seducer as a kind of devil and the woman emerging as the more familiar version of Eve. From the entrance of the seducer Wendoll in scene iv, the action organizes itself around this antiromantic configuration. The figure in *Hamlet* who is described as "The serpent that did sting thy father's life" (*H*, I. v. 39) becomes the rather more obvious demon of Heywood's Nick: "Zounds! I could fight with him, yet know not why;/The Devil and he are all one in my eye" (iv. 87–88).

But Heywood goes beyond this crude level of characterization to depict his male adulterer; he goes to another old concern of the Renaissance love tragedy—the courtly lover, archfiend to husbands. When we first see

Wendoll after his acceptance into the Frankford household, he enters with the stage direction, *"Enter* WENDOLL *melancholy"* (vi), clearly suffering from the old lover's malady of the courtly romance. He tries holy meditation, but his prayers lead him only to the images of the religion of love:

> Why, prayers are meditations,
> And when I meditate—O God, forgive me—
> It is on her divine perfections.   (vi. 9–11)

He also reminds himself of his obligations to Frankford:

> He hath plac'd me in the height of all his thoughts,
> Made me companion with the best and chiefest
> In Yorkshire.   (vi. 38–40)

But it is all for nothing; like a debased Tristram he feels fate pushing him like a pawn:

> O God! O God! with what a violence
> I am hurry'd to my own destruction.
> .   .   .   .
>   What sad destiny
> Hath such command upon my yielding thoughts?
> I will not. Ha! some fury pricks me on;
> The swift Fates drag me at their chariot wheel
> And hurry me to mischief.   (vi. 17–18, 98–102)

Heywood elaborates on this corrupt romanticism in Wendoll's speeches to Anne during the seduction scene; there is, for instance, this famous passage:

> O speak no more,
> For more than this I know and have recorded
> Within the red-leav'd table of my heart.   (vi. 125–27)

The overstrained metaphor perfectly suggests that over-ripeness or decadence of feeling which Heywood as a partisan of marriage would find offensive in Romance rhetoric. The same is true of the main body of Wendoll's plea. With a gallant's casuistry he turns his fault (to Frankford) into a lover's virtue, makes his economic dependence on Frankford into evidence of the greatness of his passion for Anne:

> Go, tell your husband; he will turn me off,
> And I am then undone. I care not, I—
> 'Twas for your sake.   (vi. 131–33)

and (the ultimate gesture) places passion above life itself: "For you I'll hazard all. What care I?/For you I'll live, and in your love I'll die" (vi. 138–39).

Thus Wendoll becomes a Romance hero exalting, with his special use of love-death language, the individual, unlawful passion over the common, ordinary joys of marriage. There is more than a little bit of Troilus in the uneasy extremism of his love language and also some of Diomedes' cunning and hypocrisy:

> I love your husband too,
>
> . . . .
> Mistake me not, the augmentation
> Of my sincere affection borne to you
> Do no whit lessen my regard of him.   (vi. 142, 144–46)

Heywood is aware too of the potential corruption inherent in secrecy. Diomedes would have Cressida "secretly open"; likewise, Wendoll will be discreet: "I will be secret, lady, close as night" (vi. 147). The whole stew is spiced by the unlawful nature of it, the sense of getting away with something: "Your husband is from home, your bed's no blab—/Nay, look not down and blush" (vi. 165–66). Even her shame is an aphrodisiac. As a final touch we are not allowed to forget that the courtly romancer in gentleman's clothing is also the Devil:

> NICH: I never look'd for better of that rascal
> Since he came miching first into our house.
> It is that Satan hath corrupted her, . . .   (vi. 177–79)

The problem of the quickness of Anne's seduction—that is, why Heywood thought he could reasonably show a wife's fall from virtuous protestation to guilty blushing in about sixty lines—has plagued Heywood criticism. T. S. Eliot minimizes the problem: "The speech is perfect for the situation; the most persuasive that Wendoll could have made to Mrs. Frankford; and it persuades us into accepting her surrender."[6] Despite objections to this,[7] scholarly investigation of the reading matter of Heywood's audience[8] indicates the justice of Eliot's confident judgment, for it appears to be perfectly in line with commonplace Elizabethan conceptions of woman that Anne should be moved by Wendoll's superficial romanticism. As Hallett Smith has shown, a long minor tradition of pathetic stories about such Royal mistresses as Jane Shore is both agent and product of this conventional point of view: that woman falls not for any good reason which requires psychological probing but because of natural malleability and

6. Eliot, "Thomas Heywood," 176.
7. For a brief review of opposing opinions, see R. W. Van Fossen, "Introduction," *A Woman Killed with Kindness* (the Revels Plays), xlvi–xlviii.
8. Smith, "*A Woman Killed*," *PMLA*, 143–44.

ingrained sensuality. Smith quotes this passage from Heywood's own Jane
Shore episode. The queen is speaking to Jane:

> Jane, I forgive thee. What fort is so strong
> But with besieging, he will batter it?
> Weep not (sweet Jane) Alas I know thy sex,
> Toucht with the self-same weakness that thou art. [9]

Even Shakespeare appears to have been operating on the same principle in
Hamlet, for at no time is Gertrude's momentous act of betrayal given objective psychological exploration; indeed, so shadowy are her own motives
that those modern critics who condemn her are limited to the vague use of
such terms as "lust," "rankness," and "grossness" [10] (all Hamlet judg-
ments) to make the play comprehensible. Applied to the comfortable,
good-natured matron Shakespeare actually shows us on stage, they seem
overblown. We are forced to assume lust without the fact of it ever becoming manifest in the character presented in the play.

   In the final analysis what Heywood really asks us to do is accept as the
basis for Mrs. Frankford's fall the same kind of stereotype that Iago provides for Othello. Our resistance—if we do resist—comes from the same
skepticism of the stereotype that makes us so furious with Othello for
accepting Iago's. The difference, however, between the Shakespeare of
Othello and Heywood is that Shakespeare places the Iago Eve within a
larger context that shows us its falsity; for Heywood the Iago vision of
woman—softened in transit through Heywood's milder intelligence—
becomes the playwright's vision.

   One result of this limitation of Heywood's perception is the failure to give
Anne Frankford—at least before her fall—any kind of genuine personality.
Iago by the power of his imagination made Desdemona seem a typical
"Venetian wife"; Heywood makes Anne Frankford into a manor house
equivalent. During the earlier parts of the play she is always seen from the
outside, in terms of her role rather than her self:

> But the chief
> Of all the sweet felicities on earth,
> I have a fair, a chaste, and loving wife.   (iv. 9–11)

This exterior view even applies to her own vision of herself, for she can
define herself only in relation to her husband:

---

9. Heywood, *Edward IV*, quoted in Smith, *"A Woman Killed," PMLA*, 146.
10. Wilson, *What Happens in Hamlet*, 42.

> Can you unblushing speak this to the face
> Of the espous'd wife of so dear a friend?
> It is my husband that maintains your state;
> Will you dishonour him? I am his wife
> That in your power hath left his whole affairs;
> It is to me you speak?   (vi. 120–25)

and Wendoll's offense only in terms of her husband:

> My husband loves you.
>
> · · · · · · · · · · · · · ·
>   He esteems you
> Even as his brain, his eyeball, or his heart.   (vi. 114–15)

Because Heywood accepts his own stereotype, he robs his audience of the kind of insight into humanity that *Othello*, clashing stereotype against reality, so perfectly provides.

There is one possibility to be mentioned though: it might be said (if it didn't seem a subtlety past Heywood's reach) that Anne's lack of a personal identity is in fact the psychological reason for her fall. Wendoll's romanticism—debased or no—reaches to her as herself, not as an adjunct to Frankford; to a person, not a role. His refrain is always on *you*:

> I love you. Start not, speak not, answer not.
> I love you—
>
> · · · · · · · · · · · · · ·
>   I was not fearful
> Bluntly to give my life into your hand,
>
> · · · · · · · · · · · · · ·
> 'Twas for your sake.
> . . . 'twas for you.
>
> · · · · · · · · · · · · · ·
> For you I'll hazard all. What care I?
> For you I'll live, and in your love I'll die.
>   (vi, 107–108, 128–29, 133–34, 138–39)

She says, "My soul is wand'ring and hath lost her way" (vi. 151). It is the kind of insight into the self that, in the right context, would have a Shakespearean resonance (like Achilles' "My mind is troubled like a fountain stirred, / And I myself see not the bottom of it" [*T & C*, III. iii. 308–309]). But the context is not firm, and Heywood's inkling of an insight remains cloudy because he remains attached to his Gertrude figure, his Eve.

That Heywood's imagination responds vividly to the idea of the corrupted woman can hardly be doubted. Anne comes alive once bereft of grace and with her, the play does also. The two most creative pieces of pure theater in the middle part of the play are concerned with sexual corruption and its revelation. Heywood's own fascination is converted into stage *coups* that are fascinating in themselves because they force us to look on along with Frankford at the spectacle of his wife's depravity.

The first is the famous card game. Frankford has already been acquainted with his wife's adultery by his unvillainous Iago, Nick; he looks on at the game with a knowing eye and adds his own double entendres to those of the wife and lover, who think their bawdry is private. The card-playing scene also gives us what is rare in Heywood but frequent in Shakespeare, Tourneur, Middleton, and Webster—a sense of how vast our subversive erotic language is, how many ideas, words and activities can be appropriated to sexual innuendo.

The other scene I refer to is very much in the tradition of the love tragedy: the revelation or discovery scene which channels the full flow of love into hatred. We think at once of Tancred emerging from his daughter's bedroom; Balthazar and Lorenzo peeping on above Bel-imperia and Horatio, going mad with fury; Tybalt overhearing Romeo; Antonio watching in disguise as court moths court his Mellida; Troilus watching Cressida surrendering to Diomedes and needing the restraint of Ulysses to hold him from outburst; and, of course, the inverted version, the surrogate revelation scenes conducted in the imagination of Iago and Othello. These scenes form a genuine tradition and, in its insistence on seeing, a uniquely theatrical one. Heywood was obviously much taken with it, for it shapes the climax in both *A Woman Killed* and *The English Traveller*.

In *A Woman Killed* Heywood uses the mechanism of the convention to organize a most theatrically effective scene, but he also perceives that it is here at the moment of loss that he must give his play its distinctive emotional feel. The result is that this conventional scene takes on a tone unlike any in the previous drama. It is set by Frankford's horror at knowing in advance what he will find and being therefore conscious of all its psychological, even mythic implications: "It leads to my polluted bedchamber,/ Once my terrestrial heaven, now my earth's hell" (xiii. 14–15). Unlike other cuckolded husbands he feels no rage even as he pauses at the door. Instead,

> Astonishment,
> Fear, and amazement play against my heart,
> Even as a madman beats upon a drum.   (xiii, 23–25)

Psychologically, he pulls back from the sight even as he enters to face it;

when he has seen, he emerges not a raging lunatic but more a man who has had to face a terrible sadness:

FRANK: O, O!
NICH: Master, 'sblood, master, master!
FRANK: O me unhappy, I have found them lying
        Close in each other's arms, and fast asleep.

(xiii, 40–43)

Even the adulterous couple seem almost conventional and certainly peaceful. This quietness leads into the greatest speech of the play:[11]

O God, O God, that it were possible
To undo things done, to call back yesterday;
That Time could turn up his swift sandy glass,
To untell the days, and to redeem these hours;
Or that the Sun
Could, rising from the west, draw his coach backward,
Take from the account of time so many minutes,
Till he had all these seasons call'd again,
Those minutes and those actions done in them,
Even from her first offence; that I might take her
As spotless as an angel in my arms.
But O! I talk of things impossible,
And cast beyond the moon.

(xiii, 52–64)

The speech is great because it sums up without a false touch the mood with which Heywood would invest adultery and the significance he would give it. This mood is one of deep sadness and melancholy at the human loss involved and has none of the moral and mental turgidity that normally accompanies this kind of revelation.

The clarity and gentleness of tone that Heywood achieves here open the way for his most original contribution to the tradition of the scene. Heywood, of course, knows that this kind of revelation scene is normally an occasion for the venting of aggressive fury, for the violent triumph of the death motive over the love motive. But he modifies the scene in such a way as to allow for separation without death. The maid with an "angel's hand" who stops Frankford on his way to becoming a Balthazar or Othello opens the way for love to reintroduce itself at the end. That this is a direct rebuke to the usual morality of the revenge play is obvious. And in terms of the

---

11. T. S. Eliot's tribute is worth recording: "His nearest approach to those deeper emotions which shake the veil of Time is in that fine speech of Frankford which surely no men or women past youth can read without a twinge of personal feeling." "Thomas Heywood," 181.

dramatic form of the play, it prepares for the transformation of the anti-romantic marriage motif into a modified version of the romantic. This is accomplished with another familiar love-death device, the Deadly Nuptial design.

T. S. Eliot has said that in Heywood "the interest is always sentimental, and never ethical." [12] The end of *A Woman Killed* seems to me an interesting example of the sentimental that goes beyond sentimentality. There is no question that the last-minute death room forgiveness is profoundly senti-mental; nevertheless, it achieves ethical weight of a kind that the end of *The English Traveller* fails to. The reason, I think, is that the sentiment in *A Woman Killed* is shaped and related to the movement of the whole play by the balancing of love motive and death motive. Symmetry combines with psy-chological realism to bring Anne back onto the stage in the bed that is wed-ding bed, adulterous bed, and deathbed, and Heywood's compassion is given a form in which it can work simultaneously with his homileticist's need for justice. Frankford's love comes out in his forgiveness and gives it a highly romantic form which keeps it from seeming patronizing:

> My wife, the mother to my pretty babes,
> Both those lost names I do restore thee back,
> And with this kiss I wed thee once again.
> Though thou art wounded in thy honour'd name,
> And with that grief upon thy deathbed liest,
> Honest in heart, upon my soul, thou diest.   (xvii, 115–20)

Thus, love reaffirms itself on the human level and carries without effort the heavy, potentially crippling burden of transcendental message. What makes the homiletics work, in other words, is the romanticism, the dra-matic coupling of Christian morality with genuine human love: "New marry'd and new widowed; O, she's dead,/And a cold grave must be our nuptial bed" (xvii. 123–24). When we think how easily these words could have been spoken by, say, Romeo, we realize how powerful an image of romance in marriage Shakespeare formed, that it could roll through such a sea change as this and emerge still artistically vital.

2. The English Traveller

A Woman Killed With Kindness is the Heywood play which has remained popular since his own day and is the one upon which his reputation rightly rests. But some perceptive critics, notably Eliot, have preferred *The English*

12. *Ibid.*, 179.

Traveller: "It was in *The English Traveller* that Heywood found his best plot. . . . It is indeed a plot especially modern among Elizabethan plots; for the refinement of agony of the virtuous lover who has controlled his passion and then discovers that his lady has deceived both her husband, who is his friend, and himself, is really more poignant than the torment of the betrayed husband Frankford."[13] I cannot say I find Young Geraldine's torment quite so poignant, but Eliot rightly notes the "refinement of agony." *The English Traveller* dates from 1625, and by then Heywood had ample time to learn from such masters of subtle and complicated eroticism as Beaumont and Fletcher and Thomas Middleton. One result is that Heywood displays a more facile kind of theatrical artifice, and this in turn reflects an increased tendency to explore out-of-the-way sexual situations. But there is still much of the old Heywood left, and in *The English Traveller* his middle-class morality and psychology conflict in some interesting but finally disastrous ways with Jacobean sexual sophistication.

An example of this conflict may be seen in the play's subplot. In it Heywood shows us a gentleman's house temporarily placed in the keeping of the son, Young Lionel, who in his father's absence has filled it with gallants and prostitutes, replacing country sobriety with the practices of the lascivious court:

> . . . all that mass of wealth
> Got by my master's sweat and thrifty care,
> Havoc in prodigal uses;
>
> . . . .
> His stools, that welcomed none but civil guests,
> Now only free for pandars, whores and bawds,
> Strumpets, and such.   (I. ii. p. 165)

These unthrifty habits are then linked to the central concern: the unrestricted license of sexual freedom. Heywood lets his young wildhead make the case against himself, and he makes it in very traditional terms, linking his own ruin metaphorically to that of his estate:

> To what may young men best compare themselves?
> Better to what, than to a house new built,
>
> . . . .
> But when that lazy tenant, Love, steps in,
> And in his train brings sloth and negligence,
> Lust, disobedience, and profuse excess,
> The thrift with which our fathers tiled our roofs

13. *Ibid.*, 178.

Submits to every storm and winter's blast,
And, yielding place to every riotous sin,
Gives way without to ruin what's within: . . .
(I. ii. pp. 168–69)

It is plain therefore that Heywood intends the subplot to counterpoint the main plot by showing the disruptive side of the sexual urge and the need for the imposition of wise authority on this urge. But, in fact, the subplot goes beyond this task and becomes for a time a much more distinctly Jacobean kind of sexual problem-situation. Young Lionel's whore falls in love with him, rather like Shakespeare's Bianca does with Cassio. The question then evolves into a test between her bawd's exhortation to infidelity—"Doth the mill grind only when the wind sits in one corner. . . ? To affect one, and despise all other, becomes the precise matron, not the prostitute; the loyal wife, not the loose wanton" (I. ii. p. 170)—and love's natural tendency towards fidelity. The situation has a moral and emotional potential not unlike that of Dekker and Middleton's *Honest Whore*, for Young Lionel, moved by his whore's rejection of the bawd's advice, vows his eternal fidelity:

> But unto thee a new indenture sealed
> Of an affection fixed and permanent.
> I'll love thee still, be't but to give the lie
> To this old cankered worm.   (I. ii. p. 171)

At the end, however, the problem raised is not allowed to develop. The girls are banished by the father, who represents wise and prudent old age. Young Lionel's vow is never given a second thought, and a situation which some writers might have used to explore a challenging moral problem is submerged under a weight of moralizing rhetoric and male solidarity:

> Y. LIO: I have but done
> Like misspent youth, which, after wit
>   dear-bought,
> Turns his eyes inward, sorry and ashamed.
> These things in which I have offended most,
> Had I not proved, I should have thought them
>   still
> Essential things, delights perdurable;
> Which now I find mere shadows, toys and dreams,
> Now hated more than erst I doted on.[14]

14. The phrasing here seems reminiscent of Shakespeare's Sonnet 129 and the message and mood are much the same.

. . . .
O. LIO: . . . only that wanton,
Her and her company, abandon quite;
So doing, we are friends.
Y. LIO: A just condition, and willingly subscribed to.
                                              (IV. vi. pp. 235–36)

The ease of this conclusion provides an insight into the working of masculine prejudice and its link with conventional morality. But what makes it important is not that it spoils this simple-minded subplot but that we find it at work in the much more elaborate and morally complex main plot, where it results in egregious moral and artistic evasions.

It is a testimony to the facility of Heywood's artistry that for a long time we are conscious of none of these complexities. In the first act, indeed, we are treated to such a barrage of mutual affection that Heywood appears to have fallen over into total sentimentality. Delavil praises Young Geraldine for his traveler's knowledge of the world. Young Geraldine, the hero-gentleman, praises old Wincott, the husband: "Oh 'tis a good old man" (I. i. p. 159). Delavil praises Mrs. Wincott:

> And she a lady
> For beauty and for virtue unparalleled,
> Nor can you name that thing to grace a woman
> She has not in a full perfection.   (I. i. p. 159)

Both rhapsodize at the pair she and Wincott make:

DEL: Betwixt them there's so sweet a sympathy
As crowns a noble marriage.

. . . .
GER: Heaven hath supplied in this your virtuous wife,
Both fair, and full of all accomplishments;
My father is a widower, and herein
Your happiness transcends him.   (I. i. pp. 159–60)

The clown praises both Geraldine and Delavil, and they for no great reason praise him. This extraordinary flow of good feeling is the equivalent to the festive banter of Frankford's wedding and persists not just through this act but throughout the play, providing a background of the joys of frank and open human affection against which the secret betrayals are set. But slowly and with considerable subtlety, Heywood lifts the corners of this happiness to reveal what lies beneath it.

The first hint of what is to come is given by a piece of bawdry from the clown: "Small doings at home, sir, in regard that the age of my master corresponds not with the youth of my mistress, and you know cold January and lusty May seldom meet in conjunction" (I. i. p. 158). But the question raised by this remark is left undeveloped until Act II, i, when the friends are again gathered. They exchange jests and amusing stories; then as the evening grows late, Old Wincott begins to nod, then goes to bed:

> You are all young, and you may sit up late;
> My eyes begin to summon me to sleep,
> And nothing's more offensive unto age
> Than to watch long and late.   (II. i. p. 180)

This hint is taken up by Delavil in a bit of jesting directed at Old Wincott's young wife, who has remained behind:

> Maids and widows,
> And we young bachelors, such as indeed
> Are forced to lie in solitary beds,
> And sleep without disturbance—we, methinks,
> Should desire later hours than married wives,
> That in their amorous arms hug their delights!
> To often wakings subject, their more haste
> May better be excused.   (II. i. p. 180)

The erotic scenes Delavil alludes to are hardly, we realize, an everyday occurrence for Mrs. Wincott, and the whole problem of the sexual aspect of marriage is thus raised in a jesting but acute form. Prudentilla takes him up in turn—keeping the theme alive:

> How can you,
> That are, as you confess, a single man,
> Enter so far into these mystical secrets
> Of marriage, which as yet you never proved?   (II. i. p. 180)

And Delavil comes back with an answer surprisingly profound in its absolute simplicity and absolute truth:

> There's, lady, an instinct innate in man,
> Which prompts us to the apprehensions
> Of the uses we were born to: such we are
> Aptest to learn, ambitious most to know,
> Of which our chief is marriage.   (II. i. p. 180)

For "marriage," of course, we read sex; just as we do for the "mystical secrets" that Pru refers to. Pru and Delavil leave for their single beds with a bit more jesting on sex and we have Young Geraldine—the husband's closest, most beloved male friend and surrogate son—left alone with the wife. It is one of those quiet, significant moments that Heywood creates so well. Young Geraldine's simple remark—"We now are left alone" (II. i. p. 181)—

loads the moment with feeling and surprise. It creates a new perspective, hints at an unseen relationship. And sure enough, a whole hidden history emerges in the next lines.

It is both an odd relationship and a moving one. Begun in childhood, ". . . when our tongues but clipped/Our mother's-tongue, and could not speak it plain" (II. i. p. 181), it extended through adolescence and should have, we learn, resulted in their marriage:

> WIFE: It was once voiced that we two should have
> matched;
> The world so thought, and many tongues so
> spake;
> But Heaven hath now disposed us otherways;
> And being as it is, (a thing in me
> Which, I protest, was never wished nor sought),
> Now done, I not repent it.
> Y. GER: In those times,
> Of all the treasures of my hopes and love,
> You were the exchequer, they were stored in you;
> And, had not my unfortunate travel crossed them,
> They had been here reserved still.
> WIFE: Troth, they had;
> I should have been your trusty treasurer.   (II. i. p. 182)

As they speak we see the remains of a young love that was snapped off by an Arranged Marriage before it could ripen. And the quiet dignity with which the two speak of it gives the moment considerable pathos. Heywood has succeeded, in other words, in turning the January-May marriage convention into the beginnings of a psychological problem play—as he had started to do with the "honest whore" motif in the subplot.

The play moves on from this revelation to show the process of deflected emotion finding expression in a genuinely chaste version of courtly love:

> . . . through my husband's love,
> Midnight hath been as mid-day, and my bed-chamber
> As free to you as your own father's house,
> And you as welcome to't.   (II. i. p. 181)

The problem is to maintain the balance between chastity and desire, and the attempt to do this is fraught with difficulties that find expression in those peculiarities of tone that come from the lovers' necessary conflict of interest:

> Y. GER: You deserve,
> Even for his sake, to be for ever young;
> And he, for yours, to have his youth renewed,

> So mutual is your true conjugal love;
> Yet, had the Fates so pleased—   (II. i. p. 181)

He wishes the old man long life, for he is his friend; but he must with part of himself wish him well dead, or at the very least wish he and Mrs. Wincott had never married. The same kind of conflict may be seen here:

> Y. GER: However, let us love still, I entreat:
> That, neighbourhood and breeding will allow;
> So much the laws divine and human both
> 'Twixt brother and a sister will approve;
> Heaven then forbid that they should limit us
> Wish well to one another!   (II. i. p. 182)

Young Geraldine is beginning to suffer from a confusion of roles. ''Wish well to one another" is a poor equivocation for romantic attachment leading to marriage. And to be romantic lover and brother, even while physically chaste, verges on what Othello called "hypocrisy against the devil" (IV. i. 6). This hypocrisy becomes even more acute as the two swear secret troth-plight; whether Heywood fully intends it or not there is something necro-philiac in Young Geraldine's proposal:

> Your husband's old, to whom my soul doth wish
> A Nestor's age, so much he merits from me;
> Yet if (as proof and Nature daily teach
> Men cannot always live, especially
> Such as are old and crazed) he be called hence,
> Fairly, in full maturity of time,
> And we two be reserved to after-life,
> Will you confer your widowhood on me?   (II. i. pp. 182–83)

The strain is more easily handled by the wife, who throughout the scene has shown considerable aplomb in guiding Young Geraldine into her fu-ture, but her control cannot hide the conflict of allegiances and affection:

> Till that day come, you shall reserve yourself
> A single man; converse nor company
> With any woman, contract nor combine
> With maid or widow; which expected hour,
> As I do wish not haste, so when it happens
> It shall not come unwelcome. You hear all;
> Vow this.   (II. i. p. 183)

"It shall not come unwelcome": a chilling sentence, for nothing could more effectively underline how empty this January-May marriage is beneath the surface pleasantries. This is Heywood writing at his very best.

Looking at the situation in terms of the other plays of love and death, we can see both similarities and basic differences. Shakespeare, for instance, would have indicated the ambiguities of the relationship by the use of metaphors which combine images of love in some manner with images of death. But Heywood doesn't have Shakespeare's richness of language; tonal effects within almost image-free lines are his major linguistic resource. But this simplicity of language does at least allow clear examination of the situation itself, and this is plainly one in which love motives and death motives are deeply wound together. The love motive is in the situation of the two young lovers plighting their troth despite an Arranged Marriage. But the death motive must necessarily intrude, for their love can have no fruition until another man dies.

The line between chaste admiration and spiritual bigamy is a very thin one. Thomas Middleton's De Flores (*The Changeling, c.* 1622) interprets it harshly when he tells Beatrice-Joanna:

> Though thou writ'st maid, thou whore in thy affection!
> 'Twas chang'd from thy first love, and that's a kind
> Of whoredom in thy heart; . . .   (C. III. iv. 142–44)

Such is the case with the much admired Young Geraldine, though Heywood's hero never shows any signs of recognizing it. Indeed the play's great recognition scene is framed in a manner which suggests that—despite Heywood's obvious total identification with him—Geraldine (no less than the adultress) has more than a little whoredom of the affections to account for.

This emotional crux becomes extremely acute one night when Young Geraldine has—unbeknownst to anyone but his friend Old Wincott—come to visit, and then to spend the night. As he lies in his bed, the night thoughts of love steal into him—outflanking the social restraints of his ordinary behavior:

> I find no sleep can fasten on mine eyes,
> There are in this disturbèd brain of mine
> So many mutinous fancies.   (IV. iii. p. 222)

The nature of these mutinous fancies becomes clear when he tries to think of some way to wile away the night:

> Oh, what more wishèd company can I find,
> Suiting the apt occasion, time, and place,
> Than the sweet contemplation of her beauty; . . .
>   (IV. iii. p. 222)

He is plainly nearing the dangerous brink to which his attempt at middle-class platonism has carried him. Here, if I read right, he tips over: "And the fruition too, time may produce,/Of what is yet lent out?" (IV. iii. p. 222). When he gets to her room, however, he finds—just as Frankford had in the earlier play—that his beloved woman has taken another man. Heywood's efforts to maintain Young Geraldine in the mold of Frankford are determined and obvious, even down to the instinctive—but again happily frustrated—lunge for his sword:

> Unchaste, impious woman,
> False to all faith and true conjugal love;
> There's met a serpent and a crocodile,
> A Sinon and a Circe. Oh, to what
> May I compare you?—Out, my sword!
> I'll act a noble execution
> On two unmatched for sordid villany—
> I left it in my chamber, and thank Heaven
> That I did so! it hath prevented me
> From playing a base hangman.   (IV. iii. p. 223)

But the writing here is crude and perfunctory when compared to the analogous scene in the earlier play. Fourteen impassioned words clog the gap between the impulse to draw and the discovery that he had forgotten his blade. Also, he gets his metaphors a bit confused; one's sword has nothing to do with one's being or not being a hangman. Loose writing is not confined to this scene, however. It presages the lax and evasive moral thinking that undermines the play's conclusion.

Heywood's technique is again to give his hero revenge not by the sword but by the word. To make this revenge credible, however, Geraldine must be painted as having a stern moral position. Since, as I have tried to suggest, he does not in fact have one, there is much intellectual straining, and much clotted thought and language, beginning here:

> To make your brazen impudence to blush—
> Damn on—revenge too great; and, to suppress
> Your souls yet lower, without hope to rise,
> Heap Ossa upon Pelion. You have made me
> To hate my very country, because here bred
> Near two such monsters.   (IV. iii. p. 223)

Heywood's Frankford had far greater cause for anguish than Young Geraldine, and because his moral position was genuinely strong he could assert it more gracefully, even lovingly. With Young Geraldine, Heywood has to force the issue, and the first quality to be lost is love, leaving only the hate that will burst out later. Thus, the paradox: the illicit lovers when they emerge sound morally healthy because they are more loving:

> DEL: Sweet, retire you
> To your warm sheets; I now to fill my own,
> That have this night been empty.
> WIFE: You advise well:
> Oh, might this kiss dwell ever on thy lips
> In my remembrance!   (IV. iv. pp. 224–25)

Devoid of love, moral sternness threatens to become nothing more than a function of the death motive. This is a point to keep in mind when considering Young Geraldine's part in the play's thundering homiletic conclusion.

We have at this point two rather interesting versions of the death of love set up to make potentially interesting psychological studies. The first, quite fully developed, was that of deflected love and the possibilities of a genuinely moral bourgeois love code, one which would result in marriage yet not break marriage up. But, having set the problem, with his gentleman hero in the problem position, Heywood fails to bring it to its logical conclusion. Indeed he evades the problem entirely by directing attention to the second, Mrs. Wincott's adultery, and thus to another problem of equal Jacobean interest: that of sexual satisfaction for woman. The trouble here, though, is the same that weakened the middle part of *A Woman Killed*: an absolute inability to deal realistically and directly with female motivation.

This failure on Heywood's part does not stem from any lack of dramatic talent. It seems instead to be a failure of sensibility. In the passages with the wife in them, there are many instances of superficial realism and theatrical panache far in advance of similar ones in *A Woman Killed*. But the greater facility of Heywood's later art only throws into greater relief the psychological emptiness of it. Between the scene in which Young Geraldine and Wincott's wife secretly pledge troth and that in which he discovers that she is secretly betraying both her wedding vows and trothplight to him, there is not a single scene showing Delavil and Mrs. Wincott together, no hint of the why or wherefore of their relationship, just the *coup de théâtre* of the discovery itself. With Mrs. Frankford, Heywood at least delineated an elaborate and fairly convincing seduction. Here, no such thing exists, and the reason is this: Heywood has gone completely over to the kind of Jacobean sexual extremism that we find in *Hamlet*, in Tourneur, in Middleton. Woman is either saint (as is the heroine of Heywood's own *Lucrece*) or (more commonly) whore. The stereotype[15] Eve figure reigns without challenge.

With this stereotype dominant in the play's fifth act, all the subtleties of the first four are forgotten, and the whole is wound up on a spool of punitive masculine rhetoric. Heywood forgets Young Geraldine's own highly ambiguous moral state so far as to allow him to be the central agent of male revenge. Encountering Mrs. Wincott at one of their ubiquitous social gatherings he blares forth all the clichés of postlapserian misogyny:

> I had thought
> Long since the sirens had been all destroyed;
> But one of them I find survives in her:
> She almost makes me question what I know,
> A heretic unto my own belief:—
> O thou mankind's seducer!
>
> . . . .
> Yes, thou hast spoke to me in showers; I will
> Reply in thunder: thou adulteress,
> Thou hast more poison in thee than the serpent
> Who was the first that did corrupt thy sex,
> The devil!
>
> . . . .
> Monday the ninth
> Of the last month—canst thou remember that,
> That night more black in thy abhorrèd sin
> Than in the gloomy darkness?
>
> . . . .
> How hath thy black sins changed thee! Thou Medusa!
> Those hairs that late appeared like golden wires
> Now crawl with snakes and adders. Thou art ugly.
>
> (V. ii. pp. 243–44)

Touches of preposterous egotism almost make us think Heywood is being ironical: "But think what thou hast lost/To forfeit me!" (V. ii. p. 244). But such is not the case: blood-and-thunder sermonizing is the order of the day, and Heywood buries all his problems, his ambiguities, his very sensitivity—and thus his art—in bombast and piety.

The possibility that Young Geraldine has been as much a whore in his affections as the wife has, or that there is some vein of untapped psychological interest in the fact that Young Geraldine's fury comes from his own jealousy while his words address the problem of his old friend's cuckoldry, does not divert Heywood from his moralizing fury. The wife is forced to

15. So stereotyped is she that she is never even given a name (unlike Anne Frankford); she is just "wife."

repent in tears and dies of a broken heart. It is difficult to imagine sentimental male egotism enjoying a more complete triumph than this:

WINCOTT: But all my best of wishes wait on you,
           As my chief friend! This meeting, that was
               made
           Only to take of you a parting leave,
           Shall now be made a marriage of our love,
           Which none save only death shall separate.
Y. GER: It calls me from all travel, and from hence-
               forth
           With my country I am friends.
WINCOTT: The lands that I have left,
           You lend me for the short space of my life;
           As soon as Heaven calls me, they call you
               lord.—
           First feast, and after mourn; we'll, like
               some gallants
           That bury thrifty fathers, think't no sin
           To wear blacks without, but other thoughts
               within.   (V. ii. p. 248)

Womanless at last, both these betrayed Adams are gratefully safe with their property and a kind of calm and sexless marriage, decked with hypocrisy.

3.

The difference between Heywood's two major tragedies is most evident in the endings. The earlier play posited a love between Anne and Frankford even though Heywood's talents gave him little scope for making it a living thing upon the stage or the page. But it was love, and this fact came out in a variety of ways throughout the play—even during the adultery itself. Thus, the basis for the symmetry of the ending was firmly grounded in human emotion and the play gained artistic strength from this because its form did not violate reality; indeed, it gave emphasis to it, as artistic form should. Thus, *A Woman Killed* managed to express a firm idea of human love, strong enough to overcome Heywood's orthodox preconceptions of the natural sexual looseness of woman.

In the interim between this play and *The English Traveller* two things have happened. One, Heywood has become increasingly conscious of complicated erotic relationships; two, he has become less confident that love can survive the weakness inherent in its sexual manifestations. In this he moves to a position which is best described by some such term as *orthodox* or *conservative*. In *The English Traveller* the relationships he tries to explore are complex, but his answer to them is brutal and obtuse. The terrible thing about the ending of *The English Traveller* is that despite the multiple levels of sex and marriage and betrothal in the play, there is not a single residue of love left at the end—except between the two men.

This points the way to what continues as a strong tendency in Jacobean tragedy: the inability to believe that love and sexuality may be united, even in marriage. This is the problem that wore Hamlet into emotional tatters, but in Hamlet's case a residue of love did persist. Heywood in *The English Traveller* does not have that much even, and it is for this reason that he can be so uncompromisingly vengeful at the end.

For the striking thing which unites all the plays in which human love is divorced from sexuality—and this includes *Hamlet*, the parent of them—is that they inevitably take the form of acts of vengeance against woman, or nature, or sexuality, all of which are seen as evil. Good is seen to reside only with chastity and to be a quality imposed and enforced from outside, from above. Such is the case in *The English Traveller*, and it recurs as a theme in important plays to come.

In light of this it is necessary that we radically limit and redefine the term *prose Shakespeare* as it can be applied to Heywood. Irving Ribner sees Heywood "as one whose imitation of Shakespeare led him to reflect in more prosaic terms a moral viewpoint which we associate with the greatest plays of his master. Like Shakespeare, Heywood was conservative. He saw the universe as the ordered creation of a loving God, every part of which was related to every other, and all joined together in a great cosmic harmony." [16] Seen in these loose and sweeping terms the only difference between the two is that whereas Shakespeare conveys this vision "in striking emotional terms," Heywood does it "in terms of the Elizabethan devotional and homiletic tract." [17] But this difference is a great deal more significant than Professor Ribner makes it out to be. Because Shakespeare depicts life in "striking emotional terms" he is able to free himself from crippling orthodox (and *conservative*) misconceptions about human nature. Because Heywood is tied to the terms of the devotional tract, he is barred from a vast range of Shakespearean perceptions and therefore from his freedom from cant. If we compare the way in which Delavil teases Old Geraldine into immediate and fantastic imaginings about female lust with Shakespeare's treatment of this in *Othello*, the huge gulf between the two becomes ap-

16. Irving Ribner, *Jacobean Tragedy* (London: Methuen & Co. Ltd., 1962), 51.
17. *Ibid*.

parent. Heywood confirms his character's most asinine assumptions by the action of his play; Shakespeare—most unconservatively free of the old Eve nonsense which has plagued Christian moral philosophy for so long—places these assumptions in the wider context of the existence of love and shows the fatuity and the destructiveness of them.

A Woman Killed with Kindness is the only Heywood tragedy which deserves the epithet *prose Shakespearean,* for it embodies the Shakespearean touchstone of human love as a source of good generated out of the actual conditions of human life on earth and in time.

11   Cyril Tourneur

The two plays attributed to Cyril Tourneur—*The Revenger's Tragedy* and *The Atheist's Tragedy*—are very much in the tradition of love-death tragedy. What sets them apart from any others, however, and yet links the two together, is a distinctive style and mode of treating erotic matters, the product of an equally distinctive erotic sensibility. T. S. Eliot—in one of his finest Elizabethan essays—indicates something of this special Tourneur style in discussing *The Atheist's Tragedy*: "Not that the scenes of *The Atheist's Tragedy* are altogether conventional; or, at least, he trespasses beyond the convention in a personal way. There was nothing remarkable in setting a graveyard scene at midnight; but we feel that to set it for the action of a low assignation and an attempted rape at the same time seems more to be expected of the author of *The Revenger's Tragedy* than of anyone else." [1] When we recall that in this same long scene there is also an attempted murder, a duel, and a killing, what becomes most striking is the extremism of these juxtapositions, the almost comic violence of the yoking of love and death. Unlike Middleton's plays, which share with Tourneur's a profound anti-romantic sexual skepticism, these two have few characters of any psychological interest; so extreme is Tourneur's vision of the place of sexuality in human nature that it almost precludes the possibility of realistic portrayal of what we think of as character. Tourneur's people are either symbols of some abstract quality or they are spokesmen for some idea, but they are persons only in a very rudimentary sense. Instead, they exist as pieces of worlds that are organized almost totally around Tourneur's erotic vision and are designed to project that vision.

1. Eliot, "Cyril Tourneur," (1930) in *Selected Essays*, 187.

197

198   *Love and Death in Renaissance Tragedy*

The nature of the vision may be stated simply: Tourneur sees a world in which erotic life and the death motive are one and the same; or at least they are so closely intertwined as to be inextricable. In Tourneur, anything connected with sexual love is connected with death, and vice versa. Only chastity leads to life, and that life is the eternal life. Tourneur is uncompromising on these points and thus extreme. Whether he expresses them in a revenge structure or in the less concentrated romantic tragedy structure of *The Atheist's Tragedy*, a powerful vision of temporal life dominates—one in which the very sources of that life are tainted by death.

1. *The Revenger's Tragedy*

The first act of *The Revenger's Tragedy* displays the world as a vast panorama of sexual depravity, and Tourneur's method throughout is to link sexual love with the death motive in one or—as is often the case—several of its manifestations. The opening speech is an instance. Tourneur sets one part of our attention on the revenger holding a death's head and the other part on a courtly train of characters, each characterized by some aspect of sexual license:

> Duke; royal lecher; go, grey-hair'd adultery;
> And thou his son, as impious steep'd as he;
> And thou his bastard, true-begot in evil;
> And thou his duchess, that will do with devil.
> Four excellent characters—[2]   (I. i. 1–5)

The skull and rampant sexuality remain the twin poles around which Tourneur organizes both his verse and theater poetry. But this long speech becomes both more particular and more inclusive in its listing of love-death horrors: a) the incompatability of old age—so close to the grave—enjoying the sexual urge:

> O, that marrowless age
> Would stuff the hollow bones with damn'd desires,
> And 'stead of heat, kindle infernal fires
> Within the spendthrift veins of a dry duke,
> A parch'd and juiceless luxur. O God!—one
> That has scarce blood enough to live upon,
> And he to riot it like a son and heir?
> O, the thought of that
> Turns my abused heart-strings into fret.   (I. i. 5–13)

---

2. Cyril Tourneur, *The Revenger's Tragedy*, ed. R. A. Foakes, the Revels Plays (London: Methuen & Co. Ltd., 1966). All quotations from the play are from this text.

b) actual murders committed by men under driving passion—in this case the murder of Vindice's own beloved:

> Thee when thou wert apparel'd in thy flesh
> The old duke poison'd,
> Because thy purer part would not consent
> Unto his palsy-lust; for old men lustful
> Do show like young men, angry, eager, violent,
> Outbid like their limited performances.
> O 'ware an old man hot and vicious:
> *Age, as in gold, in lust is covetous.*   (I. i. 31–38)

c) or even the involuntary depredations caused by innocent beauty, the mere sight of which was such

> That the uprightest man (if such there be
> That sin but seven times a day) broke custom,
> And made up eight with looking after her.   (I. i. 23–25)

The speech comes to an end with the sardonic advance of the skull—

>   . . . be merry, merry,
> Advance thee, O thou terror to fat folks,
> To have their costly three-pil'd flesh worn off
> As bare as this— . . .   (I. i. 44–47)

This is the final denuding, the stripping away of all fleshly pleasures to reveal the *memento mori* and celebrate the merger of the revenge motif and monastic morality, both linked by their common negation of the value of earthly life.

Although—as critics have noted—Vindice and Tourneur do grow apart from each other by the end of the play,[3] it is clear that in the beginning, at any rate, Vindice does see and say those things which Tourneur himself would have seen and said about the world. For even when Vindice has stepped aside as commentator, the characters he has introduced confirm the worst epithets he puts on them. As scene succeeds scene, virtually all the relationships of character to character and character to action are organized in terms of love-death imagery. In the exchange between the Duchess and Spurio, for instance, the adulterous courtly liaison is linked not merely with incest ("I'll call foul incest but a venial sin" [I. ii. 171]) but with

3. Robert Ornstein, *The Moral Vision of Jacobean Tragedy* (Madison: University of Wisconsin Press, 1960), 110–16, and Ribner, *Jacobean Tragedy*, 80.

premeditated sadism. The death motive, the desire to injure, is built into the very terms with which the Duchess courts him:

> DUCH: . . . but to our love.
> Let it stand firm both in thy thought and mind
> That the duke was thy father, as no doubt then
> He bid fair for 't: thy injury is the more,
> For had he cut thee a right diamond,
> Thou hadst been next set in the dukedom's ring,
> When his worn self, like age's easy slave,
> Had dropp'd out of the collet into th' grave.
> What wrong can equal this? canst thou be tame
> And think upon 't?
> SPUR: No, mad and think upon 't.
> DUCH: Who would not be reveng'd of such a father,
> E'en in the worst way?   (I. ii. 146–57)

Indeed vengeance is wound into the Duchess's own lust; because her husband would not free her son (his stepson),

> . . . wedlock faith shall be forgot.
> I'll kill him in his forehead, hate there feed;
> That wound is deepest, though it never bleed.
>   (I. ii. 107–109)

And it is to this hatred that Spurio himself responds in imagery that gives hatred an aphrodisiac quality:

> I feel it swell me; my revenge is just;
> I was begot in impudent wine and lust.
> Step-mother, I consent to thy desires,
> I love thy mischief well, but I hate thee, . . .
>   (I. ii. 191–94)

But the subtlest eroticist of all is that remarkable creation Lussurioso, whose lust has become so sophisticated that it can find requital only through the most complicated arabesques of seduction and humiliation. We can see this in the style of his questions to Vindice-Piato:

> Thou hast been scrivener to much knavery then?
> · · · · · · · · · · · · · · · · ·
>   Then thou know'st
> I' th' world strange lust?   (I. iii. 48, 55–56)

and in the obvious relish of his response to Vindice's fulsome answers: "He's e'en shap'd for my purpose" (I. iii. 55). Lussurioso's ambition is not the seduction of an ordinary courtly dame but rather a chaste, retiring virgin for whom seduction is not just physical debasement but moral debasement as well.

> Bewitch her ears, and cozen her of all grace;
> Enter upon the portion of her soul,
> Her honour, which she calls her chastity,
> And bring it into expense; . . .   (I. iii. 112–15)

Even this level of humiliation is insufficient though, for in the process he must also triumph over his own hirelings:

LUSS: That was her brother that did prefer thee to us.
VIND: My lord, I think so; I knew I had seen him
           somewhere—
LUSS: And therefore prithee let thy heart to him
      Be as a virgin, close.
VIND: O, my good lord.
LUSS: We may laugh at that simple age within him.
VIND: Ha, ha, ha.
LUSS: Himself being made the subtle instrument
      To wind up a good fellow—
VIND: That's I, my lord.
LUSS: That's thou.
      To entice and work his sister.
VIND: A pure novice!
LUSS: 'Twas finely manag'd.
VIND: Gallantly carried; . . .
                         (I. iii. 135–45)

The mocking, doubly ironic tone of this dialogue makes all the clearer how much Lussurioso enjoys not just the act of sex but the complexities of triumph and imposed humiliation of others. Most of this is summed up in his pat, mock-sententious credo:

> I am one of that number can defend
> Marriage is good; yet rather keep a friend.
> Give me my bed by stealth, there's true delight;
> What breeds a loathing in't, but night by night?
>   (I. iii. 103–106)

Tourneur's irony exposes two death motives packed into one theory of sexuality: the institutionalized transience of the courtly religion of love ("A very fine religion!" [I. iii. 107] Vindice ironically calls it) raised to a way of life, and the motif of sadist's triumph and mockery.

L. G. Salingar, in an interesting article, suggests that the rise of a money economy and the consequent dislocation of traditional society is the main butt of Tourneur's attack in this play.[4] My own feeling, however, is that Tourneur's enmity goes far beyond this. There is, in fact, relatively little in the play that suggests class troubles at all,[5] but there is a great deal that strikes at such universal aspects of humanity as the various animal functions. Vindice—like Iago—is vivid in the extreme with his highly emotive insistence on the biological facts of existence. An instance is this striking pun:

> LUSS: What hast been, of what profession?
> VIND: A bone-setter.
> LUSS: A bone-setter?
> VIND: A bawd, my lord; one that sets bones together.
> LUSS: Notable bluntness!   (I. iii. 42–46)

But others abound, and one feels everywhere in Tourneur the bare skull pushing through the flesh or the flesh itself thrusting out in all its offensiveness into the foreground of attention:

1) DON: Madonna, there is one, as they say, a thing of flesh and blood, a man I take him by his beard, that would very desirously mouth to mouth with you.
    CAST: What's that?
    DON: Show his teeth in your company.
    CAST: I understand thee not.
    DON: Why, speak with you, Madonna.
    CAST: Why, say so, madman, and cut off a great deal of dirty way; . . .
                                                      (II. i. 10–18)

2) DUKE: My teeth are eaten out.
    VIND: Hadst any left?
    DUKE: I think but few.
    VIND: Then those that did eat are eaten.
    DUKE: O, my tongue!
    VIND: Your tongue? 'twill teach you to kiss closer,
          Not like a slobbering Dutchman.   (III. v. 161–65)

3)   Go to, then;
    The small'st advantage fattens wronged men.
    It may point out Occasion; if I meet her,
    I'll hold her by the foretop fast enough,
    Or, like the French mole, heave up hair and all.
                                                      (I. i. 97–101)

---

4. L. G. Salingar, "*The Revenger's Tragedy* and the Morality Tradition," *Scrutiny*, VI (March, 1938), 402–24.
5. And all of it is linked to sexual evil of one sort or another.

Even on those occasions when flesh and bone are not meant to seem so blatantly horrible, Tourneur's death-haunted imagination puts them to odd and unnatural juxtapositions:

> No, I would raise my state upon her breast,
> And call her eyes my tenants; I would count
> My yearly maintenance upon her cheeks,
> Take coach upon her lip, and all her parts
> Should keep men after men, and I would ride
> In pleasure upon pleasure.   (II. i. 95–100)

or into a teasing, erotic tension with other biological necessities such as eating and drinking and sexuality itself:

> Faith, if the truth were known, I was begot
> After some gluttonous dinner, some stirring dish
> Was my first father, when deep healths went round,
> And ladies' cheeks were painted red with wine,
> Their tongues as short and nimble as their heels,
> Uttering words sweet and thick; . . .   (I. ii. 180–85)

To such a mind as Tourneur's, even language takes on a kind of physical reality, words becoming like after-dinner sweets and everything—food, language, drink, sex—being implicitly condemned by a process of guilt by association. Asked by the judges who are about to condemn him to death for rape "What mov'd you to 't?" the Junior Brother answers: "Why, flesh and blood, my lord;/What should move men unto a woman else?" (I. ii. 47–48). This universal flaw—the flaw of Eden, Eve, and the fall—transcends questions of social class such as Salingar discusses, and it fits Tourneur's medieval tenor of mind more perfectly. The result is a vision of evil that can express itself by taking something as morally neutral as night and seeing in it a whole world of sexuality, decay, and death:

> Now 'tis full sea abed over the world;
> There's juggling of all sides. Some that were maids
> E'en at sunset are now perhaps i' th' toll-book.
> This woman in immodest thin apparel
> Lets in her friend by water; here a dame,
> Cunning, nails leather hinges to a door,
> To avoid proclamation; now cuckolds are
> A-coining, apace, apace, apace, apace; . . .
>   (II. ii. 136–43)

Sociology will not explain this perverse imaginative reach; for that, one must turn to philosophy.

As one might expect, primal guilt goes back to the problem of woman.

The Revenger's Tragedy is remarkable even among antiromantic plays for the number, polish, and glibness of its antifeminist aphorisms and assumptions:

1)   Most women have small waist the world throughout,
        But their desires are thousand miles about.
                                                    (IV. iii. 15–16)
2)   My fault was sweet sport, which the world approves;
        I die for that which every woman loves.
                                                    (III. iv. 80–81)
3)   'Women with women can work best alone.'
                                                    (II. ii. 64)
4) LUSS: Is she a woman?
   VIND: In all but in desire.
   LUSS: Then she's in nothing—
                                                    (II. ii. 23–24)
5)   Faith now, old duke, my vengeance shall reach high;
        I'll arm thy brow with woman's heraldry.
                                                    (I. ii. 176–77)

These are all from subordinate characters. Vindice provides many others; speaking of his mother and sister, he tells Hippolito:

                        We must coin.
        Women are apt, you know, to take false money;
        But I dare stake my soul for these two creatures,
        Only excuse excepted—that they'll swallow
        Because their sex is easy in belief.   (I. i. 103–107)

And talking to his mother, he sharpens his phrasing:

VIND: . . . 'lack, you know all,
        You were his midnight secretary.
GRAT: No.
        He was too wise to trust me with his thoughts.
VIND: I'faith, then, father, thou wast wise indeed;
        Wives are but made to go to bed and feed.
                                                    (I. i. 128–32)

Compared to such a barrage, Hamlet's "Frailty, thy name is woman!" seems modest and understated. But the ease with which Tourneur can turn out these statements shows how correspondingly easy he found it to accept the stereotype Eve. Where Shakespeare struggled on with the question of what life was really like after great expressions of discontent in the sonnets and *Hamlet*, Tourneur accepts the basic disillusionment with grim jocularity. The result of this surety secure is a reenactment of the temptation and fall of Eve that has a surface of great wit and aphoristic brilliance. Vindice comes in disguise to seduce his sister's honor into Lussurioso's use, but he has been advised that if she prove chaste, he should "venture upon the mother":

VIND: O fie, fie, that's the wrong end, my lord. 'Tis mere impossible that a mother by any gifts should become a bawd to her own daughter.

LUSS: Nay then, I see thou'rt but a puny in the subtle mystery of a woman; why, 'tis held now no dainty dish. The name
Is so in league with age that nowadays
It does eclipse three quarters of a mother.

(I. iii. 150–57)

This could be read as a comment on *Hamlet* and on the whole problem of mothers and human sexual origins. But Vindice hardly needs such advice. As he says, *"That woman is all male, whom none can enter"* (II. i. 112).

The Tourneur style of dramatic presentation does, of course, fit the aphorisms; the ironic polish is so brilliant that it is impossible to become emotionally involved with the mother's fall. The natural response to the following exchange is rueful delight:

VIND: Thus it said:
The daughter's fall lifts up the mother's head.
Did it not, madam? But I'll swear it does:
In many places, tut, this age fears no man;
'Tis no shame to be bad, because 'tis common.

GRAT: Ay, that's the comfort on't.   (II. i. 114–19)

The same is only slightly less true of the fall itself; Vindice gives the mother pieces of gold:

GRAT: Ay, these are they—

VIND: O!

GRAT: —that enchant our sex, these are
The means that govern our affections.
That woman
Will not be troubled with the mother long,
That sees the comfortable shine of you;
I blush to think what for your sakes I'll do.

(II. i. 122–28)

Thus, instead of human involvement in a powerful scene of degradation, one is given great surface clarity and wit and, therefore, above all else, superb entertainment. But, there is another and much more important gain from this emotional distancing of Tourneur's. Despite the repeated insistence that

Were 't not for gold and women, there would be no damnation;
Hell would look like a lord's great kitchen without fire in 't:

But 'twas decreed before the world began,
That they should be the hooks to catch at man.

(II. i. 257–61)

there is not a trace in this play of the masculine self-pity that marred Heywood's *The English Traveller*. Despite all the aphorisms and jesting about women there is also the cool, logical acceptance that both sexes are damned equally. This understanding does not make Tourneur any less pessimistic, but it keeps him from being pessimistic in a ludicrous, self-pitying, self-justifying manner.

For the characters in this play there are three courses of action in life. One is to participate in the world of sensual pleasures and be damned for it. The other two are those taken respectively by Castiza and Vindice—chastity and vengeance. To understand how these two courses relate to the theme of love and death and the whole problem of human sexuality is to understand the Tourneurean ethic and its consequences.

Tourneur's Castiza is probably the central moral agent in the play. She exemplifies Tourneur's ideal of withdrawal from the world by the preservation of her maidenhead and by her refusal to frequent the court. But when Vindice comes disguised as Lussurioso's pander, she is offered the opportunity for an active denial:

CAST: Whence this?
VIND: O, from a dear and worthy friend,
       Mighty!
CAST: From whom?
VIND: The duke's son.
CAST: Receive that!
       A box o' th' ear to her brother.

(II. i. 30–31)

Nor is her vigor expressed only by her fists; it finds its way into her wit, giving her a strong line of bitter irony. When solicited by her fallen mother, she turns the thrust:

I cry you mercy, lady, I mistook you;
Pray, did you see my mother? Which way went she?
Pray God I have not lost her.   (II. i. 161–63)

Tourneur sets her virgin strength against the sensual susceptibilities of her sexually experienced mother to create a double temptation scene. The temptations are the active enticements of the sensual life, vividly evoked in some of Tourneur's finest verse:

> O, think upon the pleasure of the palace;
> Secured ease and state; the stirring meats,
> Ready to move out of the dishes, that
> E'en now quicken when they're eaten;
> Banquets abroad by torch-light, music, sports,
> Bare-headed vassals, that had ne'er the fortune
> To keep on their own hats, but let horns wear 'em;
> Nine coaches waiting,—hurry, hurry, hurry. (II. i. 199–206)

But Castiza—unlike her mother—sees life through the "eternal eye,/That sees through flesh and all" (I. iii. 65–66). Her sharp vision immediately reveals the true adversary nature of the man pretending to be her benefactor: "Ay, to the devil" (II. i. 207).

This strength and sharpness of vision—united with her uncompromising chastity—places her, in terms of the play's symbolism and ethic, outside and indeed above the world. If—as Vindice would have it—it was decreed before the world began that women should be hooks to catch at man, Castiza's refusal to be a woman moves her towards the realm of heavenly beings: "O angels, clap your wings upon the skies,/And give this virgin crystal plaudities!" (II. i. 245–46). Hamlet, reacting against a world of sexual evil, told Ophelia "Get thee to a nunnery"; Tourneur, giving a full dramatic exposition to the Hamlet state of mind, follows his injunction rigidly for those women who are his heroines. The result is a harsh split between those who do, as it were, and those who don't. A woman is either a virgin or a whore. And for an honest woman who is tainted by sexual violation—even when it is forced—the antiromantic taboo on sexuality is so great that the only honorable result must be voluntary death. Thus, Antonio's raped wife is allowed to take her place with Castiza as a woman to be praised:

> ANT: Violent rape
> Has play'd a glorious act; behold, my lords,
> A sight that strikes man out of me.
> PIER: That virtuous lady!
> ANT: Precedent for wives!
>
> (I. iv. 3–6)

Such praise is more than a little chilling, however, for it represents the triumph of an abstract, sexless admiration over any warm, genuine love.

Antonio thus praises his wife in these odd terms—as a woman who "ever liv'd/As cold in lust as she is now in death" (I. iv. 34–35). When coldness becomes a term of praise in love between man and woman, the antiromantic dry rot has spread very far indeed. But Tourneur's moral men are inflexible. There is no middle ground of experience which can rightly be called love. Even grief becomes a function of the moralist's ego:

> That is my comfort, gentlemen, and I joy
> In this one happiness above the rest,
> Which will be call'd a miracle at last;
> That, being an old man, I'd a wife so chaste.
>
> (I. iv. 74–77)

And the death motive triumphs even in goodness.

This brings us to Vindice's reaction to the world; if Castiza's was to show contempt for it by withdrawal, Vindice's is just the opposite: to show contempt by active involvement, by vengeance. Because this vengeance is directed against a world in which the central symbol of corruption is sexual love, it is logical that the play should find some powerful way of bringing these things into a definitive conjunction. Such is the case in the justly celebrated Act III. v, the most elaborately orchestrated long scene in the play and one of the masterpieces of the unwed versions of the Deadly Nuptial.

We learn at the beginning of the scene that the duke has put himself in Vindice's power because of the prodding of his own lust. But Vindice completes the circuit begun years before with the duke's murder of his betrothed by unveiling the girl he has brought for the duke's pleasure to show the masked and decked-out skull of that same girl. The moment of unmasking becomes the occasion for one of Vindice's most elaborate sermons. His basic text is again the gulf between the human eye with its self-seducing ability to see beauty in woman and the eternal eye that sees through flesh. The skull of the formerly beautiful Gloriana is the vehicle by which we perceive the insights of the eternal eye:

> Here's an eye
> Able to tempt a great man—to serve God;
> A pretty hanging lip, that has forgot how to dissemble:
> Methinks this mouth should make a swearer tremble, . . .
>
> (III. v. 54–57)

Hippolito underlines the irony with his awed rhetorical question: "Is this the form that living shone so bright?" (III. v. 67). Vindice uses it to give his own personal recantation:

> The very same.
> And now methinks I could e'en chide myself
> For doting on her beauty,though her death
> Shall be reveng'd after no common action.   (III. v. 68–71)

He then sails off into one of the play's most famous speeches:

> Does the silk-worm expend her yellow labours
> For thee? for thee does she undo herself?
> Are lordships sold to maintain ladyships
> For the poor benefit of a bewitching minute?
> Why does yon fellow falsify high-ways,
> And put his life between the judge's lips,
> To refine such a thing? keeps horse and men
> To beat their valours for her?   (III. v. 72–79)

The probing, controlled disgust in this passage is very close to that of Shakespeare's Sonnet 129 and is Tourneur's most wide-reaching rejection of sensual pleasure, primarily because it uses the physical fact of the skull as the springboard to a more Olympian view of the human condition. From this lofty position he can visualize the sexual urge not just as a disease of the flesh but as a disease of the spirit and the will that even corrupts—in the image of the silkworm's mindless labor—the impersonal functioning of nature itself.

The logic of revenge demands the total—or as near total as possible—suppression of love, for love militates against murder even as it often prompts man towards it. The result of this contrary action is a tumultuous mental state like that of Hamlet or Othello or even Romeo in the brief seconds during which his attempts to act towards Tybalt in the spirit of love are frustrated and mischanneled by the greater force of loss of Mercutio. In Vindice, however, there is no love left. The impulse behind his vengeance was the loss of his own love, so there is personal force behind his hatred. But this force is drained of any of the residual human affections that so hampered Hamlet's progress from lover to killer by Vindice's total contempt for humanity and the world. In consequence Vindice's whole wit is released to design a death scene that is indeed "no common action." He becomes a portrait of the artist given coolly and completely over to destruction. In the whole body of Jacobean tragedy his only equivalent in philosophic direction and ability to translate philosophy into action is Iago.

To see Vindice in this way is to understand why he is so resolutely theatrical. The whole of Act III. v. is like a morality masque. There is the superb theater of the bringing in of the lady:

> Madam, his grace will not be absent long.
> Secret? Ne'er doubt us, madam; 'twill be worth
> Three velvet gowns to your ladyship. Known?
> Few ladies respect that! Disgrace? a poor thin shell;
> 'Tis the best grace you have to do it well.
> I'll save your hand that labour; I'll unmask you.
>
> (III. v. 43–48)

and the deliberate use of theater imagery:

> Now to my tragic business; look you, brother,
> I have not fashion'd this only for show
> And useless property; no it shall bear a part. . . .
>
> (III. v. 99–101)

Audience appreciation comes throughout from the astonished Hippolito:

> Why, brother, brother!
> . . . .
> Brother, y' have spoke that right.
> . . . .
>   . . . most dreadfully digested.
> . . . .
> Brother, I do applaud thy constant vengeance,
> The quaintness of thy malice, above thought.
>
> (III. v. 49, 66, 25, 108–109)

Even the killing itself is done with theatrical verve. There are puns and asides:

> Brother, fall you back
> A little, with the bony lady.
> . . . .
> . . . sh' has somewhat a grave look with her, . . .
>
> (III. v. 120–21, 137)

The method of the murder itself seems to be a parody of Juliet's attempt to kiss poison off Romeo's lips. And the dying man is even shown a real-life morality play involving his wife and his bastard son:

> SPURIO: Had not that kiss a taste of sin, 'twere
>   sweet.
> DUCH: Why, there's no pleasure sweet but it is
>   sinful.
> SPURIO: True, such a bitter sweetness fate hath given,
>   Best side to us is the worst side to heaven.
> DUCH: Push, come; 'tis the old duke thy doubtful
>   father,

> The thought of him rubs heaven in thy way.
> But I protest, by yonder waxen fire,
> Forget him, or I'll poison him.   (III. v. 207–14)

What we have in Tourneur, therefore, is a peculiar merging of dramatic traditions. The morality tradition and the revenge tradition are two, but these are joined by that of the tragedy of love. Behind this play's elaborate and fantastic verbal and visual puns on love and death lies the powerful influence of the tomb scene at the end of *Romeo and Juliet*. But the sensibility that guides their use belongs to the two first-mentioned traditions. For Shakespeare, love has the power to transfigure death: "For here lies Juliet, and her beauty makes/This vault a feasting presence full of light" (*R & J*, V. iii. 85–86). For Tourneur, this would be the grossest kind of heresy. His own emphasis goes in the exact opposite direction: "—see, ladies, with false forms/You deceive men, but cannot deceive worms" (III. v. 97–98). Tourneur's vision of the world of sensual beauty and of the relationship of art to this world is embodied perfectly in Vindice, about whom Lussurioso is finally the most acute commentator: "A parlous melancholy! 'Has wit enough/To murder any man, . . ." (IV. ii. 106–107). Creativity linked to the death motive: it is a formula that helps explain many aspects to Jacobean literature—from the satires of Hall or Marston to the deadly shrewdness of Iago or Hamlet's manic rages.

The final question for interpretation from the point of view of the love-death theme is why Vindice himself is dammed by his author to a death as ironic as any he himself has perpetrated. One of the main messages of this play is ironically stated by the Duchess: "Why, there's no pleasure sweet but it is sinful" (III. v. 208). This touches Vindice directly, for if nothing else he has enjoyed his vengeance immensely. Deprived of the ordinary imaginative and sensual delights of love, he gets them from murder. I spoke earlier of the complicated forms of lust necessary to satisfy Lussurioso's jaded palate. Vindice's own pleasures are very similar— subtly attenuated through arabesques of irony:

LUSS: Thy name, I have forgot it.
VIND: Vindice, my lord.
LUSS: 'Tis a good name, that.
VIND: Ay, a revenger.
LUSS: It does betoken courage; thou shouldst be valiant,
       And kill thine enemies.
VIND: That's my hope, my lord.
                                           (IV. ii. 173–76)

And when Vindice comes to the great Act III. v, the moment of the consummation of revenge, he is like a man going to a lover:

> O sweet, delectable, rare, happy, ravishing!
> . . . .
>   O, 'tis able
> To make a man spring up, and knock his forehead
> Against yon silver ceiling.   (III. v. 1–4)

When Hippolito complains about being left out, the same continues:

> VIND: True, but the violence of my joy forgot it.
> HIPP: Ay, but where's that lady now?
> VIND: O, at that word
> I'm lost again, you cannot find me yet;
> I'm in a throng of happy apprehensions.
> (III. v. 27–30)

It is therefore no idle irony that his vengeances all involve pleasure, and usually sexual pleasure. To turn pleasure into death for the sinners satisfies his (and the author's) love of poetic justice. To show Vindice and Hippolito enjoying themselves like this:

> DUKE: O, Hippolito! call treason.
> HIPP: Yes, my good lord; treason, treason, treason!
>   *Stamping on him.*
> (III. v. 156–57)

is to prepare the ground for their own downfall. In this, Tourneur is taking the insight of Marston and Seneca (see Chapter VI) that vengeance can be elaborated by art into a kind of rape but, unlike Marston, carrying it to its logical conclusion—that vengeance may be just one more version of sensual and even sexual pleasure, no matter how disguised. By this means Tourneur projects a vision of phallic evil that has its basis in such jesting as that which opened *Romeo and Juliet*: " 'Tis all one; I will show myself a tyrant: when I have fought with the men, I will be cruel with the maids; I will cut off their heads" (*R & J*, I. i. 21–23) and serves for Tourneur as the final damning male complement to the usual antiromantic conception of female evil. And like the other impenitent and witty rapist in the play—Junior Brother—Vindice goes off to his own death as jauntily as he had sent his victims to theirs.

2. *The Atheist's Tragedy*

The Revenger's Tragedy is one of those happy works of art whose genre perfectly embodies its emotional content and its philosophy; the play therefore achieves a limited perfection. Tourneur's other play—*The Atheist's Tragedy* —does not achieve this marriage of form and content. The reason, it seems to me, is that Tourneur tries the impossible—to force the conventions of the early romantic version of the love tragedy into the service of a violently antiromantic vision of life and the world. The result is a play that is interesting rather than excellent, and one that helps define more clearly the struggle of the antiromantic myth against the romantic in post-*Hamlet* tragedy.

Tourneur's borrowings from romantic tragedy fall into two basic categories: character types and elements of plot structure. For his embodiments of truth and beauty, Tourneur chooses a young pair borrowed from the tradition of *Romeo and Juliet* and *Antonio and Mellida*. Their characteristics: beauty and honesty in the woman (the name *Castabella* combines beauty and chastity), courtliness and honor in the young man, and a mutual love. Even in this love, however, we can detect Tourneur's native antiromanticism in the way romantic passion is cooled into something prudent, formalized, and a bit distant. Charlemont, when departing for the wars, almost totally submerges feeling under a weight of nice rhetoric:

> My noble mistress, this accompliment
> Is like an elegant and moving speech
> Compos'd of many sweet persuasive points
> Which second one another with a fluent
> Increase and confirmation of their force,
>
> . . . .
> But you, dear mistress, being the last and best
> That speaks my farewell, like th' imperious close
> Of a most sweet oration, wholly have
> Possess'd my liking and shall ever live
> Within the soul of my true memory.
> So, mistress, with this kiss I take my leave.[6]
>
> (I. ii. 68–72, 82–87)

Nevertheless, the situation itself sets up expectations familiar from the romantic plays: that lovers belong together and that they will try to come together, even over obstacles thrown up by schemers and rivals.

Just as his lovers come from the romantic tradition, so come Tourneur's blocking characters, the main analogues being the triad of girl's father, rival lover, and third party who feeds the father's lust for dominance. For in-

6. Cyril Tourneur, *The Atheist's Tragedy*, ed. Irving Ribner, the Revels Plays (London: Methuen & Co. Ltd., 1964). All quotations from the play are from this text.

stance, we recall in *The Spanish Tragedy* the king's advice to Bel-imperia's father Castile:

> Now brother, you must take some little pains
> To win fair Bel-imperia from her will:
> Young virgins must be ruled by their friends.
> The prince is amiable and loves her well,
> If she neglect him and forgo his love,
> She both will wrong her own estate and ours:
>
> (*ST*, II. iii. 41–46)

and Castile's own attitude:

> Although she coy it as becomes her kind,
> And yet dissemble that she loves the prince,
> I doubt not, I, but she will stoop in time.
> And were she froward, which she will not be,
> Yet herein shall she follow my advice,
> Which is to love him or forgo my love.
>
> (*ST*, II. iii. 3–8)

and think at once of this scene from *The Atheist's Tragedy* in which Castabella's father reports his daughter's negative attitude to D'Amville's son Rousard, the proposed rival suitor, and is chidden by D'Amville's agent: "Verily, that disobedience doth not become a child. It proceedeth from an unsanctified liberty. You will be accessory to your own dishonour if you suffer it" (I. iv. 15–17). This bit of ego-stoking quickly converts Belforest into a blindly tyrannous father in the tradition of Castile and, of course, Shakespeare's old Capulet:

> Your honest wisdom has advis'd me well.
> Once more I'll move her by persuasive means.
> If she resist, all mildness set apart,
> I will make use of my authority.   (I. iv. 18–21)

The kinship with old Capulet becomes more notable still when Belforest compresses the time span, thus increasing the impact of the Enforced Marriage situation:

> LANG: And instantly, lest fearing your constraint her
>   contrary affection teach her some device that may
>   prevent you.
> BEL: To cut off ev'ry opportunity
>   Procrastination may assist her with,
>   This instant night she shall be married.
>
> (I. iv. 22–26)

Even old Capulet's early liberalism turns up, providing an ironical mask for D'Amville, while his late blustering is given to Belforest:

D'AM: My Lord Belforest,
    I would not have her forc'd against her choice.
BEL: Passion o' me, thou peevish girl. I charge
    Thee by my blessing and th' authority
    I have to claim th' obedience, marry him.

                                                        (I. iv. 121–25)

We feel the pressure of an established set of conventions and conventional responses very strongly here, and it is clear that Tourneur did also. So conscious, in fact, have these conventions become that one of Tourneur's notable minor characters, the raffish brother of Rousard, can energetically redefine the Enforced Marriage custom in terms both romantic and profeminist in ideology:

SEB: A rape, a rape, a rape!
BEL: How now?
                                    What's that?
SEB: Why what is't but a rape to force a wench
    To marry, since it forces her to lie
    With him she would not?   (I. iv. 128–31)

Tourneur owes much then to the *Romeo and Juliet* tradition, but these similarities also point up distinctions and differences. For instance, in the true romantic play the heroine refuses to bow to paternal pressure. In this play she bows. Also, in the romantic plays, the Enforced Marriage theme (which makes the lovers its central concern) normally continues to follow the lovers and thus evolves into some verison of the related and complementary motif of the Deadly Nuptial, as in *The Spanish Tragedy* and *Romeo and Juliet*. In *The Atheist's Tragedy*, however, there is no Deadly Nuptial motif because the focus of the play makes frequent shifts to the corrupt world in which the lovers must exist. Thus, the Deadly Nuptial motif gives way to a satiric variant, the Deadly Fornication familiar from *The Revenger's Tragedy* and used in *The Atheist's Tragedy* for the same purpose: to serve as the chief polemic vehicle for Tourneur's basically medieval, antiromantic philosophy, that of *contemptus mundi*. Thus, both plays show their central figures attempting to survive in a world riddled by lust and murder. And in both plays, sexuality and death are equated and mutually stigmatized.

    A few examples will demonstrate the frequent force and ingeniousness of the method even in this less forceful and less ingenious play. For instance, the case of Languebeau Snuffe: in the early scenes of the play, a certain amount of crude but conventional comedy is concocted out of the gulf between Snuffe's pious mask and his submerged desire. But once desire is inflamed to the point where it becomes action, the comedy deepens; it becomes black comedy in the sense we know it today and projects an image of "lust in action" that is —despite its clownish absurdity—just as "Mad in pursuit, and in possession so;/Had, having, and in quest to have, extreme" as Shakespeare's Sonnet 129 makes it out to be. Tourneur accomplishes the transformation by means of a series of perverse (yet farcical) images of eros and death. Thus, for his lovemaking, Snuffe chooses a graveyard and, to avoid identification, disguises himself as a ghost risen from the dead. Crudely absurd complications result that (together with the disguise) show the deadness at the heart of the man and at the heart of Tourneur's conception of the sexual urge: "I will try how I can kiss in this beard.—A, fie, fie, fie. I will put it off, and then kiss, and then put it on. I can do the rest without kissing" (IV. iii. 67–69). In a later incident Tourneur uses hints of sodomy and necrophilia to give us another brief allegory of the blindness of lust and its movement towards death: *"He* [SNUFFE] *mistakes the body of* BORACHIO *for* SOQUETTE! 'Verily thou liest in a fine premeditate readiness for the purpose. Come, kiss me, sweet Soquette.—Now purity defend me from the sin of Sodom! This is a creature of the masculine gender.—Verily the man is blasted.—Yea, cold and stiff!—Murder, murder, murder'" (IV. iii. 206–10).

With Levidulcia, Tourneur casts the net of deadly eros much wider by giving her an elaborate and not uninteresting naturalistic philosophy to justify her activities. In *The Revenger's Tragedy* a mother tries to seduce her virgin daughter into a shameful sexual contact; here Levidulcia plays that role, trying to seduce her stepdaughter Castabella into a shameful marriage. Instead of using wealth as the basis for her appeal, however, Levidulcia has a philosophy, a set of arguments that have their origins in certain trends of sixteenth-century naturalistic thought:[7]

> Prefer'st th' affection of an absent love
> Before the sweet possession of a man,
> The barren mind before the fruitful body,
> Where our creation has no reference
> To man but in his body, being made

7. See Robert Ornstein, *"The Atheist's Tragedy* and Renaissance Naturalism," *Studies in Philology,* LI (April, 1954), 194–207.

Only for generation which, unless
Our children can be gotten by conceit,
Must from the body come. If reason were
Our counsellor, we would neglect the work
Of generation for the prodigal
Expense it draws us to of that which is
The wealth of life. Wise Nature, therefore, hath
Reserv'd for an inducement to our sense
Our greatest pleasure in that greatest work, . . .

(I. iv. 79–92)

It is clear that, to Tourneur, Levidulcia's rejection of reason for sensuality is the way of death, despite the biological common sense of her link between the sexual urge and the need to preserve the species. Indeed, the preservation of the species is nowhere in Tourneur's work a goal of very potent force, the way it becomes, for instance, in such otherwise disparate plays as *The Duchess of Malfi* and *The Winter's Tale*. The death-dealing side of eros far outweighs its life-giving capacities in Tourneur's work, and the predominance of this motif is the link between the philosophical naturalism and materialism of both Levidulcia and D'Amville and the unintellectualized lusts of Snuffe, Sebastian, and a host of figures in *The Revenger's Tragedy*.

This is, of course, the reason that Levidulcia's own lust is followed through the play in such detail, becoming finally a cautionary *exemplum* of the havoc eros can wreak on the most hallowed conventional restraints (marriage, kinship, class), resulting in social violation, personal misery, and death. Seeing Rousard unable to perform the act with Castabella, she begins to think of love herself. As she does, all the old pejorative metaphors for passion—like itching and heat—become real physiological symptoms:

When my affection even with their cold bloods,
As snow rubb'd through an active hand does make
The flesh to burn, by agitation is
Inflam'd! I could unbrace and entertain
The air to cool it.   (II. iii. 40–44)

She plans an assignation with Sebastian; unable to wait she tries to seduce a friend's lowborn servant; caught with both she escapes her husband's suspicion with a trick as old as European folklore.[8] By this time she is hardly more than a schoolboy's fantasy-nymphomaniac, the grossest kind of caricature Eve-Gertrude-Woman figure, and the resulting low farce debases everyone involved, adding powerful brush strokes to Tourneur's continu-

8. Ribner (ed.), "Introduction" to Cyril Tourneur, *The Atheist's Tragedy*, xliii.

ing portrait of a world riddled by the disease of sexual desire. The final touch to this part of the picture is the literal transformation of erotic motive into death motive, as both husband and lover kill each other and Levidulcia commits suicide after pointing up the moral of her story in powerful love-death imagery:

> Dear husband, let
> Not thy departed spirit be displeas'd
> If with adult'rate lips I kiss thy cheek.
> Here I behold the hatefulness of lust,
> Which brings me kneeling to embrace him dead,
> Whose body living I did loathe to touch.   (IV. v. 65–70)

D'Amville differs from Levidulcia mainly in his cooler, more generalized and rational-seeming intellectual stance. He is one of the first Renaissance characters to look explicitly into the void of death and spell out conclusions based on what he has seen there. The fact of endless nullity prompts both his hedonism:

> Then if death casts up
> Our total sum of joy and happiness,
> Let me have all my senses feasted in
> Th' abundant fulness of delight at once,
> And with a sweet insensible increase
> Of pleasing surfeit melt into my dust.   (I. i. 16–21)

and his revisionist theory of immortality:

> Here are my sons. . . .
> There's my eternity. My life in them
> And their succession shall for ever live, . . .
>
>   (I. i. 123–25)

But to Tourneur, obviously, the denial of the existence of the supernatural means the rejection of all the conventional restraints upon the rampant human will. In the trickery played on Charlemont, the murder of Montferrers, the Enforced Marriage of Castabella, and the attempted incestuous rape of Castabella, D'Amville breaks all social and familial bonds.

The last of these offenses is, of course, the most unholy of all, and to portray it and to display the latent horror of the human sexual will, Tourneur employs a full range of love-death conjunctions. The setting for the rape is the aforementioned graveyard, again a perfect image for the perverse union of eros and death. The dialogue between Castabella and D'Amville reinforces the identification of the two motives:

CAST: The poison of
        Your breath, evaporated from so foul a soul,
        Infects the air more than the damps that rise
        From bodies but half rotten in their graves.
D'AM: Kiss me. I warrant thee my breath is sweet.
        These dead men's bones lie here of purpose to
        Invite us to supply the number of
        The living.
        . . . .
CAST: O would this grave might open, and my body
        Were bound to the dead carcass of a man
        For ever, ere it entertain the lust
        Of this detested villain.   (IV. iii. 150–57, 170–73)

The stigma placed on unrestrained erotic desire by such eros-death images is plainly a very powerful polemic device. With it, Tourneur teaches by horror that eros has its roots in horror and death. He also teaches—as he did in the final acts of *The Revenger's Tragedy*—that murder has its erotic component. Such, at any rate, is the import of this deservedly famous passage:

                    And that bawd,
        The sky there, she could shut the windows and
        The doors of this great chamber of the world,
        And draw the curtains of the clouds between
        Those lights and me about this bed of earth,
        When that same strumpet, Murder, and myself
        Committed sin together.   (IV. iii. 215–21)

In this vision, the sky becomes a bawd, the whole earth is transformed into a lustful bed, and murder is seen as both a whore and the act of lovemaking itself. A vision such as this testifies again to the range of emotion that the poetic conjunction of eros and death could inspire in these writers. Even in repenting of murder, D'Amville looks to the imagery of sexual disgust for his comparison (IV. iii. 221–26).

This then is Tourneur's pessimistic image of the world of natural human will and desire. The question to be asked is, how is one to live in this world? The answer of *The Revenger's Tragedy* is embodied in Castiza: hard, stony rejection of the world. In *The Atheist's Tragedy*, where the young hero and heroine are involved in the world by the machinations of others, a different kind of rejection is offered: complete passivity and patience, both being expressions of a genuine trust in divine providence. (Tourneur's subtitle, we recall, is "The Honest Man's Revenge." He might have added a second subtitle—"The Honest Girl's Romanticism"—for passivity in love is as integral a part of his message as passivity in vengeance.) While D'Amville's atheism leads him to challenge and reject all authority but his own will, the lovers never challenge authority of any kind.

For instance: the Enforced Marriage. Castabella puts forward the usual romantic objections to it:

> *Kneel*[s] *from one to another.*
> [*To* BELFOREST] Dear father, let me but examine my
> Affection. [*To* D'AMVILLE] Sir, your prudent judgment can
> Persuade your son that 'tis improvident
> To marry one whose disposition he
> Did ne'er observe.   (I. iv. 114–18)

But when the time comes, she makes no rebellion, tries no stratagems. The why of this passive obedience is to be found in her theory of love: "O love, thou chaste affection of the soul,/Without th' adult'rate mixture of the blood" (II. iii. 1–2). Love to Castabella is pure spirit; there is no blood, that is, no sexual energy or desire in it, thus nothing of the fuel of rebellion. With such a concept, her easy capitulation is in no sense illogical, though it may be both unrealistic and dispiriting: "Yet, since thy pleasure hath inflicted it,/If not my heart, my duty shall submit" (II. iii. 13–14). Like Ophelia she chooses to obey rather than assert. Only the imposition of a tragi-comic ending saves her from a fate even worse than Ophelia's.

Charlemont's situation in the revenge plot parallels Castabella's in the love plot. Like Hamlet, he has ample reason for revenge. He also has the emotional impulse to it, as he demonstrates when he battles Sebastian (III. ii. 31). But Charlemont's ghostly father brings a message very different in content from that of Hamlet's:

> Hold, Charlemont!
> Let him revenge my murder and thy wrongs
> To whom the justice of revenge belongs.   (III. ii. 32–34)

Here, the human will is subordinated, snuffed out indeed, and all is left to the divine will. The key lines defining this conflict are Charlemont's: "You torture me between the passion of/My blood and the religion of my soul" (III. ii. 35–36). The key word again is *blood*, the symbol Tourneur and the other Renaissance dramatists use frequently to merge the erotic and the death motive in the human will. Charlemont, like Castabella, chooses duty, obedience, the religion of his soul.

Inaction and obedience then are Tourneur's moral positives, all action being suspect because tainted by the perversities of desire. As a result, Tourneur's hero and heroine—in scenes that carry to its farthest extreme Tourneur's rigidly Christian logic—reject the world, reject any action that might save them, and turn themselves over to a civil authority they know to be dominated by the corrupt D'Amville. Then, after his inevitable conviction and sentencing, Charlemont leaps to the scaffold with alacrity, smiles on the dead bodies of D'Amville's sons, and explains his rationale in a speech that teaches that this life is not the true one, that the true one is the one beyond the body's corruption:

> Thus, like a warlike navy on the sea,
> Bound for the conquest of some wealthy land,
> Pass'd through the stormy troubles of this life
> And now arriv'd upon the armed coast,
> In expectation of the victory
> Whose honour lies beyond this exigent,
> Through mortal danger, with an active spirit,
> Thus I aspire to undergo my death.   (V. ii. 123–30)

Life on earth equals the "stormy troubles"; death is the door to the victory, honor, and wealth of the afterlife. Death therefore becomes the good. Castabella seconds this; her cheerful explanation of why death is welcome provides a measure of Tourneur's great pessimism concerning this life:

> Be cheerful, Charlemont. Our lives cut off
> In our young prime of years are like green herbs
> Wherewith we strew the hearses of our friends,
> For as their virtue gather'd when th' are green,
> Before they wither or corrupt, is best,
> So we in virtue are the best for death
> While yet we have not liv'd to such an age
> That the increasing canker of our sins
> Hath spread too far upon us.   (V. ii. 132–40)

To Castabella and to Tourneur, merely to live is to be corrupted; it is better then to die young and innocent. This rejection of earthly experience in favor of death is central to Tourneur's philosophy and his dramatic mode.

It is also, of course, the reason Tourneur's attempt at a romantic tragedy fails as a coherent work of dramatic art. And with this problem we return to the subject of my opening remarks on *The Atheist's Tragedy*, the fatal gulf between its form and its didactic content.

In *The Revenger's Tragedy* there is no gulf because Tourneur's morality play mind works hand in glove with his revenge tragedy form. Both are in

222 *Love and Death in Renaissance Tragedy*

essence antilife and antilove; the morality play prompts one to fearful contemplation of the afterlife, the revenge play sends its characters to the afterlife. In addition, both are essentially punitive in motive. Irving Ribner has
said "most Elizabethan revenge tragedies . . . are moral,"[9] but to make
them moral one has to posit a medieval God with his just vengeance upon
sin. In the idea of the avenging God the morality play and revenge play
come together, and the death motive gets divine sanction, even though the
revenger may condemn himself (the case in *The Revenger's Tragedy*). Here,
of course, Tourneur has a hero who follows doctrine and will not commit
the deed his human emotions tell him to. Thus, to save his pair and show
God's justice, Tourneur must resort to one of the crudest *deus ex machina*
endings in seventeenth-century drama, a triumph of old doctrine over the
subtle art that dedicated and innovative theater men had labored decades
to develop:

> D'AM: I ha' the trick on 't, nephew. You shall see
> How eas'ly I can put you out of pain.—O.
> *As he raises up the axe [he] strikes out his own
> brains, [and then] staggers off the scaffold.*
> EXEC: In lifting up the axe, I think h' has knock'd
> His brains out. (V. ii. 240–43)

A retreat in other words, to the intellectual and artistic level of *Cambyses*.
   As a love play, the failure of *The Atheist's Tragedy* is even more radical, for
the romantic tragedy is founded on a vision of human nature and life on
this earth that stands in complete opposition to the morality play ethos. The
romantic tragedy presupposes, first of all, that sexual love is a source of life
and therefore of good, thus rejecting any one to one equation of sexuality
and evil. One cannot imagine a Castabella or Castiza giving voice to such
sentiments as Juliet's

> Spread thy close curtain, love-performing night,
> That runaways' eyes may wink, and Romeo
> Leap to these arms untalked of and unseen.
> Lovers can see to do their amorous rites
> By their own beauties; . . . (*R & J*, III. ii. 5–9)

Juliet's love has a most definite admixture of blood to it, and this admixture
of blood is the energizing force behind her terrific vitality, her resolution,
her ability to act, rebel, and above all to command her audience's emotional
involvement. It is obvious that Tourneur saw this as well as Shakespeare,

9. *Ibid.*, l.i.

but unlike Shakespeare, Tourneur rejects the pleasures of the senses and thus the Shakespearean vision of love. Instead—possibly as a rebuke to Juliet—he gives us a heroine totally without erotic energy, as she herself states to Rousard:

> Believe me, sir, it never troubles me.
> I am as much respectless to enjoy
> Such pleasure as ignorant what it is.   (III. iv. 70–72)

and thus without the will to act or even, at the end, to live. The result makes good doctrine, perhaps, but bad romantic tragedy, for it robs the romantic tragedy conventions of the very power that animates them. Shakespeare set the energy of love and life against the contrary energy of hatred and death. Tourneur sets the undeniable, but self-defeating energy of lust and death against a love so rarified that it disdains to express itself in bodies. The result, paradoxically, is a double triumph of the death motive.

12 John Webster

Moving to Webster one feels a conflict between the general antiromantic bias of most Jacobean love tragedy and Webster's distinctive treatment of the themes of love and death, a treatment in several important respects clearly in opposition to that of all his contemporaries except Shakespeare and Ford.

One can see, for instance, that although Webster builds both of his great tragedies on stock antiromantic situations (murderous adultery in one; remarriage of a widow in the other—both *Hamlet* themes) he evolves his plots and develops his characters in a way that derives from the plays of the early romantic convention, with their rebellious young lovers and conservative blocking characters. Thus it is that in both plays the chief interest proves not to be the destructive power of eros but the attempts of a pair of lovers to carve out a world of their own in defiance of a hostile society. The fact that Webster's lovers bear burdens of guilt (Vittoria and Bracciano) or adult knowledge (Antonio and the Duchess) does not invalidate the comparison. The first decade of the seventeenth century seems to have been a growing-up period for the serious dramatist, and the troubling gift left to those who followed Shakespeare through his great period was a level of knowledge about love and human nature that made naïve, innocent lovers all but obsolete as vehicles for the serious expression of that knowledge. One task of this book, therefore, is to clarify the relationship between Webster and his post-*Hamlet* contemporaries, and Shakespeare himself.

One significant point, however, had best be named now, for out of it come most of the qualities of mind and art that link Webster to Shakespeare and set him apart from Heywood, Tourneur, and Middleton. This is his appreciative fascination with women. Fascination with woman is

224

probably the basis of the whole complex evolution that made love a central concern of English Renaissance drama. But Webster is appreciatively
fascinated, almost to the point of being a feminist. No dramatist of his
time (except, again, Shakespeare in *Antony and Cleopatra*) so persistently
and effectively made women the dominant figures in great tragedy. Because Webster lived in a time when the reaction of most of his best contemporaries to women was either woeful moralizing or satiric dismissal,
his attitude needs pondering, particularly since he is also a master of
misogynous rhetoric.

1. *The White Devil*

Most critics would agree, I think, that the morality of *The White Devil* is
highly ambiguous. Robert Ornstein's comparison between it and *The
Duchess of Malfi* expresses the prevailing feeling:

> Still we ask from tragedy more than an unwearying display of human
> vitality or a thrilling clash of personalities. We expect a depth of vision
> that penetrates the surface violence or anarchy of life to illumine the
> underlying pattern and meaning of man's fate. Despite its errors and
> inconsistencies of plot, the *Duchess* is a greater play than *The White Devil*
> because it offers a more coherent and profound interpretation of expe-
> rience. Its action has a rightness and inevitability that makes the unflag-
> ging energy of *The White Devil* seem, by comparison, artistically
> unpurposed.[1]

The basic problem in *The White Devil* is that energy and morality are divorced from each other just as effectively as the heroine Vittoria (representing energy) is from her foolish, conventional husband. The best way to
understand this split, how it came about, and what it means, is to see it as
the product of strong contrary movements of feeling and thought: that is to
say, Webster in *The White Devil* takes a stock antiromantic theme—murderous adultery, the stuff of *Hamlet* and *The Revenger's Tragedy*—and uses it
in ways which produce by the end a play about the victimization of a pair of
unconventional but genuine lovers. This is plainly a difficult problem—as
difficult as Tourneur's unsuccessful attempt to use the conventions of naïve
romantic tragedy to write a play against eros and atheism. Nor can it be said
that Webster is entirely successful. One thing to insist on, though, is that
there is a moral and artistic consciousness constantly at work in the play. It
is an unconventional consciousness but not a moral blank, as some (here,
L. G. Salingar) would have it: "Webster, unable to come to rest on any atti-

1. Ornstein, *Moral Vision*, 129.

tude, from which to value his people, more stable or more penetrating than a pose of stoical bravado, could not write coherent drama at all."[2] Better, I think, to see Webster as a moral adventurer and a psychologist of the darker side of eros—a man, in other words, who can hold more than one attitude to the phenomena of human passion and thus open up new possibilities for response in his audience.

The opening scenes of the play paint mainly an antiromantic picture of eros. The first thing we hear of Bracciano is that he is trying "by close pandarism" to "prostitute/The honour of Vittoria Corombona" (I. i. 41–42),[3] and we hear it from the banished murderer who at the end of the play is one of their killers. Thus, the conjunction of eros and murder is present even before the lovers take the stage. When they do come before us we see that the murderer's words are true. Bracciano longs for Vittoria. Because she is married, the passion is adulterous; because he is married, it is doubly adulterous. Furthermore, there is a pander, creating a situation that *David and Bethsabe*, *Troilus and Cressida*, and *The Revenger's Tragedy* have taught us to see as death-haunted, full of the potential for personal and moral blight. The fact that the pander is Vittoria's own brother, and in the affair for personal gain, turns the screw of corruption a notch tighter.

The authorial attitude towards all this seems definite enough. It is expressed partly through Vittoria's mother, a choral figure giving us the point of view of conventional morality:

> . . . now I find our house
> Sinking to ruin. Earthquakes leave behind,
> Where they have tyrannized, iron, or lead, or stone,
> But—woe to ruin—violent lust leaves none.   (I. ii. 217–20)

But Webster never relies primarily on overt moralizing to indicate his moral weighting; he reveals the latent flaws of character and how these produce flawed acts. Thus, Bracciano's language is frequently the obtusely flowery language that the Renaissance dramatist so frequently mistrusted, and Vittoria's unconscious (as revealed in her dream) is a murky compound of death and desire:

> . . . my husband straight
> With pick-axe gan to dig, and your fell duchess
> With shovel, like a Fury, voided out
> The earth and scattered bones,—

2. Salingar, "Morality Tradition," 223.
3. John Webster, *The White Devil*, ed. John Russell Brown, the Revels Plays (London: Methuen & Co. Ltd., 1960). All quotations from the play are from this text.

. . . .
When to my rescue there arose methought
A whirlwind, which let fall a massy arm
From that strong plant,
And both were struck dead by that sacred yew
In that base shallow grave that was their due.
                                        (I. ii. 244–47, 251–55)

All this death imagery in the midst of love (not set in opposition to it) clearly indicates a union of love and death of the destructive kind—the tradition of Claudius and Gertrude—and so Webster presents it.

One feels the full force of this presentation in Bracciano's treatment of his wife. His unmerited harshness is emphasized rather than blurred by Webster's use of the imagery of love and the death of love. Thus, Bracciano descends from the verbal negation of the symbols of love:

          Your hand I'll kiss,—
This is the latest ceremony of my love,
Henceforth I'll never lie with thee, by this,
This wedding-ring: I'll ne'er more lie with thee.
                                        (II. i. 192–95)

(and all that is associated with them—marriage, religion, the earthly fruition of children   [II. i. 190–91]) to actual murder: "*Enter* ISABELLA *in her nightgown as to bed-ward* . . . *she kneels down as to prayers, then draws the curtain of the* [poisoned picture of her husband], *does three reverences to it, and kisses it thrice, she faints and will not suffer them to come near it, dies (II. ii. A dumb show)." The love-death convention has its own forms of moral readjustment, and— as here—its own forms of moral exposure and revelation. In Bracciano's case they underline (for us, if not for him) his betrayal, and in the case of Isabella they underline her innocence. We recall from *Othello*, for instance, that Desdemona's love for Othello persisted even to death, when she attempted to protect him by taking the guilt on herself. Isabella twice attempts the same kind of self-sacrificial act: once by taking the blame for an argument with Bracciano (to protect him from her brothers) and here, the second time, by waving her attendants away from her husband's poisoned picture so they will not know how she was poisoned and thus by whom. Professor Salingar and others notwithstanding, Webster is not in any essential state of moral confusion about the specific actions of his characters even though he gives explicit moral commentary relatively little scope.

I stress this point for two reasons: the first, obviously, being to answer critics who find Webster morally deficient. The second, though, is to readjust the findings of some of his defenders, particularly those who find in

Flamineo a commentator whose assessments of character and motive represent Webster's own point of view.[4] This attempt to find some reliable moral voice—in view of the seeming amorality of most of Webster's characters—is natural and understandable, but it must be insisted that in Webster as in Shakespeare, no character ever speaks out of character; all represent partial views. And of no one may this be more truly said than Flamineo, particularly since his supposed acuteness is little more than the marriage of his envy with an obsessive, conventional, knee-jerk antifeminism. Flamineo's commentary on love and woman will indicate what I mean. From the beginning it is evident that what Bracciano feels for Vittoria is more than transient lust, despite its frank carnality. He is, in fact, completely taken out of himself with a vision of beauty. It is to answer this mood that Flamineo gives us his conception of female psychology: "'Bove merit! we may now talk freely: 'bove merit; what is't you doubt? her coyness? that's but the superficies of lust most women have; yet why should ladies blush to hear that nam'd, which they do not fear to handle? O they are politic, they know our desire is increas'd by the difficulty of enjoying; whereas satiety is a blunt, weary and drowsy passion" (I. ii. 17–23). Whatever else this may be, it is not moral penetration, nor pertinent, original thought. It is instead a retailing of the stale clichés of traditional misogyny, expressed with force but no more penetrating for that.

James Smith, in *Scrutiny*, suggests that Flamineo has a conscious, politic reason for his obsessive denigration of love: *i.e.*, that as long as Bracciano regards his sister as an object of lust she will have little influence over him, whereas Flamineo will maintain his.[5] This is an interesting, acute idea in the context of this play, but one can reach wider and see Flamineo's general attitude as the common property of a whole tradition of murderous egoists whose power depends on their ability to reduce all human activity to its lowest denominator and thus keep the self detached, always in a position to manipulate, never to love. How a character so much akin to Iago, and so full of the death-ridden, stereotyped "wisdom" of Iago, can gain eminence as a moral commentator is obscure, but it has happened: "In many ways the most interesting figure in *The White Devil* is Flamineo. He is of all men the least deceived. . . . We have seen how Webster uses Flamineo as a chorus. We remember that Iago is the sharpest-visioned man in the play of *Othello*,

---

4. This is particularly true of Travis Bogard, *The Tragic Satire of John Webster* (Berkeley and Los Angeles: University of California Press, 1955), and Clifford Leech, *John Webster: A Critical Study* (London: Hogarth Press, 1951).
5. James Smith, "The Tragedy of Blood," *Scrutiny*, VIII (December, 1939), 273.

and his soliloquized comments on the other characters are almost alone trustworthy."[6] Clearly this trust is misplaced; far from being a sharp analyst of human nature, Flamineo is in fact the most deceived of men, as was Iago. The plain truth is that neither understands passion, only weakness; faced with passion they are ciphers—able to satirize but unable finally to control or comprehend.

Passion, however, is Webster's special field, and he depicts it on a much wider canvas than Flamineo or any other character in the play can fully understand. What is fascinating in Webster, therefore, is not the small insights of the satirist but the larger insights into the transformations that passion can bring to the most superficial, sordid kind of affair. It is in his analysis of these that the conventions of the romantic love myths begin to work against the grain of the anti-romantic situation.

We see this in the way Bracciano ignores Flamineo's cynicism and goes on speaking to himself in sighs and exclamations, as if he has been elevated to a new level of consciousness:

> Quite lost Flamineo.
>
> . . . .
> Are we so happy?
>
> . . . .
> We are happy above thought, because 'bove merit.
>
> . . . .
> O should she fail to come,—   (I. ii. 3, 10, 16, 38)

The same kind of transformation can be seen in his conversations with Vittoria. When she speaks of her dream, her language rises above the ordinary and becomes allegorical in intent, its full import meant only for Bracciano, who is enrapt and answers appropriately. Flamineo—partly an insider because of his function as pander—is limited to a functionary's understanding, and thus is also very much an outsider. He sees nothing but a simple invitation to murder where Bracciano sees an invitation to a new life for himself and Vittoria:

> Sweetly shall I interpret this your dream—
> You are lodged within his arms who shall protect you,
> From all the fevers of a jealous husband,
> From the poor envy of our phlegmatic duchess,—
> I'll seat you above law and above scandal,
> Give to your thoughts the invention of delight
> And the fruition,—nor shall government

6. Leech, *John Webster*, 47, 49–50. See also Bogard, *Tragic Satire*, 107–108.

Divide me from you longer than a care
To keep you great: you shall to me at once
Be dukedom, health, wife, children, friends and all.
                                                    (I. ii. 259–68)

These additional qualities—the shared protectiveness, the shared ideal of escape from conventionality—become the foundation for a kind of sustaining romantic idealism, despite the brutal and unconscionable means needed to reach the promised end.

The introduction of elements from the romantic convention complicates matters in other ways. There is, for instance, the relationship of Vittoria to her husband Camillo. The old romantic tragedies had a stock situation: an unmarried girl was sought by an unmarried young man; separating them was the old father, conventional, often comic, inevitably jealous. Webster transforms this stock situation by making the pair of lovers into separately married adults and the father figure into the girl's husband. The effect of this—and certainly Webster's point in doing it—is to make what might have been a simple melodrama of adultery into a sexual problem play by showing a fully sexed young woman mated to a partner no more fit to be her husband than her old father would have been. Thus Flamineo strongly and crudely intimates that Camillo is impotent: "So unable to please a woman that like a Dutch doublet all his back is shrunk into his breeches" (I. ii. 32–34). And nothing Camillo says about their relations suggests a large, or even a small, flow of libido: "I do not well remember I protest/When I last lay with her" (I. ii. 55–56). Euphemism calls this kind of marriage the "marriage in name only"; the romantic convention—with its roots in Juliet's pointed rhetorical query "What's in a name?"—puts this kind of dry relationship in a critical perspective, one which had considerable standing within living dramatic tradition and rose from the oldest known tradition of poetic imagery and ritual—that of fertility and sterility.

With this in mind we can go back to the charnel imagery of Vittoria's dream and understand it somewhat more sympathetically:

As I sat sadly leaning on a grave,
Chequered with cross-sticks, there came stealing in
Your duchess and my husband, one of them
A pick-axe bore, th' other a rusty spade,
And in rough terms they gan to challenge me,
About this yew.   (I. ii. 235–40)

The full meaning of the dream is vague, but two related ideas are clearly expressed: one, Vittoria's despair at having to endure a marriage that is death-in-life (the grave is quite possibly her own life); two, an identification of the lover (the "yew"/"you") with what she sees to be nature and life-renewing strength.[7] This imagery is solidly in the romantic tradition, and if we ignore the emptiness of Vittoria's married life merely to condemn her lust, we miss the major complexity in the play. Nor, incidentally, is it just physical satisfaction that Vittoria misses and seeks. There is no level of mental, spiritual, or imaginative life on which Camillo is a near companion, not to say an equal.

In the older romantic tragedies, innocent young lovers rejected name, fortune, society in order to escape social repression and form—most of them—their love marriages. Here again we see this tradition at work, though not innocently. Mainly, indeed, the romantic convention manifests itself in this play in the heroic conception that the lovers have of each other and of themselves. They believe themselves romantic lovers, and by running off together they try to make the belief become the truth. But, because of the human cost of their relationship, imperfection—the death motive—is built into their love and emerges repeatedly throughout the play. Still, the conception they have of themselves is itself interesting, for it is built out of their own pride of life, and it gives form to their spirit. A classic instance is, of course, the great trial scene—the arraignment of Vittoria.

It is a classic clash of legal repressiveness and institutionalized retribution against irresponsible romanticism. To support the conventions of social order Monticelso evokes a conventional female stereotype, the destructive Eve of the antiromantic tradition:

> I am resolved
> Were there a second paradise to lose
> This devil would betray it.   (III. ii. 68–70)

And he goes on to expand the image, playing powerful variations on death-eros imagery:

> What are whores?
> They are those flattering bells have all one tune,
> At weddings, and at funerals: your rich whores
> Are only treasuries by extortion fill'd,

---

7. The yew tree is, of course, a two-sided symbol. It is traditionally associated with graveyards and death. Yet, as an evergreen, it has often been seen as a symbol for life or immortality. Webster, here, seems to be making use of both meanings at once. See Arnold Whittick, *Symbols, Signs and Their Meaning* (Newton 59, Mass.: Charles T. Branford Company, 1961), 296.

And empty'd by curs'd riot. They are worse,
Worse than dead bodies, which are begg'd at gallows
And wrought upon by surgeons, to teach man
Wherein he is imperfect.   (III. ii. 91–98)

Against this Vittoria sets her own determination not to be bullied, her strength of character and quickness of wit. Her answers obviously have little to do with morality, but they have a great deal to do with intellectual and physical energy. It appears to be these qualities, these marks of her unfeminine independence, that offend the judges most, particularly since she cannot be directly implicated in any murder. Thus it is that her accusers hit hardest at her sexuality, what they call her lust. Their punishment, sending her to "a house/Of penitent whores" (III. ii. 266–67), has a nice ironic symmetry, particularly as Vittoria remains impenitent to the last and even displays a fine erotic wit at the sentence. Of the house of penitent whores, she asks: "Do the noblemen in Rome/Erect it for their wives" (III. ii. 267–68). From *The Atheist's Tragedy*, Webster borrows Sebastian's spirited lines on enforced marriages to apply to this new instance of sexual repression:

vit: A rape, a rape.
mont: How?
vit: Yes you have ravish'd justice,
       Forc'd her to do your pleasure.
                                        (III. ii. 274–75)

When faced with these flashes of spirit, critics have commented that Vittoria almost hoaxes us into believing her innocent.[8] Certainly they make us wish she were. And this phenomenon itself suggests several things: first, how conventional morality seems to pale before the imaginative expression of some greatness of spirit. The yea of admiration seems in such cases to push ahead of our moral nays. Second, how dismissive stereotypes like the antiromantic Eve—even when presented with some power—fade before the presence of the living human being in all her complexity. Third, how Vittoria's confidence seems built on inner conviction and not mere hypocrisy. Her last ringing challenge has terrific authority: "Know this, and let it somewhat raise your spite,/Through darkness diamonds spread their richest light" (III. ii. 293–94). The point is that Webster in this scene is not being morally evasive; he is being psychologically true. Vittoria cannot be shamed into taking the title of whore because in her own mind she is not

8. See Ribner, *Jacobean Tragedy*, 101–102, and M. C. Bradbrook, *Themes and Conventions of Elizabethan Tragedy* (Cambridge: The University Press, 1964 reprint of 1935 edition), 186–87.

one; she is the faithful beloved, soon-to-be wife, of the Duke of Bracciano. Webster is recapitulating in darker, more terrible tones the psychological lesson of *Romeo and Juliet*: that lovers make their own world and as long as they remain true to it and to each other they maintain a spiritual center that cannot be touched by the larger world outside.

This is why the strongest threat to the love of Vittoria and Bracciano is not Vittoria's trial but the subsequent jealousy of Bracciano himself. The feigned love letter from Francisco to Vittoria is thus a very subtle revenge, for it plays on the residue of suspicion of woman in nearly every male ego and in this case gains perverse credibility from the betrayal which has come before. What we have, in other words, is a psychological parallel to the *Othello* situation, with Francisco playing both Iago and Cassio. To remember Othello in the "brothel scene" is to feel the psychological kinship of Bracciano's rage:

> BRAC: Can you read mistress? look upon that letter;
> There are no characters nor hieroglyphics.
> You need no comment, I am grown your receiver,—
> God's precious, you shall be a brave great lady,
> A stately and advanced whore.
> VIT: Say sir?
> BRAC: Come, come, let's see your cabinet, discover
> Your treasury of love-letters. Death and furies,
> I'll see them all.

> (IV. ii. 72–79)

Webster develops the scene at considerable length, with much acute observation on the dynamics of the sex war, its fear, distrust, resentment, both in man and in woman. Reconciliation is, however, the final note, and in this the scene follows *Antony and Cleopatra*. The jealous accusation is recanted— "I have drunk Lethe" (IV. ii. 129)—and healed by an unequivocating reaffirmation of the bond for which both have taken so many spiritual and physical risks: "Be thou at peace with me; let all the world/Threaten the cannon" (IV. ii. 173–74). The reconciliation is followed by that classic romantic gesture—elopement and the romantic marriage.

Again it is worth noting that what moral ambiguity exists in the play is not due to confusion on Webster's part but rather to his exploratory, iconoclastic turn of mind. Without forgiving or excusing the lovers for murder, he, at the same time, takes a classic antiromantic premise and shows in it more than is dreamt of in a narrow antiromantic philosophy. For Webster is more interested in being a psychologist of eros than a moralist or a satirist, and the acuteness of his insight is shown in his final treatment of both the lovers and the revengers. As the play moves to its close, the lovers in their tight, solipsistic world renounce allegiance to society at large and judge themselves only on their actions toward each other: their fidelity to the love bond even in the face of death. The phenomenon here would be defined as love arising out of death. The revengers show the opposite principle at work: death emerging from love.

Both motifs are, of course, familiar from the tradition of love-death opposites, and the result of their clash is another familiar organizing structure— the Deadly Nuptial. The revengers are led to their sister's murderer by the intuitions of brotherly love, prodded by Monticelso's beautifully pregnant love-death imagery:

> Come, come my lord, untie your folded thoughts
> And let them dangle loose as a bride's hair.
> Your sister's poisoned.   (IV. i. 1–3)

and nourished by Francisco's tormenting visions:

> Call for her picture: no; I'll close mine eyes,
> And in a melancholic thought I'll frame
> Her figure 'fore me.
> > *Enter* ISABELLA's *Ghost.*
> Now I ha't—how strong
> Imagination works! how she can frame
> Things which are not! methinks she stands afore me; . . .
> > (IV. i. 100–104)

Whatever Webster touches he humanizes; the bloody revenger becomes no vehicle for a sermon but instead a moving study in the psychology of loss, despair, and the rage born out of love's frustration. True to the exploratory style that has typified the play, Webster's audience is asked to understand before judging.

The deaths of the lovers are treated with the same complexity as their lives. The messiness of their end is never temporized. Bracciano falls raving from the corrosive effects of a poisoned helmet, and by an ironically symmetrical twist he cannot even kiss Vittoria as he sinks for fear of poisoning her with his own infection just as his poisoned image killed his wife. For most of his lingering decline he is out of his wits entirely, making bawdy, mad remarks. Vittoria and Flamineo die after a melange of cross purposes and betrayals. But Webster never gratuitously degrades, and he never deprives his people in death of the substance that drove them in life. Bracciano defines the meaning of his death in terms of his love:

> Where's this good woman? had I infinite worlds
> They were too little for thee. Must I leave thee?
> What say yon screech-owls, is the venom mortal?
> (V. iii. 17–19)

and calls Vittoria's name as his last word. Vittoria meets her killers' blades with the same determination with which she faced life:

> Yes I shall welcome death
> As princes do some great ambassadors;
> I'll meet thy weapon half way.   (V. vi. 219–21)

and something of the same wit:

> 'Twas a manly blow—
> The next thou giv'st, murder some sucking infant,
> And then thou wilt be famous.   (V. vi. 232–34)

And she gets the accolade finally from her misogynous brother:

> Th'art a noble sister—
> I love thee now; if woman do breed man
> She ought to teach him manhood: fare thee well.
> (V. vi. 241–43)

Irving Ribner, among others, maintains that it is in the idea of "integrity of life"[9] that Webster finds the sources of human value and moral energy. In Vittoria and Bracciano this integrity of life is not to be divorced from the erotic attraction and energy which brought them together. The flaw in this eros was its early involvement with death, but what value there was in it is given due and measured (and appropriately qualified) expression. The play, therefore, seems to be a liberating act, a deliberately iconoclastic piece of romantic analysis of a stock antiromantic situation, not morally confused, just morally adventurous. In his next play Webster again sets love against social repression, but in this love, there is no death motive. It is all life.

2. *The Duchess of Malfi*

I pointed out at the beginning of this chapter that critics find in *The Duchess of Malfi* the firmness of moral perception they missed in the earlier play. The reason appears to be that Webster has come to a decision concerning

---

9. Ribner, *Jacobean Tragedy*, 105.

the relative weight to be given to the antiromantic and romantic visions of nature and human existence. This does by no means give him a rose-colored view of life, but it does give him a more just comprehension of the sources of good and evil, of the death motive and love motive.

Of Shakespeare's plays, the most influential in this context would appear to be *Othello*. In that play the sources of life and of good are to be found in their most complete form in the generosity and freedom of love between person and person, particularly man and woman. Such is the case in *The Duchess*. Nothing could make a more perfect contrast to Ferdinand's all-consuming egotism: "Why do you laugh? Methinks you that are courtiers should be my touch-wood, take fire, when I give fire; that is, laugh when I laugh, were the subject never so witty—"[10] (I. i. 122–25) than the open praise and admiration that Antonio shows for the Duchess well before she reveals her love for him:

> For her discourse, it is so full of rapture
> You only will begin then to be sorry
> When she doth end her speech; and wish, in wonder,
> She held it less vain-glory to talk much,
> Than you penance to hear her: whilst she speaks,
> She throws upon a man so sweet a look,
> That it were able raise one to a galliard
> That lay in a dead palsy, . . .   (I. i. 190–97)

The scene in which the Duchess declares her love and she and Antonio plight their troth expands these themes of generosity and love into the context of the romantic marriage. As in *Romeo and Juliet* and *Othello* it is the woman who steers the way into love when man, with his greater sensitivity to the pressures of external social relationships, seems to falter. Juliet had directly said: "If that thy bent of love be honourable,/Thy purpose marriage, send me word tomorrow" (*R & J*, II. ii. 143–44). Desdemona had been "half a wooer." Webster shows the same process. He builds the scene on love-death imagery ("I am making my will," the Duchess says, employing both meanings of that word), but this imagery turns insistently towards love and life away from death. Antonio urges her towards a renewal of life:

> ANT: Begin with that first good deed began i'th' world
> After man's creation, the sacrament of marriage—
> I'd have you first provide for a good husband,
> Give him all.

10. John Webster, *The Duchess of Malfi*, ed. John Russell Brown, the Revels Plays (London: Methuen & Co. Ltd., 1964). All quotations from the play are from this text.

DUCH:	All?
ANT:	Yes, your excellent self.
DUCH:	In a winding sheet?
ANT:	In a couple. (I. i. 385–89)

After all the antiromantic denigrations of marriage as man's primal curse, this reference to it as "that first good deed" after creation comes like a piece of happy emotional heresy. All the small details of Antonio's formulation of the idea of marriage are right too: the insistence on the idea of the couple and the emphasis on "all" being "your excellent self" rather than a good dowry. The Duchess' wooing reinforces these themes by laying special emphasis on her own humanity, her existence as a loving, sentient being, rather than as a cold symbol:

> This is flesh and blood, sir;
> 'Tis not the figure cut in alabaster
> Kneels at my husband's tomb. Awake, awake, man!
> (I. i. 453–55)

But flesh must still battle social convention, the barrier of rank. Antonio's love had been wholly disinterested, had worked towards her happiness, not his own. As he says himself: "I have long serv'd virtue,/And ne'er ta'en wages of her" (I. i. 439–40). When to his shock she says "Now she pays it!" (I. i. 440) and the reward is that which he desires most but never looked to have, all the old social repressions represented by the rigid adherence to class barriers and class pride so thoroughly embodied in the Arragonian brothers become deadening forces on the mind. He falls to his knees; he tries to find excuses; he puts his fears in hackneyed political saws like "Ambition, madam, is a great man's madness" (I. i. 420). The Duchess then must take on a task women have always had to perform—inspiriting, giving life to, the egos of those they love:

> . . . I must tell you
> If you will know where breathes a complete man—
> I speak it without flattery—turn your eyes
> And progress through yourself.   (I. i. 434–37)

We know, of course, that she is not exaggerating; no other man Webster shows us is his equal in virtue. Love in this case sees with one kind of wisdom even while it discards another kind of "wisdom," that associated with the term *policy*.

The central movement of this scene creates a union of love, life, generosity, personal value that stands in direct opposition to the clotted, oppressive will to dominance exemplified by the brothers. As in *Romeo and Juliet* or

Othello love is shown as a force which frees people from rigid, lifeless barriers that separate them; the Duchess says, "I do here put off all vain ceremony" (I. i. 456), echoing Juliet and Desdemona. And the whole movement culminates in the beautiful vows of marriage, which set the bond of love against the death motive: "Bless, heaven, this sacred Gordian, which let violence/Never untwine"(I. i. 480–81) and reassert the romantic idea of the love marriage as the source of earthly harmony and fruition:

> ANT: And may our sweet affections, like the spheres,
>   Be still in motion.
> DUCH: Quickening, and make
>   The like soft music.
> ANT: That we may imitate the loving palms,
>   Best emblem of a peaceful marriage,
>   That ne'er bore fruit, divided.   (I. i. 482–87)

Sex and spirit are again brought into conjunction. And this is done successfully because Webster himself is able to give the combination dramatic life by showing on stage two people genuinely, sexually in love, as here:

> I would have you lead your fortune by the hand,
> Unto your marriage bed:—
> (You speak in me this, for we now are one)
> We'll only lie, and talk together, and plot
> T' appease my humorous kindred; and if you please,
> Like the old tale, in 'Alexander and Lodowick',
> Lay a naked sword between us, keep us chaste:—
> O, let me shroud my blushes in your bosom, . . .
>   (I. i. 495–502)

Nor, as the play unfolds, does the romanticism ever float off into sentimentality or hollowness. Webster's wit and his free acknowledgment of love's sexual content prevent this. At one point, a jealous subordinate says of Antonio, "Some said he was an hermaphrodite, for he could not abide a woman" (III. ii. 220–21). But nothing could be more carefully calculated to discredit that remark or the larger antiromantic denigrations of eros than the good-natured and witty bawdry that passes in the following exchange between Antonio, the Duchess, and Cariola. I give it at length because outside of Shakespeare and the earlier Elizabethans no other passage exists that so naturally and convincingly presents sexuality as the basis for a bond that includes but goes beyond the physical:

> DUCH: Bring me the casket hither, and the glass:—
>   You get no lodging here tonight, my lord.
> ANT: Indeed, I must persuade one:—

DUCH: Very good:
      I hope in time 'twill grow into a custom
      That noblemen shall come with cap and knee,
      To purchase a night's lodging of their wives.
ANT: I must lie here.
DUCH: Must? you are a lord of mis-rule.
ANT: Indeed, my rule is only in the night.
DUCH: To what use will you put me?
ANT: We'll sleep together:—
DUCH: Alas, what pleasure can two lovers find in sleep?
CAR: My lord, I lie with her often; and I know
      She'll much disquiet you:—
ANT: See, you are complain'd of.
CAR: For she's the sprawling'st bedfellow.
ANT: I shall like her the better for that.
CAR: Sir, shall I ask you a question?
ANT: I pray thee, Cariola.
CAR: Wherefore still when you lie with my lady
      Do you rise so early?
ANT: Labouring men
      Count the clock oft'nest Cariola,
      Are glad when their task's ended.
DUCH: I'll stop your mouth.
                          [*Kisses him.*]
                          (III. ii. 1–20)

The living fruits of this union of love and sex are, of course, the three children that play a much greater symbolic role in the play than their infre-
quent appearances (first, in effigy during the Duchess' torture, and finally,
at the conclusion of the play, when the eldest becomes ruler of a society
purged of evil) suggest.

For the depiction of the Arragonian brothers, two studies in the complexities of evil that must rank with any, the influence of Tourneur would appear to join with Shakespeare's. In Ferdinand the psychology of the male
ego seems to be drawn from *Othello*; for the obsessive phallicism of its manifestation, *The Revenger's Tragedy* would be the relevant comparison. Taken
together, the brothers may be said to represent the principle of masculine
dominance run mad.

Webster uses this principle to tie together a striking number of antiromantic social and psychological phenomena. The first is the taboo on the
remarriage of widows with which the Arragonian brotherhood browbeat
the Duchess long before they have any reason (other than the assumed
looseness of women) to suspect her of wanting a husband. The question of
second marriages was, of course, a vexed one in Elizabethan England. That

widows frequently did remarry has been shown in convincing detail by
Frank W. Wadsworth,[11] but against practice we must also set theory: "The
church never condemned second marriages, but there was a considerable
body of feeling against them. Indeed it is easy to amass a series of passages
from sixteenth- and seventeenth-century works of all kinds to show the
strength of the feeling." [12] The gulf here seems to be less a question of high
principle versus low practice than one of male jealousy versus female independence—another skirmish in the sex war, in other words. Seen in this
way, the question of second marriage for widows parallels that of enforced
marriage. Fathers rail against daughters because they want to maintain
their extensive masculine prerogatives. A vast tribe of preachers and satir-
ists rail indiscriminately against widows (but not, of course, widowers) and
are moved to do so by the same will to ascendancy.

It is in this context, I think, that the brothers' parting exhortations in
Act I. i should be read. An abstract but highly emotional suspicion of
woman motivates them, and the result is a long recital of the clichés of
antifeminism; their theme is Hamlet's theme (though they have far less
excuse for disturbance):

FERD: You are a widow:
        You know already what man is; and therefore
        Let not youth, high promotion, eloquence—
CARD: No, nor anything without the addition, honour,
        Sway your high blood.
FERD: Marry! they are most luxurious
        Will wed twice.
CARD: O fie!
FERD: Their livers are more spotted
        Than Laban's sheep.

        . . . .

FERD: . . . be not cunning:
        For they whose faces do belie their hearts
        Are witches, ere they arrive at twenty years—
        Ay: and give the devil suck.   (I. i. 293–99, 308–11)

And the conjunction of animal imagery, witchcraft imagery, and the theme
of female depravity strongly suggests in the beginning what we find all
through the play: that the Cardinal and Duke Ferdinand are—on the ques-

11. Frank W. Wadsworth, "Webster's *Duchess of Malfi* in the Light of Some Contemporary
Ideas on Marriage and Remarriage," *Philological Quarterly*, XXXV (October, 1956), 394–407.
12. Clifford Leech, *Webster: The Duchess of Malfi*, Studies in English Literature, No. 8 (London: Edward Arnold Ltd., 1963), 55.

tion of woman—perpetually in the *Hamlet* state of mind: cynical in the extreme concerning them, yet feeling themselves inextricably involved in what their women do. The fact that events justify their fears of the Duchess' remarriage does not blind us to the fact that they are wrong to forbid her in the first place and to force her into a secret marriage and secret life.

Webster simultaneously deepens both the psychological and the moral insights of the situation as the play advances. From mere moral exhortation the brothers move—by a logical extension of the will to power—to overt threats, converting the sterility implicit in their moralizing into overt expressions of the death motive:

> CARD: You may flatter yourself,
> And take your own choice: privately be married
> Under the eaves of night.
>
> .   .   .   .
> FERD: . . . but observe,
> Such weddings may more properly be said
> To be executed, than celebrated.   (I. i. 316–18, 321–23)

The male will to power takes as its province not just the Duchess' love life but her very existence. By the end of the scene—when only Ferdinand remains to urge her—the focus narrows down to the explicit linking of murder to destructive phallicism:

>   You are my sister—
> This was my father's poniard: do you see?
> I'd be loth to see't look rusty, 'cause 'twas his:—
> I would have you to give o'er these chargeable revels;
> A visor and a mask are whispering-rooms
> That were ne'er built for goodness: fare ye well:—
> And women like that part which, like the lamprey,
> Hath ne'er a bone in't.   (I. i. 330–37)

The discovery that the Duchess has in fact taken a husband touches deeper chords—particularly in Ferdinand—but the tune remains the same. The Cardinal tends to be phlegmatic and even scientific, giving irrational prejudice a pseudoanatomical foundation:

>   Curs'd creature!
> Unequal nature, to place women's hearts
> So far upon the left side!   (II. v. 31–33)

But Ferdinand's rage is deeply personal and it comes to dominate and pervert his imagination. It is through Ferdinand that Webster reveals the masochistic fantasies that form the underside of antiromantic and misogynous satire:

FERD: Methinks I see her laughing—
          Excellent hyena!—talk to me somewhat, quickly,
          Or my imagination will carry me
          To see her, in the shameful act of sin.
CARD: With whom?
FERD: Happily with some strong thigh'd bargeman;
          Or one o'th' wood-yard, that can quoit the sledge,
          Or toss the bar, or else some lovely squire
          That carries coals up to her privy lodgings.

                                             (II. v. 38–45)

and the manner in which such fantasies translate themselves into sadistic aggression:

                              I would have their bodies
          Burnt in a coal-pit, with the ventage stopp'd,
          That their curs'd smoke might not ascend to heaven:
          Or dip the sheets they lie in, in pitch or sulphur,
          Wrap them in't, and then light them like a match;
          Or else to boil their bastard to a cullis,
          And giv't his lecherous father, to renew
          The sin of his back.   (II. v. 66–73)

Obscenity, beast metaphor, forced devouring of offspring, mutilation: these are the classic symptoms of the psyche torn simultaneously by love motive and hate motive, and they can be observed in tragedies as widely separated in time and style as *Gismond of Salern, Antonio's Revenge, Othello,* and *The Revenger's Tragedy*. Behind Ferdinand are—in particular—Tancred, Brabantio, Hamlet, Vindice, and Othello, for the extreme nature of their passion brought out the conflict in extreme manifestations. When Tancred mutilated Gismond's lover he put into action the feelings which Ferdinand has here put into words and will later also act on.

The chief point to make about Ferdinand is that his rage and his subsequent actions and madness are both the product of his irrational distrust of woman and his fanatically antiromantic attitude towards woman, love, indeed, life itself. When this is accepted, two things follow. One is that his persecution of the Duchess, particularly the long, tortuous death scene of Act IV, results from the union of a highly emotional misogyny with an equally emotional will towards phallic dominance. The second is that this death-ridden state of mind is finally most destructive to himself.

Act IV takes its power primarily from the conflict between the fanatical,

antiromantic Ferdinand (with his satirical mouthpiece Bosola) and the
Duchess, whose whole set of personal valuations and actions are inextricably tied to her powerfully romantic vision of life. Ferdinand, of course,
holds the power over physical life and death, but what he really wants from
her is spiritual capitulation, the abandonment of romanticism. Thus, the
full force of Ferdinand's revenge comes into play only when Bosola confirms his own observation that "Her melancholy" (his term for her persis-
tence in loving her husband) "seems to be fortify'd/With a strange disdain"
(IV. i. 11–12). To break her down from this, Ferdinand turns his wit to
grossly satirical practical jokes that revolve around the theme of love and
death, such as offering her his hand to kiss in love but revealing it to be a
dead man's hand. The same diseased wit provides the tableau of her murdered loved ones. But all the comfort Ferdinand gets from this is to see her
retreat further from him into her love. Bosola suggests politic wisdom:

> He doth present you this sad spectacle
> That now you know directly they are dead—
> Hereafter you may wisely cease to grieve
> For that which cannot be recovered.   (IV. i. 57–60)

But she turns this back on them by giving testimony to the power of the
small world she had built with Antonio and her family by wanting to join
them in death.

The final stage of Ferdinand's mocking torture is the long masque-like
scene which Inga-Stina Ekeblad in a brilliant piece of scholarly spadework
and analysis has related to the European *charivari*, used by Webster as the
formal basis for still one more Deadly Nuptial motif:

> The *charivari* as such was a French *ludus*, or marriage-baiting custom,
> dating from the latter part of the Middle Ages, "originally common af-
> ter all weddings, then directed at unpopular or unequal matches as a
> form of public censure." But the practice which the word stands for was
> not limited to France. English folk-customs and folk-drama knew the
> equivalent of the French *charivari*—indeed a descendant of it was still
> known when Hardy put his skimmington-ride into *The Mayor of Caster-
> bridge*.[13]

Miss Ekeblad goes on to say that a seventeenth-century audience "would
then have seen a meaning in Ferdinand's (and Webster's) device which totally escapes us when we see it as just one Bedlam episode among many.
For, if seen as related to the *charivari* tradition, the madmen's masque be-

---

13. Inga-Stina Ekeblad, "The 'Impure Art' of John Webster," *Review of English Studies*, IX
(1958), 261.

comes a contrivance of cruel irony on the part of Ferdinand: in a sense, the Duchess is here being given her belated wedding entertainment."[14] Her article goes on to discuss various aspects of the love-death interaction: the ironic counterpoint of the *charivari* scene with the wooing scene and the subordinate love-death ironies that result from this.[15] Most important for my own present purposes is her suggestion that the entrance of Bosola, disguised *"like an old man,"* is intended to evoke such themes as the Dance of Death and *memento mori*,[16] for the attitude implicit in these themes— contempt of the world—is precisely that which Bosola employs to break down the Duchess' will to life. Thus, when she asks "Who am I?" Bosola urges on her a penitential, self-mortifying, self-denying contempt for the flesh: "Thou art a box of worm-seed, at best, but a salvatory of green mummy:—what's this flesh? a little crudded milk, fantastical puff-paste; our bodies are weaker than those paper prisons boys use to keep flies in; more contemptible, since ours is to preserve earth-worms" (IV. ii. 124–28). These persistent attempts to break down her love of life and the world are what she rebukes with the great and simple statement, "I am Duchess of Malfi still" (IV. ii. 142). The statement is itself an act of romantic self-assertion. She disowns nothing in her past actions or her love and marriage, for to do so would be to disown a part of herself. Ferdinand had designed these torments to bring her to "despair." The despair to which he referred has religious connotations, but it is a despair not of Christian faith but of romantic faith that he tries consistently to effect. His final weapon—the denigration of the body—is the same which animated *The Revenger's Tragedy* of Tourneur, for what Tourneur was trying to do to Renaissance humanism Ferdinand is trying to do to the Duchess. Ferdinand, of course, fails. The Duchess dies with unrepentant scorn for her oppressors: "Go tell my brothers, when I am laid out,/They then may feed in quiet" (IV. ii. 236–37). And we are not allowed to forget that this spirit is intimately linked to the erotic energy which first moved her to defy her brothers and marry. Her last word affirms everything that Ferdinand has tried to subvert or erase: "Antonio!" (IV. ii. 350). Bosola sees by this time who has won the contest of wills between Ferdinand and the Duchess and, like a referee awarding a prize, gives her the last and best gift she is capable of receiving:

14. *Ibid.*, 262.
15. *Ibid.*, 261–66.
16. *Ibid.*, 262–63.

BOS: Yes, madam, he is living—
          The dead bodies you saw were but feign'd statues;
          He's reconciled to your brothers; the Pope hath
              wrought
          The atonement.
DUCH: Mercy!   (IV. ii. 350–53)

Bosola's transformation from agent of Ferdinand to the Duchess'
avenger is clearly to be interpreted as punctuation to the main theme.
Bosola had impersonally but with great force wielded the lash of satire
against women; early in the play he says to an "old lady": "—to behold thee
not painted inclines somewhat near a miracle: these, in thy face here, were
deep ruts and foul sloughs the last progress. There was a lady in France,
that having had the smallpox, flayed the skin off her face to make it more
level; and whereas before she looked like a nutmeg-grater, after she re-
sembled an abortive hedgehog" (II. i. 23–29). He had underlined with disgust the physical aspects of pregnancy:

                    I observe our duchess
          Is sick o' days, she pukes, her stomach seethes,
          The fins of her eyelids look most teeming blue,
          She wanes i'th' cheek, and waxes fat i'th' flank; . . .
                                         (II. i. 63–66)

All of these things touch the antiromantic convention directly. But—in an
expansion of Flamineo's last-minute conversion—Bosola too recants: "O
sacred innocence, that sweetly sleeps" (IV. ii. 355). We may read this not as
just a piece of personal characterization but a *placing* of the satiric spirit, of
the whole antiromantic convention, partly for its implicit egotism and
cruelty to others. There is another reason, however.
    As Shakespeare had shown in *Hamlet*, the hatred and fear of female sex-
uality is of its very nature self-destructive. The male ego can soothe itself
with flattering unctions, but what is inescapable finally is the fact of nature
that all blood is the same. Ferdinand, because of the greater passion of his
emotions for his sister, feels this instinctively and wildly even early in the
play, and his lust to kill threatens even then to rebound upon himself:

                    I could kill her now,
          In you, or in myself, for I do think
          It is some sin in us, heaven doth revenge
          By her.   (II. v. 63–66)

Added to this is the unquestionable fact that Ferdinand did love his sister profoundly. Whether it was repressed incest or not must remain uncertain, but the love was so powerful that it could seem like incest:

> Damn her! that body of hers,
> While that my blood ran pure in't, was more worth
> Than that which thou wouldst comfort, call'd a soul—
> (IV. i. 121–23)

Thus Ferdinand is trapped between hating the body and the beauty that he at the same time strongly loved. The end of this must be madness, and proves to be so. In killing his sister he has killed something of himself:

> Cover her face: mine eyes dazzle: she died young.
> . . . .
> She and I were twins:
> And should I die this instant, I had liv'd
> Her time to a minute.   (IV. ii. 264, 267–69)

Thus his madness takes a penitential, self-lacerating form that is suicidal in intent:

> One met the duke, 'bout midnight in a lane
> Behind Saint Mark's church, with the leg of a man
> Upon his shoulder; and he howl'd fearfully;
> Said he was a wolf, only the difference
> Was, a wolf's skin was hairy on the outside,
> His on the inside; bade them take their swords,
> Rip up his flesh, and try: . . .   (V. ii. 13–19)

This is the ultimate judgment on the antiromantic vision, that it is condemned to destroy the only things which can bring it pleasure.

13   Thomas Middleton

In a commendatory verse prefixed to the 1623 printing of *The Duchess of Malfi*, Thomas Middleton gives Webster tribute for his "masterpiece of tragedy." The poem ends with these lines:

> Thy epitaph only the title be—
> Write 'Duchess', that will fetch a tear for thee,
> For who e'er saw this duchess live, and die,
> That could get off under a bleeding eye?[1]

Few things in Jacobean theater strike one more strangely than the thought of a self-evident rationalist and skeptic like Middleton shedding a tear over a romantic tragedy, for one hallmark of his work in both comedy and tragedy is a penchant for reductive analysis of the motives behind words and actions.

In this connection, let me argue with the assessment of Una Ellis-Fermor: "A wide and keen observer, he covered a range of mood and material only equalled by Shakespeare among his contemporaries and, like him again, could so identify himself with any given mood or matter as to make it his own and proper to him. No one ever explains a failure of Middleton's on the ground that the theme was uncongenial; few of us would care to guarantee any theme impossible to him."[2] Judging from the plays he actually did write, I would suggest that the theme of *The Duchess of Malfi* was impossible to him, and so were those of such Shakespearean plays as *Othello*, *Antony and Cleopatra*, and *The Winter's Tale*. Despite T. S. Eliot's assertion

---

1. Quoted in the Revels Plays edition of *The Duchess of Malfi*, 4.
2. Una Ellis-Fermor, *The Jacobean Drama: An Interpretation* (5th ed.; London: Methuen & Co. Ltd., 1965), 128.

that next to Shakespeare Middleton portrayed women best in tragedy,[3] one kind of woman seems beyond his reach—that is, one who could be both sexually alive and, at the same time, good. What Middleton is supremely good at is bad, vain, or amoral women—the Cressidas and Gertrudes. With these he did indeed surpass any but Shakespeare.

Middleton's tragedies have a special place in this study for two reasons. First, they represent the most consistent and penetrating post-Shakespearean critique of the romantic vision of erotic experience and the romantic patterns of tragedy. Second (and this point complements Middleton's portrayal of women), he offers the most passionate and moving attempt of any to analyze the plight—and to some degree the proper response—of the male in his necessary and inescapable confrontations with these women.

1. *The Changeling*

The typical pattern of a Middleton tragedy is the following: to set up some situation of romantic love tragedy and then subvert it by means of determinedly antiromantic analysis of the nature of woman and the nature of love.

In *The Changeling* Middleton takes for his central focus the idea of the romantic marriage, opening his play with a situation that bears many resemblances to *Romeo and Juliet*.[4] Alsemero, the young male lover, is smitten at first sight of Beatrice-Joanna and filled with a sense of love so pure that it can find expression only in the images of religion:

> 'Twas in the temple where I first beheld her,
> And now again the same; what omen yet
> Follows of that? None but imaginary;
> Why should my hopes or fate be timorous?
> The place is holy, so is my intent:
> I love her beauties to the holy purpose,
> And that, methinks, admits comparison
> With man's first creation, the place blest,
> And is his right home back, if he achieve it.
> The church hath first begun our interview,
> And that's the place must join us into one,
> So there's beginning and perfection too.[5]   (I. i. 1–12)

---

3. Eliot, "Thomas Middleton," (1927) in *Selected Essays*, 166.
4. Ornstein, *Moral Vision*, 180–89. Mr. Ornstein considers some of these resemblances, though his discussion has a somewhat different general emphasis.
5. Thomas Middleton and William Rowley, *The Changeling*, ed. N. W. Bawcutt, the Revels Plays (London: Methuen & Co. Ltd., 1961). All quotations from the play are from this text.

In keeping with this purity of affection Alsemero immediately thinks of marriage, and his reference to "man's first creation" puts forth the typically romantic idea (we recall it from Shakespeare, Webster, and the early part of each of Heywood's plays) that marriage is a retrieval of the Edenic union of earthly pleasure and spiritual bliss fragmented by the fall.

Other romantic conventions are given prominence in Act I. For instance, *Romeo and Juliet* gave dramatic sanction to the idea that love at first sight is a revelation that transcends in truth the pedestrian valuations of common sense. To a rationalist like Middleton this is obviously an assumption to be questioned. It is with nicely judged irony that he makes Beatrice-Joanna the first spokesman for reason and judgment. She tells the love-sick Alsemero:

> Our eyes are sentinels unto our judgments,
> And should give certain judgment what they see;
> But they are rash sometimes, and tell us wonders
> Of common things, which when our judgments find,
> They can then check the eyes, and call them blind.
>
> (I. i. 72–76)

The irony is in the fact that Beatrice-Joanna's own judgment is subordinate to her own self-love:

> How wise is Alsemero in his friend!
> It is a sign he makes his choice with judgment.
> Then I appear in nothing more approv'd,
> Than making choice of him;
> For 'tis a principle, he that can choose
> That bosom well, who of his thoughts partakes,
> Proves most discreet in every choice he makes.
> Methinks I love now with the eyes of judgment,
> And see the way to merit, clearly see it.   (II. i. 6–14)

She could never imagine the possibility that "judgment" would fail to choose her, and by a circular argument (Alsemero's wise choice of friends includes not only Jasperino, who is the explicit subject of conversation, but by implication herself) she is led to complacently affirm her own judgment.

Behind the high comedy of such speeches, though, lie Middleton's real reservations concerning the blindness of romantic love to its own motives and objects. There is, for instance, nothing comic in the treatment of the betrothed whom Beatrice-Joanna wishes to reject in favor of Alsemero. Piracquo's brother—who is not in love and therefore can judge objectively

—sees that Beatrice-Joanna does not love his brother, and he is eloquently realistic about the long-term consequences of such a marriage:

> Come, your faith's cozened in her, strongly cozened;
> Unsettle your affection with all speed
> Wisdom can bring it to, your peace is ruin'd else.
> Think what a torment 'tis to marry one
> Whose heart is leap'd into another's bosom:
> If ever pleasure she receive from thee,
> It comes not in thy name, or of thy gift;
> She lies but with another in thine arms, . . .
>   (II. i. 128–35)

The psychological perception of this passage is strong indeed, but it meets with nothing but naïve romantic bravado, the defense of an image of woman, not a fully perceived person:

> I should depart
> An enemy, a dangerous, deadly one
> To any but thyself, that should but think
> She knew the meaning of inconstancy,
> Much less the use and practice;   (II. i. 145–49)

The lesson is a complex one: love, Middleton seems to be saying, idealizes and blinds, but never in Middleton is it trivial. If it were, the "torment"— and torment is the primary emotion of all of Middleton's truly romantic male lovers—would be eliminated, as would love itself.

Middleton also takes up the theme of the Enforced Marriage, though rather perfunctorily, as if it had importance to him primarily because of its status as a stock romantic convention. Nevertheless, his treatment of the motif does have interest. We know, for instance, that Middleton and Rowley had earlier pondered the problem of fatherly pressures. One result is a passage like this from *A Fair Quarrel*:

> Defend and keep me from a father's rage,
> Whose love yet infinite, not knowing this,
> Might, knowing, turn a hate as infinite;
> Sure, he would throw me ever from his blessings,
> And cast his curses on me![6]
>   (*A Fair Quarrel*, III. ii. 52–56)

The theme here is also the main theme of *Gismond of Salern*, and subtheme in many earlier plays, but in none of these was it explicated with such dis-

---

6. Quoted by N. W. Bawcutt in the Revels Plays edition of *The Changeling*, 26.

cursive directness. In *The Changeling* the theme is transformed back into drama, as in this exchange between Beatrice-Joanna, who wishes out of her engagement to Piracquo, and her father Vermandero, who insists on proceeding as scheduled:

VER: He shall be bound to me,
As fast as this tie can hold him; I'll want
My will else.
BEA: [*aside*]   I shall want mine if you do it.
                                                          (I. i. 218–20)

This is dramatic in that all residue of discursiveness is dissolved, but it also displays Middleton's rationalistic bias in that he refuses the potential emotionalism of the scene and directs our attention instead to the key word *will* and the concept behind it, linking father and daughter without taking sides.

Not all of Middleton's writing is so coolly dispassionate, however. As he moves away from the ironies of his mock-romantic premises and into the antiromantic development of them, passion and analysis merge to produce his most remarkable writing. The animating force behind it is the myth of the fall and the betrayal of man by the serpent and the eternal Eve. The chief virtue of it—at least in *The Changeling*—is an attention to language that raises the linguistics of love and death to a new level of semantic self-awareness.[7]

The two great scenes between Beatrice-Joanna and De Flores are the most important products of this awareness. Both are based on puns implicit in certain words which can refer to either love or death.

In Act II. ii Middleton demonstrates various ways that the language of love can be made to mask the hidden motive of death. Beatrice-Joanna disguises her loathing of De Flores in words which have their customary function in the language of love:

                              What ha' you done
To your face a-late? Y'have met with some good
          physician;
Y'have prun'd yourself, methinks, you were not wont
To look so amorously.   (II. ii. 72–75)

7. Every student of Middleton's language owes a special debt to Christopher Ricks's two fine articles: "The Moral and Poetic Structure of *The Changeling*," *Essays in Criticism*, X (July, 1960), 290–306; and "Word-Play in *Women Beware Women*," *Review of English Studies*, XII (1961), 238–50. Even where the instances I cite differ from Ricks's, his analysis is the basis from which I have worked.

The words are augmented by meaningful sighs and exclamations—"Oh my De Flores! . . . Oh!" (II. ii. 98, 101)—which disguise the death motive that she reveals in an aside:

> Why, put case I loath'd him
> As much as youth and beauty hates a sepulchre,
> Must I needs show it? Cannot I keep that secret,
> And serve my turn upon him?   (II. ii. 66–69)

Duplicity thus is one way of punning, of opening up the gap between word and fact that gives rise to ambiguity. Another is euphemism, in this case the euphemisms of courtly love. One of the distinctive features of courtly language is that it provides a framework for talking in traditional and elevated terms about very brutal matters. Thus De Flores and Beatrice-Joanna can use the word *service* to negotiate the murder of an actual living human being as if the victim had no living actuality, for he has none in the language:

> BEA: Hardness becomes the visage of a man well,
>   It argues service, resolution, manhood,
>   If cause were of employment.
>
>   . . . .
>
> DE F: It's a service that I kneel for to you.
> BEA: You are too violent to mean faithfully;
>   There's horror in my service, blood and danger,
>   Can those be things to sue for?
> DE F: If you knew
>   How sweet it were to me to be employed
>   In any act of yours, you would say then
>   I fail'd and us'd not reverence enough
>   When I receive the charge on't.
>   (II. ii. 92–94, 117–24)

The language of honor and service masks the bloodiness of fact until Middleton sweeps the punctilious conversation to a powerful, orgiastic close in which the rhythm of the will breaks through the distancing effect of the formality of the language:

> BEA: Then take him to thy fury.
> DE F: I thirst for him.
> BEA: Alonzo de Piracquo.
> DE F: His end's upon him;
>   He shall be seen no more.   (II. ii. 133–35)

But the additional twist is that it is not just the death motive which is hiding behind the courtly language of the scene ("service," "act") but also a deeply hidden erotic motive—De Flores' obliquely expressed carnality.

If—in the scene just described—Middleton shows language in its evasive character, in the superb Act III. iv he does the opposite. He brings
words and deeds together again. This is accomplished by having De Flores
equate *service* with *blood* and *death*, first with the excised finger:

> BEA: Bless me! What hast thou done?
> DE F: Why, is that more
> Than killing the whole man? I cut his heartstrings.
>   (III. iv. 29–30)

and then with the seemingly inexplicable rejection of gold for his *service*:

> Do you place me in the rank of verminous fellows,
> To destroy things for wages? Offer gold?
> The life blood of man! Is anything
> Valued too precious for my recompense?   (III. iv. 64–67)

What he wants is payment in kind, that is, in flesh; and it is on this basis
that the love-death puns carry their real bite. Death is made the very basis
for this new erotic coupling as De Flores uses the language of betrothal and
romantic marriage to insist on the bond between them: "Nor is it fit we two,
engag'd so jointly,/Should part and live asunder" (III. iv. 88–89). When
Beatrice-Joanna balks at this confusion of meanings, he plays upon *blood*:
"Justice invites your blood to understand me" (III. iv. 100). Beatrice-
Joanna's romantic faith in herself is predicated on a strict separation of love
motive and death motive:

> Why 'tis impossible thou canst be so wicked,
> Or shelter such a cunning cruelty,
> To make his death the murderer of my honour!
> Thy language is so bold and vicious,
> I cannot see which way I can forgive it
> With any modesty.   (III. iv. 120–25)

But De Flores insists on their absolute equivalence: "Push, you forget yourself!/A woman dipp'd in blood, and talk of modesty?" (III. iv. 125–26). He
then goes on to expand this equivalence in terms of the primal love-death
myth:

> Y'are the deed's creature; by that name
> You lost your first condition, and I challenge you,
> As peace and innocency has turn'd you out,
> And made you one with me.   (III. iv. 137–40)

And in this play De Flores is absolutely right. As Professor Ricks has shown, the word *deed* refers to the act of murder and the act of love.[8] When Middleton gives De Flores the universalizing language of the myth of man's first fall, he is making a link between sexual love and the death motive as firm as that of Tourneur's, although in very different style. Where Tourneur had made the link by emotionally charged metaphor, Middleton does it with deliberate rationalism—by linking deeds to key abstract words, and by this means to the myths and conceptions behind them.

One result of this determination to have absolute linguistic clarity is that there is no room in Middleton for the kind of moral ambiguity that one finds in *The White Devil*, for instance, about the role of woman in all this evil doing. Webster's Vittoria had been kept clear of the actual killing and left in the shadowy role of accomplice by inspiration, from which she could make a case for her innocence. Middleton's Beatrice-Joanna could almost be read as a rebuke to this in Webster, for with Beatrice-Joanna there is no question where the blame lies. It comes first from her romantic determination to have her own true love no matter what the cost; she thus becomes a Juliet figure run amok:

> Oh, 'tis the soul of freedom!
> I should not then be forc'd to marry one
> I hate beyond all depths, I should have power
> Then to oppose my loathings, nay, remove 'em
> For ever from my sight.   (II. ii. 109–13)

This is the language of feminine rebellion, shown as an impulse towards evil. As for the question of complicity, Middleton's whole point is to make sure we—and eventually she—understand that despite her physical distance from the crime, she is still the deed's creature, both in fact and myth:

> Murder I see is followed by more sins.
> Was my creation in the womb so curs'd,
> It must engender with a viper first?   (III. iv. 164–66)

Eros and death are seen to be inseparable, and both are built into the very sources of being.

The action proceeds from this point by a series of turns on the familiar love-death motif of the Deadly Nuptial. Piracquo is murdered on the day before his wedding day; Diaphanta is killed for taking too long at her pleasures as Beatrice-Joanna's substitute on Alsemero's wedding night. The murder is done, needless to say, with witty turns on the love-death imagery; as Beatrice-Joanna waits anxiously for Diaphanta to be rousted out of

8. Ricks, "Moral and Poetic Structure," 295.

bed, she utters what is perhaps the primal one, the link between death and orgasm:

> . . . oh, this strumpet!
> Had she a thousand lives, he should not leave her
> Till he had destroy'd the last.   (V. i. 64–66)

The final turn on the Deadly Nuptial theme is more a kind of Deadly Assignation. Alsemero, after facing Beatrice-Joanna with her whoredom, locks her in his bed-chamber where "The bed itself's a charnel, the sheets shrouds/For murdered carcasses" (V. iii. 83–84). And then—his mind seething with clotted erotic fantasies—he forces De Flores in with her to await capture:

> I'll be your pander now; rehearse again
> Your scene of lust, that you may be perfect
> When you shall come to act it to the black audience
> Where howls and gnashings shall be music to you.
> Clip your adult'ress freely, 'tis the pilot
> Will guide you to the Mare Mortuum,
> Where you shall sink to fathoms bottomless.
>   (V. iii. 114–20)

The "clip" which De Flores gives her, though, is the point of his knife, a piece of symbolical symmetry that completes the circle of eros and death that the stabbing of Piracquo began.

Still to be defined, however, is the peculiar and unsettling effect of the contrast between Alsemero's and De Flores' behavior at the end. The latter is cool, lucid, witty, precise—rather, one feels, like the man who created him. He meets his accusers and does not flinch:

> ALSE: My wife's behindhand with you, she tells me,
>   For a brave bloody blow you gave for her sake
>   Upon Piracquo.
> DE F: Upon? 'Twas quite through him sure; . . .
>   (V. iii. 102–104)

And he dies without recantation or breast-beating, giving his passion for Beatrice-Joanna and his celebration of sensual pleasure a perverse value by the very energy of his commitment:

> DE F: I lov'd this woman in spite of her heart;
>   Her love I earn'd out of Piracquo's murder.
> TOM: Ha! My brother's murderer!
> DE F: Yes, and her honour's prize
>   Was my reward; I thank life for nothing
>   But that pleasure: it was so sweet to me

That I have drunk up all, left none behind
For any man to pledge me.
VER: Horrid villain!
Keep life in him for further tortures.
DE F: No!
I can prevent you; here's my penknife still.
It is but one thread more, [*stabs himself*]—and
    now 'tis cut.
Make haste, Joanna, by that token to thee:
Canst not forget, so lately put in mind,
I would not go to leave thee far behind.

(V. iii. 165–77)

Beside De Flores, Alsemero—with his faulty chemical tests, obtuse idealizing, and masochistic fantasies—comes off much the second best, despite his being the injured party and the man with convention on his side.

To explain this, I think we must postulate several points towards a Middletonian theory of eros. First, beautiful women are seen to be as attractive and as dangerous as the sirens on the rocks. At heart, Middleton seems to say, they have no moral or ethical center whatsoever and are capable of any depravity they can think of or be manipulated into. They are, nevertheless, vehicles for the most extreme pleasures—pleasures so great that even a thorough skeptic like De Flores will commit his life to possession of one.

What stance, then, is the man to take to the woman? Plainly, this play offers no positive norm, but from the given context one can surmise this: it is better to act out of true knowledge than out of illusion. De Flores is evil, as evil as Beatrice-Joanna, but he, at least, knows what he is doing, and under his tutelage Beatrice-Joanna comes to know herself better. To be absurd is to be Vermandero or Piracquo or Alsemero: that is—to be fooled into romantic illusions about woman and to suffer thereby. This is also the plight of the Alsemero-like hero of the next play to be discussed, *Women Beware Women*, where it is this figure, the young cuckold, that Middleton explores with remarkable passion and perception.

2. Women Beware Women

Women Beware Women is a much bleaker play even than *The Changeling*. Something in De Flores' assurance, self-knowledge, and jaunty wit gives that play active life—as does the good-humored fooling on the theme of love in Rowley's subplot. *Women Beware Women* has little of this kind of vitality, mainly because there is no character who—like De Flores—captures the author's imaginative appreciation. All of *Women Beware Women's* many

virtues—its psychological penetration, its superb irony, its fine construction—are put to destructive purposes: during the body of the play Middleton reveals and destroys illusions; at the end he orchestrates a masque that
destroys—with what appears to be a chilly contempt for character and audience—his own creations.

One cause of this bleakness is—as Muriel Bradbrook says—that "*Women
Beware Women* is a slighter play than *The Changeling*. Its themes are nearer
to a thesis."[9] One sign of this is the more schematic application of the fall
myth to the illusions of romantic young lovers. The first two acts briskly set
up—one for each plot—two absolutely fundamental conventions of romantic love tragedy and give them apparently sympathetic exposition. In
the main plot Middleton takes up the idea of the romantic marriage, showing Leantio coming home with a bride stolen, as it were, out of a social
milieu that would have normally opposed the marriage. Leantio is ecstatic
in praise of Bianca to his mother:

> Oh you have named the most unvalued'st purchase,
> That youth of man had ever knowledge of.
> As often as I look upon that treasure,
> And know it to be mine—there lies the blessing—
> It joys me that I ever was ordained
> To have a being, and to live 'mongst men; . . .[10]
>
> (I. i. 12–17)

She, in her turn, speaks like the perfect romantic bride of fairy tales:

> Kind mother, there is nothing can be wanting
> To her that does enjoy all her desires.
> Heaven send a quiet peace with this man's love,
> And I am as rich, as virtue can be poor—
> Which were enough, after the rate of mind,
> To erect temples for content placed here.
> I have forsook friends, fortunes, and my country;
> And hourly I rejoice in't.
> .   .   .   .
> I'll call this place the place of my birth now—
> And rightly too, for here my love was born,
> And that's the birthday of a woman's joys.
>
> (I. i. 125–32, 139–41)

She has—like Juliet, like Desdemona—given up all habitual pleasures of
upper-class life to consecrate herself to love and inner peace.

---

9. Bradbrook, *Elizabethan Tragedy*, 224.
10. Thomas Middleton, *Women Beware Women*, ed. Roma Gill, A Mermaid Dramabook
(New York: Hill and Wang, 1969). All quotations from the play are from this text.

The subplot tale of the plight of Isabella also originates from a conventional motif in romantic tragedy—the Enforced Marriage theme. Isabella has an obstinate Capulet-like father who would force her into a wealthy but loveless marriage with an unspeakable fool:

> How do you like him, girl? this is your husband.
> Like him or like him not, wench, you shall have him,
> And you shall love him.   (I. ii. 130–32)

And she herself is shown at first in the most pathetic possible light, on one occasion lamenting the sorrows of forced wedlock:

> Marry a fool!
> Can there be greater misery to a woman
> That means to keep her days true to her husband,
> And know no other man, so virtue wills it!
> . . . .
>   Oh the heartbreakings
> Of miserable maids, where love's enforced!
>   (I. ii. 161–64, 168–69)

and going on to larger questions of the fate of womankind:

> The best condition is but bad enough:
> When women have their choices, commonly
> They do but buy their thraldoms, and bring
>   great portions
> To men to keep 'em in subjection: . . .   (I. ii. 170–73)

In addition, she has had to fend off the sexual advances of the one man she does admire, her uncle Hippolito. It is notable that she does this with great moral earnestness:

> I'll learn to live without ye, for your dangers
> Are greater than your comforts. What's become
> Of truth in love, if such we cannot trust.
> When blood that should be love is mixed with lust!
>   (I. ii. 226–29)

Having gone to great pains to establish these romantic situations, Middleton shows himself almost impatiently brisk in demolishing them. Isabella is falsely told by her Aunt Livia—a Jacobean high priestess of the id —that the man she believes to be her uncle is in fact not. Her reaction is startling to say the least. Not only does she promptly offer to entertain Hippolito in bed but she rushes to forward the marriage with the foolish ward so as to mask the other affair. The girl who talked so sensitively and philosophically about morality, love, and marriage in Act I. ii becomes in an instant the politic sensualist of Act II. i:

ISA: I did but chide in jest; the best loves use it
   Sometimes; it sets an edge upon affection.
   When we invite our best friends to a feast
   'Tis not all sweetmeats that we set before them,
   There's somewhat sharp and salt, both to whet
     appetite,
   And make 'em taste their wine well:

   . . . .
   This marriage shall go forward.
HIP: With the ward!
   Are you in earnest?
ISA: 'Twould be ill for us else.
            (II. i. 196–201, 206–207)

The quickness of this switch from innocent to adultress is extreme even by the sternest antiromantic standards. The same is true of the seduction of Bianca in the main plot. Here Bianca is tricked by the false sociability of Livia and Guardiano into the duke's amorous clutches. She tries at first to defend herself and is shown intending the defense seriously and with real feeling:

BIAN: Oh my extremity!
   My lord, what seek you?
DUKE: Love.
BIAN: 'Tis gone already;
   I have a husband.
DUKE: That's a single comfort;
   Take a friend to him.
BIAN: That's a double mischief,
   Or else there's no religion.   (II. ii. 346–50)

But not even the duke's powerful, unyielding pressure—though it accounts well enough for the seduction—quite accounts for the Bianca who greets her husband like an unwanted relative several days later. It is with her as it was with Beatrice-Joanna, though here the process of what T. S. Eliot called "habituation to . . . sin"[11] and M. C. Bradbrook called "progressive deterioration of character"[12] occurs with much greater rapidity. Bianca has seen in her sexual betrayal something about her own nature that shocks her deeply. Middleton presents this shock in love-death imagery

11. Eliot, "Thomas Middleton," 164.
12. Bradbrook, *Elizabethan Tragedy*, 224.

that suggests this new love is not just a kind of dying but a very attractive kind:

> Now bless me from a blasting! I saw that now
> Fearful for any woman's eye to look on;
> Infectious mists and mildews hang at's eyes,
> The weather of a doomsday dwells upon him.
> Yet since mine honour's leprous, why should I
> Preserve that fair that caused the leprosy?
> Come, poison all at once!   (II. ii. 421–27)

The "poison" is the full acceptance of her own sexual evil, the taking of it as her very life's blood. But here—as with Isabella—it remains unclear precisely why she should have this reaction and not some other, some rejection of what she has gone through, for instance.

The answer, of course, is in Middleton's conception of female nature, and the play has numerous though scattered statements of it. Thus, at the beginning, even while Leantio's tendency towards idealizing rhetoric is at its greatest, the telltale phrase "Licentious swindge of her own will" intrudes in this quote:

>   . . . she's contented
> With all conditions that my fortunes bring her to:
> To keep close as a wife that loves her husband;
> To go after the rate of my ability,
> Not the licentious swindge of her own will, . . .
>   (I. i. 88–92)

and prejudices the judgment on Bianca even before there is the slightest hint of what she will become. This is not unusual. The nature of woman in a Middleton play is prejudged, her frail moral character being posited before the temptations that provide it with direction—as in this summary statement by the long-fallen Livia on the newly fallen Bianca:

> 'Tis but want of use;
> Her tender modesty is sea-sick a little,
> Being not accustomed to the breaking billow
> Of woman's wavering faith, blown with temptations.
>   (II. ii. 471–74)

Bianca—unlike Beatrice-Joanna, who required long tutoring to become aware of her natural evil—sees immediately that the "poison" of infidelity is far from being repulsive:

>   I'm made bold now,
> I thank thy treachery; sin and I'm acquainted,
> No couple greater; and I'm like that great one

Who, making politic use of a base villain,
'He likes the treason well, but hates the traitor'; . . .
(II. ii. 440–44)

Though she despises Guardiano, the professor of "ladies' rights" who betrayed her to the duke, she fully admits her relish for the sin to which she is now committed. In this, of course, she is of a kind with Isabella and with Beatrice-Joanna in the previous play. Thus, De Flores' great punning thrust at Beatrice-Joanna—"You are the deed's creature"—extends beyond the boundaries of that play and illuminates this one. For one major point of the pattern of the double adulteries of plot and subplot is that both Isabella and Bianca are the deed's creatures.

It is clear, I think, that Middleton is, after Tourneur, the Jacobean drama's most formidable critic of Elizabethan and Websterian romanticism. But he is also aware that the emotional cost of abandoning the romantic vision is great indeed. To give up the idea of love is to feel the full and bitter vertigo of the fall all over again. Such is Leantio's fate. On his way to greet his fortnight's bride after his first absence he is full of the imagery of Eden:

How near am I now to a happiness
That earth exceeds not—not another like it!
The treasures of the deep are not so precious
As are the concealed comforts of a man,
Locked up in woman's love. I scent the air
Of blessings when I come but near the house.
What a delicious breath marriage sends forth;
The violet-bed's not sweeter. Honest wedlock
Is like a banqueting-house built in a garden,
On which the spring's chaste flowers take delight
To cast their modest odours— . . .   (III. i. 82–92)

But after the first chilly blast of his fallen wife's new behavior, there is a profoundly different note:

Nay, what a quietness has he 'bove mine,
That wears his youth out in a strumpet's arms,
And never spends more care upon a woman
Than at the time of lust; but walks away,
And he finds her dead at his return,
His pity is soon done: he breaks a sigh
In many parts, and gives her but a piece on't.
(III. ii. 286–92)

This is a powerful bitterness powerfully expressed, for it reduces woman to nothing more than a body and deliberately shuts down the wellsprings of personal emotion. It could stand as the motto of the antiromantic tradition.

What makes Middleton the great dramatist he is even in this gloomy, at times perfunctory, play is his unfailing ability to reveal the psychological torments of the fallen condition. The great scenes concerned with this revelation are focused on the downfall of Leantio, for here Middleton's psychological perception operates at its highest level of genius. His particular insight into Leantio is this—that although the defeated husband wishes love could be treated as nothing more than sex, he is unable to do this himself. Love persists in manifestations of the death motive as terrible as those that tormented Hamlet and drives Leantio to the same kind of manic confrontations. The process is presented with a level of understanding and deep genuine feeling that is totally absent from Middleton's treatment of the women of the play.

This motif begins when Leantio and Livia are left together in the banqueting area (III. ii). A new couple is formed visually before our eyes, though psychologically each is very much alone. Leantio is wrapped up in his misery and loneliness and Livia is completely excluded by the magnitude of it:

> Oh, hast thou left me then, Bianca, utterly!
> Bianca! now I miss thee—Oh return,
> And save the faith of woman. I nev'r felt
> The loss of thee till now; 'tis an affliction
> Of greater weight than youth was made to bear—
> As if a punishment of after-life
> Were fallen upon man here, so new it is
> To flesh and blood; so strange, so insupportable
> A torment— . . .   (III. ii. 243–51)

Leantio's plea first evokes a generalized concept—"the faith of woman"— to define what has been lost, but it immediately deepens into a powerful statement of personal anguish. Middleton has a great apprehension of how closely together mind and body work, and Leantio's grief has a terrific bodily force that gives it substance and reality. It is this which distinguishes these speeches from the similar great one of Heywood's Frankford. When Leantio remembers, he remembers physical things:

> Canst thou forget
> The dear pains my love took, how it has watched
> Whole nights together in all weather for thee,
> Yet stood in heart more merry than the tempests

That sung about mine ears, like dangerous flatterers
That can set all their mischiefs to sweet tunes;
And then received thee from thy father's window
Into these arms at midnight, when we embraced
As if we had been statues only made for't,
To show art's life, so silent were our comforts;
And kissed as if our lips had grown together.
(III. ii. 254–64)

In the triumphant complacency of his early happiness and possession, Leantio's physical imagery was crass; here—in grief and loss—all crassness is purged and what remains is the distilled physical substance of memory and the poetic imagination.

This kind of violently self-destructive grief must have some relief, however; this is one thing which a thoughtful dramatist like Middleteon would have learned from the great plays of love and vengeance. *Othello* seems to have been one he studied, for echoes of it—and comments which could be glosses on Othello's grief—slip in as Leantio tries to gain control over himself:

She's gone for ever—utterly;

. . . .
I cannot love her now, but I must like
Her sin and my own shame too, . . .

. . . .
Then my safest course,
For health of mind and body, is to turn
My heart and hate her, most extremely hate her!
(III. ii. 330, 336–37, 339–41)

Middleton would also have learned that what Leantio proposes is easier said than done, that the emotions of love and hate in jealousy are not turned on or off like separate spigots of hot or cold water. Nor can the spirit endure the self-abasement of doing nothing. Middleton's Leantio, not being the kind of man to express the mixture of love and hatred in the act of killing the lost loved one, revenges himself by committing his own murder of love, by taking on the offered love of Livia. The death motive in this love comes out as the frank expression of mercenary greed: "Troth then, I'll love enough and take enough" (III. ii. 377). But even this does not satisfy his frustrated will and damaged pride.

The result is a series of manic attempts at confrontation with Bianca that show the great potential for theatrical power and psychological perception in the love-death opposition. Leantio must not only take a lover, but he must go to Bianca and flaunt the lover at her. This is love used as an instrument of punishment:

> And to spite thee as much, look there, there read!
> Vex! gnaw! thou shalt find there I am not
> love-starved.   (IV. i. 65–66)

The irony is, of course, that there is no residue of love left in Bianca, so she remains cool while Leantio—who loves even as he hates—stays vexed and gnawed. She would as soon never see him again, but he cannot stay away from her any more than, for instance, Hamlet could from Gertrude. It is only as he dies that the binding knot is broken:

> Rise, strumpet, by my fall! Thy lust may reign now;
> My heart-string and the marriage-knot that tied thee
> Breaks both together.   (IV. ii. 43–45)

Both those breaking strings are important, but the first perhaps is the most. The marriage knot is the social form; the other is the emotional bond that persists after forms are broken and can only be snapped by death itself.

In a sense the play ends with the death of Leantio, for it is clear that Middleton takes little personal interest in the characters that remain after. There is genuine bite in Livia's grief at hearing of Leantio's death:

> HIP: Will you but entertain a noble patience
>   Till you but hear the reason, worthy sister!
> LIV: The reason! that's a jest hell falls a-laughing at!
>   (IV. ii. 61–63)

But from this point on, entropy sets in, and a tortuously complex set of revenges is required to dispatch the rather full collection of sinning lovers that remain. The result is a Deadly Nuptial scene which is the *reductio ad absurdum* of the motif. If any sense can be made of a scene in which one lover is killed by poisoned cupid arrows, another by a lapful of poisoned gold, and still another by falling through his own carefully set trapdoor, it is this: that the state of emotional anarchy created by unrestrained passions (both of love and death) can be expressed only by an exhibition of lunatic chaos. Nevertheless, Middleton does use the few quiet moments at the end to inculcate his moral:

> Leantio, now I feel the breach of marriage
> At my heart-breaking! Oh the deadly snares
> That women set for women—without pity
> Either to soul or honour! Learn by me
> To know your foes. In this belief I die:
> Like our own sex, we have no enemy.   (V. ii. 208–13)

I suggested at the beginning of this chapter that—in agreement with most critics of Middleton—I regarded him as first and foremost a rationalist. Certainly he seems to have a rationalist's idea of love. The puns in *The Changeling*, for instance, are more than just commentaries on the actions in that play. Middleton deals in abstract words and abstract conceptions. His plays are concrete realizations of philosophical concerns. If to him the language of love could be reduced under close examination to puns on *will* and *blood* then we must draw the further conclusion that this is, in fact, what he thought love basically is. One of the characters in *Women Beware Women* offers a theory in which love and lust merge on a sliding scale. The wording here might well reflect some of Middleton's own thinking:

> Oh affinity,
> What piece of excellent workmanship art thou?
> 'Tis work clean wrought, for there's no lust,
>   but love in't,
> And that abundantly—when in stranger things,
> There is no love at all, but what lust brings.
>
> (I. ii. 69–73)

The romantic vision would accept some version of this because it accepted and celebrated a union of body and spirit and thus in some sense found potential good in *will* and *blood* and even *appetite*. The rationalist identifies these with the subhuman and anarchic tendencies in man. Thus, while Middleton accepts that love is inextricable from sexual will, he cannot accept any optimistic vision of this situation. His rationalism tells him that man is dominated by will; this fact confirms him in his pessimism. He unquestionably has pity and some affection, for no one could delineate degradation in such loving detail without it. But he has no admiration and can celebrate nothing. His erotic puns are to the language of beauty what Tourneur's skull is to the beauty of flesh. And, if in the end one finds in Middleton a rare kind of clarity and precision of statement, one misses something rarer—the real music of love.

14 John Ford and the Jacobeans

Although a summary view of the major Jacobeans will inevitably gloss over particular divergences of character and art, a few general points will be useful before putting the whole evolution of love-death tragedy back in a Shakespearean perspective: the object of the final chapter.

First, the image of woman. Louis B. Wright has noted that the nature of woman was a topic of lively popular debate during the late sixteenth and the seventeenth century.[1] With the exception of Webster, the Jacobean playwrights appear to have taken the negative side. In the plays of Heywood, Tourneur, and Middleton the central female characters suffer from moral disabilities ranging from the spiritual paralysis of Mrs. Frankford to the actively poisonous corruption of Tourneur's duchess and Middleton's Bianca. These—as well as Tourneur's Levidulcia, Middleton's Beatrice-Joanna, Isabella, and Livia, and Heywood's Mrs. Wincott—live in a world apart from the morally sensitive and conscious male hero. Their prototypes are the easy, sensual Gertrude and the sensual, changeable Cressida. And the men who become involved with them are doomed to trouble, disillusionment, even damnation. To recall Tourneur: "But 'twas decreed before the world began,/That they should be the hooks to catch at man" (*RT*. II. i. 260–61). The world of these plays is truly the fallen world; the dramatic plots are composed of repeated reenactions of the temptation and fall of Eve and the suffering and misery of Adam. And just as the wages of sin is death in that archetypal myth, so are they in these plays, most noticeably in the ascendancy of a bitter, resentful pessimism about human relations that distorts both the form and the imaginative vision of several notable plays.

1. See Louis B. Wright, "The Popular Controversy over Woman," in *Middle-Class Culture in Elizabethan England* (Chapel Hill: University of North Carolina Press, 1935), 465–507.

To suggest the nature of this distortion let me recall two comments by T. S. Eliot. In the first he defines the mood of *The Revenger's Tragedy*: "Its motive is truly the death motive, for it is the loathing and horror of life itself. To have realized this motive so well is a triumph; for the hatred of life is an important phase—even, if you like, a mystical experience—in life itself."[2] There are two stages to this statement. The first identifies "death motive" with "the loathing and horror of life itself"; the second implies that no matter how compelling this vision of death is, it is still a stage in life to be transcended. In this context, we must also recall Eliot on Hamlet's emotions toward his mother—prototype of the loose woman of the antiromantic paradigm: "Hamlet (the man) is dominated by an emotion which is inexpressible, because it is in *excess* of the facts as they appear. . . . his disgust envelops and exceeds her. It is thus a feeling which he cannot understand; he cannot objectify it, and it therefore remains to poison life and obstruct action."[3] It is my contention that certain notable plays are written in the Hamlet mood, under the curse of the death motive to such a degree that they condemn eros and the male-female bond in excess of the facts as they appear in nature; and that these feelings are inadequately objectified and poison the artistic life of the drama at crucial points—most particularly at the very important conclusion of the action.

The great plays of Heywood, Tourneur, and Middleton bring love and death finally into a significant, emotionally and intellectually satisfying state of tension and equilibrium. Thus Frankford's rejection of Anne is balanced by his love of her; thus Vindice's loathing of sexuality is balanced by his perverse joy in sexualized violence; thus De Flores' clear-sighted vision into the essential evil of Beatrice-Joanna is balanced by the equally clear-sighted passion of his attachment to her. In the lesser plays, however, this balance is lost, and the dominance of the death motive, the excessive hatred of life, emerges in such palpably distorted scenes as the absurd self-execution of D'Amville in *The Atheist's Tragedy* and the ridiculous carnage of the last moments of *Women Beware Women*. In both these instances the playwright appears to fall back on God out of exhaustion, the exhaustion of resources intrinsic to human life out of which to create a balancing term to death.

The missing resource is that which forms the central image of value in the plays of the romantic tradition—the image of human beings bound to each other by the beneficent unreason of love, the central metaphor of which is

2. Eliot, "Cyril Tourneur," 190.
3. Eliot, "*Hamlet,*" (1919) in *Selected Essays*, 145.

the mutual love of man for woman, woman for man. The nurturing, the preserving, the recovering or reestablishing of this bond is in these plays an action of deep human and humanistic value. And this indeed is how we see and interpret such gestures as Juliet's last kiss of Romeo, Othello's of Desdemona, the brief reconciliation of Lear and Cordelia, Frankford's last-moment symbolic remarriage to Anne, and the Duchess of Malfi's last cries for husband and children. Evil, in such a context, is, of course, a function of the broken bond, the betrayed trust: Old Capulet forcing his daughter to marry against her own happiness; Claudius betraying his brother; Cressida betraying Troilus; Othello betraying Desdemona; Anne betraying Frankford; Beatrice-Joanna betraying both Piracquo and Alsemero; the multiple betrayals of the Tourneur world.

The human toll of this is terrible. But a playwright totally emeshed in the antiromantic vision cannot render this human toll in any finally moving fashion because he does not admit that these man-woman bonds have reality or authenticity. For this, there must be mutuality. But what mutuality—the antiromantic would query—can be built on the shifting sands of female faith? With no stronger foundation than this, bonds *must* be transient, *must* succumb to time, to seduction, to boredom, to money. And so they do—as quickly undermined as the faith of a Mrs. Frankford or a Bianca. The diminishment of the value of the human bond accounts, I think, for the singular number of lonely, loveless male characters who remain at the end of these plays: Troilus, Tourneur's Duke Antonio, the bleakly Machiavellian assassins of Bracciano and Vittoria, the stilted, womanless men who moralize over Heywood's Mrs. Wincott and Middleton's Beatrice-Joanna and De Flores, and the severe, moralizing Cardinal who survives the holocaust of lovers and lechers at the end of *Women Beware Women*. Thus also, the strange emptiness which dogs the conclusions of these tragedies. No male-female allegiance survives, and few more melancholy messages for humans could be devised than this. But this pessimism rings as false as the forced conclusions of the plays that project it, for it fails to account for large areas of observed and felt experience.

The same is true of the question of sexual fruition. The logic of the antiromantic vision runs thus:

> *Of what is't fools make such vain keeping?*
> *Sin their conception, their birth weeping;*
> *Their life a general mist of error,*
> *Their death a hideous storm of terror.*

(Bosola: *DM*. IV. ii. 186–89)

If we accept the premise that conception is a sin, the rest follows as a most just and unforced conclusion. Life is just what Bosola—here at his most Gothic—says it is. But if conception is not in fact conceived of as sin, the way is open for the establishment of sane values which—though they do not alter the basic, terrible necessity of death and loss—do at least give biological life and the biological origins of life and futurity some claim to both pleasure and goodness. But among the major Jacobeans (excluding now Shakespeare) only Webster had any confidence in the instincts of sexual love and the idea that sexual love was a value in itself. Despite what Webster's Bosola avers at that point in the play, Webster himself does not see conception and fruition as the substance of sin. This confidence, this central optimism, shapes every aspect of his otherwise tragic art.

1. John Ford

That Ford was profoundly interested in the tradition of love-death opposition is easy enough to demonstrate. His plays abound with enforced marriages, jealous lovers, deadly nuptials, the urge of lovers towards each other. In *'Tis Pity*, when Giovanni and Annabella swear troth, they do so with a rhetorical play on love and death:

> On my knees.
> Sister, even by my mother's dust, I charge you,
> Do not betray me to your mirth or hate,
> Love me or kill me, sister.[4]   (I. ii. 252–55)

When Soranzo and Annabella are married, the jealous Hippolita's plot to kill Soranzo is organized around a murderous wedding masque, and her dying curses are in the blackest tradition of the theme:

> . . . may thy bed
> Of marriage be a rack unto thy heart,
> Burn blood and boil in vengeance— . . .   (IV. i. 94–96)

And—to move to *The Broken Heart*—Penthea's song could be a summary of this antithesis:

> *Love is dead; let lovers' eyes,*
> *Lock'd in endless dreams,*
> *Th'extremes of all extremes,*

4. John Ford, *'Tis Pity She's a Whore*, ed. N. W. Bawcutt, Regents Renaissance Drama Series (Lincoln: University of Nebraska Press, 1966). All quotations from the play are taken from this text.

> *Ope no more, for now love dies,*
> *Now love dies, implying*
> *Love's martyrs must be ever, ever dying.*[5]
>
> (IV. iii. 147–52)

The deeply sympathetic tone of the song indicates another way in which Ford fits into the line of plays covered in this study. In a way unlike any of his peers, Ford attempted to rehabilitate the innocent, naïve Elizabethan young lover as a subject for tragedy. The grouping of character types in *'Tis Pity* goes back directly to that of *Romeo and Juliet*—Annabella being Juliet; Giovanni, Romeo; Florio, Capulet; Soranzo, Paris; Putana, the Nurse. And in *The Broken Heart* there are no fewer than three young couples in the foreground of the action. In both of these plays the lovers are given lines and scenes of great natural tenderness and sympathy. Annabella and Giovanni —incestuous though they be—do not speak like anything but true, young, romantic lovers:

GIOVANNI: Kiss me: so; thus hung Jove on Leda's neck,
And suck'd divine ambrosia from her lips.
I envy not the mightiest man alive,
But hold myself in being king of thee
More great than were I king of all the world.

(II. i. 16–20)

Furthermore, the opposition to the lovers comes—in the characteristic manner—from members of the older generation. Annabella's father Florio says in Act I: "I will not force my daughter 'gainst her will" (I. iii. 3). In Act III, however, he reverts to the old manner of dominating fathers: "She shall be married ere she know the time" (III. iv. 11). And in *The Broken Heart* there is a subtle transformation of this traditional configuration. Instead of an old dominating father forcing the hand of a young suitor on his daughter, we find that a young brother (the father being dead) has forced his sister to marry an old, dominating suitor.[6] Thus in both instances the conventional opposition is set up: youthful eros versus age and authority in the traditional manner. But in Ford's plays the action does not evolve in the usual manner from these carefully established premises.

In the romantic convention, the opposition set up above produces some

---

5. John Ford, *The Broken Heart*, ed. Donald K. Anderson, Jr., Regents Renaissance Drama Series (Lincoln: University of Nebraska Press, 1968). All quotations from the play are taken from this text.
6. See G. F. Sensabaugh, *The Tragic Muse of John Ford* (Stanford, Calif.: Stanford University Press, 1944), 59–62, and H. J. Oliver, *The Problem of John Ford* (Carlton, Victoria: Melbourne University Press, 1955), 61–62 on the bases in Burtonian theories of melancholy of Bassanes' jealousy.

variation of the theme of eros-rebellion. Like romantic comedy, romantic tragedy—despite the death of lovers—celebrates even in mourning the redeeming qualities of youthful energy and fertility. In Ford, however, a peculiar formula seems to be working in which lovers are damned in rebellion and unrewarded in conformity.

In *'Tis Pity* the young lovers are damned because—against the traditional authority figures of father, priest, legitimate suitor, and the age-old pressures of the incest taboo—they conduct an energetic romantic rebellion. But in no sense does Ford let us see these feelings and actions as conducing towards life. The cards of situation—that they were born sister and brother—are so stacked against the lovers that their natural sexual energies can only be turned against life. Thus, the child (normally—as in *The Duchess of Malfi*—a life symbol) that Annabella carries in her womb is always associated with images of sickness and death rather than health. This motif begins with the ironic language used to convey Soranzo's still unknowing concern for the pregnant Annabella:

> She plainly told me that she could not love,
> And thereupon soon sicken'd, and I fear
> Her life's in danger.   (III. ii. 78–80)

And the theme is driven home with perverse force by Putana's reversal of the usual life-birth equation:

> PUT: O that ever I was born to see this day!
> GIOV: She is not dead, ha? Is she?
> PUT: Dead? No, she is quick; 'tis worse, she is with
>   child.   (III. iii. 4–6)

It is, of course, specifically the child that brings death to the pair by forcing Annabella to submit herself to a loveless marriage with another man (the wedding scene being a notably bloody variant on the Deadly Nuptial theme). The final turn on this child-death motif comes with the death of Annabella. There is no romantic double suicide here. Giovanni kills his sister and in doing so he kills his own posterity, his own future. This is truly a chilling inversion of the central theme and symbolism of the romantic drama and seems intended as a critique of the potential for self-indulgent excess that the antiromantic sees in romantic passion.

With *The Broken Heart* we move to a very different world, a world not of rebellion, but of stoical acceptance. But even here, we find that death triumphs, the slow, lingering death that emerges from a situation in which the natural movement of love is blocked or diverted so it can come to no true fruition. The main force of this theme is concentrated in the story of Orgilus and Penthea. In this pair we have—essentially—a Romeo and Juliet (that is, a pair of passionate and truly mutual young lovers) who are separated by familial authority and a family feud. Unlike Romeo and Juliet, however, they make no attempt to rebel against this authority and are thus separated forever by the enforced marriage of Penthea to an unloved husband. In both Penthea and Orgilus, then, fruition and love are balked and life is deflected towards death (the death of youth, the wasting of the energies of youth). In Orgilus, whose impulse towards death is active, the result is the revenge murder of the man who separated him from Penthea, her brother Ithocles. In keeping with the tradition of placing love and death motifs in meaningful conjunction, Ithocles is murdered immediately after Penthea's death and on the verge of his own long-hoped-for marriage to the Princess Calantha. Furthermore, Orgilus ironically congratulates Ithocles on his coming marriage in words that evoke both fertility symbolism ("The glory/Of numerous children, potency of nobles" [IV. iii. 128–29]) and play on the marriage-bed/deathbed motif:

> ITHO: We'll distinguish
> Our fortunes merely in the title, partners
> In all respects else but the bed.
> ORGIL: The bed?
> Forfend it, Jove's own jealousy!—till lastly
> We slip down in the common earth together;
> And there our beds are equal, save some monument
> To show this was the king, and this the subject.—
> (IV. iii. 132–38)

In Penthea the movement towards death is passive and self-directed. She makes one noble, selfless attempt to foster life by furthering her brother's cause with Calantha. Other than this, however, her life is a steady drift from being metaphorically "buried in a bridebed" (II. ii. 38) to actually being buried in death. This melancholy downward movement is likewise notable for its terrible evocation of lost youth and wasted fertility. This is Penthea—Ophelia-like—near the end:

> Since I was first a wife, I might have been
> Mother to many pretty prattling babes.
> They would have smil'd when I smil'd; and, for certain,
> I should have cried when they cried; truly, brother,
> My father would have pick'd me out a husband,
> And then my little ones had been no bastards.
> But 'tis too late for me to marry now,
> I am past childbearing; 'tis not my fault.
> (IV. ii. 87–94)

We may again quote a part of Penthea's song, for it captures perfectly the debilitated, pathetic, melancholy mood that surrounds her death, and later that of Calantha, with its elaborate Deadly Nuptial rite that culminates in her marriage to the corpse of her betrothed (V. iii). The summarizing lines are: *"Now love dies, implying/Love's martyrs must be ever, ever dying"* (IV. iii. 151–52). The sympathy and pity that one feels in this song have been noted; but one should also note the deep pessimism of these lines. For to the extent that we may see them as choric (which is, I think, considerable) they reflect the melancholy acceptance of a world in which death seems always to have the upper hand.

The Broken Heart is not, however, entirely consumed by melancholy and death, and the one strand of action that does show love leading to life is of considerable interest for defining the exact nature of Ford's commitment to the romantic tradition.

The particular line of action is that which traces the emerging romance of Orgilus' sister Euphranea and Ithocles' friend Prophilus. A special twist to the action is that at its very beginning, Orgilus, while still suffering from one brother's tyranny over a sister (Ithocles over Penthea), arbitrarily insists on a similar power over his own sister:

> [To EUPHRANEA]   That you will promise
> To pass never to any man, however
> Worthy, your faith, till with our father's leave
> I give a free consent.   (I. i. 92–95)

This is not, as H. J. Oliver suggests, a line of development that "does not come to anything." [7] Given the force of Orgilus' melancholy, such a request plainly sets the stage for the emergence of another death-directed, eros-frustrating act of tyranny. Indeed, in a scene strongly reminiscent of that in which Lorenzo and Balthazar of *The Spanish Tragedy* eavesdrop on Bel-imperia and Horatio, Orgilus overhears his sister exchange words of love and counterpoints them with words of death:

> PROPHIL: [To EUPHRANEA]
>   Smile, Hymen, on the growth of our desires;
>   We'll feed thy torches with eternal fires.
>   [*Exeunt.*]
>   ORGIL: Put out thy torches, Hymen, or their light
>   Shall meet a darkness of eternal night.
>   (I. iii. 173–76)

---

7. Oliver, *The Problem of John Ford*, 63.

Nevertheless, having prepared this movement, Ford goes directly against it by having Orgilus transcend his lower impulses and make a gesture towards life that parallels the gesture Penthea makes towards Ithocles. In a moving scene, Orgilus abandons the morbid egoism of the eavesdropping scene and freely gives his permission:

> Euphranea, lend thy hand.—Here, take her Prophilus.
> Live long a happy man and wife; and further,
> That these in presence may conclude an omen,
> Thus for a bridal song I close my wishes: . . .

(III. iv. 66–69)

This is accompanied by a song of Orgilus' own composition:

> *Comforts lasting, loves increasing,*
> *Like soft hours never ceasing;*
> *Plenty's pleasure, peace complying*
> *Without jars or tongues envying;*
> *Hearts by holy union wedded*
> *More than theirs by custom bedded;*
> *Fruitful issues; life so graced*
> *Not by age to be defaced,*
> *Budding, as the year ensu'th,*
> *Every spring another youth:*
> *All what thought can add beside*
> *Crown this bridegroom and this bride.*

(III. iv. 70–81)

The song has a double significance. It is first of all a moving statement of what Orgilus thinks of the condition of life Ithocles has stolen from him. Even more significantly, it is a paean to the romantic marriage that takes its impetus directly from the plays of the early romantic tradition. As such it is one of Ford's main gestures of affiliation with that tradition and with its central symbol and value—the freely made marriage for love.

But Ford does not stop here in forcing us to recognize the real and the symbolic values embodied in the romantic marriage. He introduces the theme into the early development of Calantha's otherwise blighted courtship. Here again we have a father who ponders the problem of enforced marriage:

> AMYCL: [To NEARCHUS]   As you are
> In title next, being grandchild to our aunt,
> So we in heart desire you may sit nearest
> Calantha's love, since we have ever vow'd
> Not to enforce affection by our will,
> But by her own choice to confirm it gladly.

(III. iii. 7–12)

Unlike so many of the fathers in the plays of this study, this one will in fact not attempt to enforce his own favorite. Nearchus, himself a prince and a proud man who has come with every expectation of succeeding with Calantha, gives an even stronger development of the theme of freedom in love when he realizes that he is about to lose Calantha to Ithocles:

> AMEL: But can your highness brook to be so rival'd,
>   Considering th'inequality of the persons?
> NEARCH: I can, Amelus; for affections injur'd
>   By tyranny or rigor of compulsion,
>   Like tempest-threaten'd trees unfirmly rooted,
>   Ne'er spring to timely growth. Observe, for
>   instance,
>   Life-spent Penthea and unhappy Orgilus.
>
>   (IV. ii. 203–209)

This gesture is also one of Ford's ways of showing that Nearchus will be a fit ruler of Sparta, one who will ensure the renewed health and vigor of the state. Of particular significance to this further expansion of the eros-fertility theme is Nearchus' use of the image of the "tempest-threaten'd trees" and the lack of "timely growth" that comes with "affections injur'd." For the tree image is repeated in the oracle's prophecy that

> *The plot in which the vine takes root*
> *Begins to dry from head to foot;*
> *The stock soon withering, want of sap*
> *Doth cause to quail the budding grape.*
> *But from the neighboring elm a dew*
> *Shall drop and feed the plot anew.*   (IV. iii. 11–16)

The explication by the philosopher Tecnicus makes the significance clear:

> *The plot is Sparta, the dried vine the king,*
> *The quailing grape his daugher; but the thing*
> *Of most importance, not to be reveal'd,*
> *Is a near prince, the elm; the rest conceal'd.*
>
>   (IV. iii. 19–22)

Nearchus—the promoter of true love at the expense of his own ego—is the well-rooted tree and thus a bringer of life to a moribund society. This represents a full and essentially romantic identification of eros and life.

We can see now the peculiar doubleness of Ford's relation to the plays about love that have gone before him. There is no question but that he identifies strongly with the ethos of *Romeo and Juliet*. He hates the Enforced Marriage; he sees the free, unforced marriage as the chief repository for the whole symbolism of fertility and health. And yet he stops short of a total commitment to the *Romeo and Juliet* theme on the question of eros-rebellion. In the romantic convention, the lovers' rebellion against conventional authority is the central vehicle for establishing that sexual attraction is a source of active energy for life against death. But in Ford this does not seem to be the case. He loves his romantic lovers, but in his treatment of rebellion he seems much closer to the antiromanticism of Middleton, in whom eros-rebellion is always characterized in terms of betrayal, adultery, or incest. The eros-rebellion of a Bianca or Beatrice-Joanna is the open door of a Pandora's box of death and suffering. This is certainly the case in *'Tis Pity She's a Whore*, and partly the case in that interesting though unsuccessful tragedy *Love's Sacrifice* (see the story of Ferentes as well as that of the figures of the central triangle). It is precisely this odd combination of romantic sympathy with the plight of lovers and a conservative horror of any violation of love conventions that makes Ford's most challenging plays so ambiguous and controversial.

The lovers who do not rebel against convention are plainly Ford's moral exemplars, but they are placed in the awkward and (I believe) morally enervating position of having their fate always decided by the actions of others. In *The Broken Heart* this condemns Orgilus, Penthea, and by extension, Calantha and Ithocles to sterility and death. For Prophilus and Euphranea there is fruition, but it comes as the gift of an enlightened moment in the otherwise darkened mind of Orgilus and seems almost (given the mood of melancholy and futility that pervades the play) a lucky accident. Despite, therefore, his love of his young lovers, and his moral and psychological commitment to the romantic marriage, Ford is without any faith in the primal rebellious energies of eros and it is this, I believe, that accounts for the hopelessness and despair that is the substance of Penthea's song and most of Ford's plays. We see John Ford, then, as a talented, potentially great playwright caught between two traditions, romantic and antiromantic, and unable to identify himself wholly with the ideas and conventions of either.

15   Shakespeare and the Poetry of Earth

I shall end this study by discussing briefly two of Shakespeare's greatest plays on love—*Antony and Cleopatra* and *The Winter's Tale*—in the context of the whole evolving tradition of love-death tragedy. The purpose will be mutual illumination—this despite the fact that both of these plays chronologically precede several of the non-Shakespearean works discussed earlier. The real point of the departure from time sequence is that Shakespeare had thought his way completely through the problem of what to make of sexual love whereas many of the writers discussed here proceeded only to partial conclusions or arrived at pessimistic dead ends. The key to Shakespeare's own illumination is the realization that sexual love and sexual energy have a profound, essential, and necessary connection with life itself and with human value. Lest this seem too obvious a point to make, let me quote the starting point and conclusion of an influential modern discussion of *Antony and Cleopatra*, that of Professor L. C. Knights. He starts with the recognition that "what Shakespeare infused into the love story as he found it in Plutarch was an immense energy, a sense of life so heightened that it can claim to represent an absolute value."[1] But, at the end, he abandons insight for this conventional retreat: "It is, of course, one of the signs of a great writer that he can afford to evoke sympathy or even admiration for what, in his final judgement, is discarded and condemned."[2] Shakespeare has, of course, anticipated this kind of reaction. In the intelligent generosity of its initial perception and the critical rejection of it at the end, it is quintes-

---

1. L. C. Knights, *Some Shakespearean Themes* (1959) in *Some Shakespearean Themes and An Approach to Hamlet*, Peregrine Book (Harmondsworth: Penguin Books Ltd., 1966), 123–24.
2. *Ibid.*, 127.

sentially the Enobarbus point of view. But Enobarbus ended up in a ditch, dead of a broken heart. Perhaps Professor Knights's formulation would be better stated this way: it is, of course, one of the signs of a great writer that he can afford to show all the strains and flaws in something which, in his final judgment, is accepted and celebrated.

1. *Antony and Cleopatra*

The tradition of love tragedy to which *Antony and Cleopatra* belongs may be traced back to Marlowe's *Dido of Carthage*. In both plays there is the clash between the values of empire and the values of love, of private experience. In both plays we find a rich and fertile erotic language; in both, a pair of lovers capable of great passion. But there is one major difference between the two. In *Dido*, the male lover vacillates and chooses empire. In *Antony and Cleopatra*, Antony vacillates, seeming at times to choose peace with Caesar and thus political safety (as when he marries Octavia), yet at the same time remaining under the influence of a powerful, unconscious choice made long before. As Robert Ornstein acutely notes: "At the beginning of the play it is obvious that . . . he does not yet know what is evident to the audience, that his only desire is to be with [Cleopatra]."[3] What we really wait and watch for in this play is the moment when Antony's rational, conscious self acknowledges the unconscious one and gives it the legitimacy it deserves. Of course, this acknowledgment is fatally long in coming, and it is in this long delay that the real interest and drama of the play lie.

The disabling division of consciousness in Antony is defined quite explicitly in terms of the opposing ideologies of love that have dominated this study—the romantic and the antiromantic. Thus, the vision of eros that we see in *Antony and Cleopatra* as distinctively *Roman* is also the typical Renaissance antiromanticism that manifests itself elsewhere in the drama. Here, it ranges from the crude sarcasm of Philo:

> Take but good note, and you shall see in him
> The triple pillar of the world transformed
> Into a strumpet's fool. Behold and see.   (I. i. 11–13)

---

3. Robert Ornstein, "The Ethic of the Imagination: Love and Art in *Antony and Cleopatra*," *Later Shakespeare*, ed. T. R. Brown and Bernard Harris, Stratford-upon-Avon Studies (London: Edward Arnold Ltd., 1966); reprinted in *Shakespeare: Modern Essays in Criticism*, 398.

to the more subtle denigrations of Pompey:

> But, first or last, your fine Egyptian cookery
> Shall have the fame. I have heard that Julius Caesar—
> Grew fat with feasting there.   (II. vi. 63–65)

to the politic wisdom of the worldly Caesar: "Women are not/In their best fortunes strong, but want will perjure/The ne'er-touched vestal" (III. xii. 29–31). The particular expressions differ in style, but the general tenor is clear enough—rational and antiromantic, suavely misogynous. Eros is put firmly in a diminutive, even demeaning place. This tendency extends, of course, to the kind of woman the Romans admire (*i.e.*, would marry), as opposed to the sort they see exemplified in Cleopatra. I shall come back later to the question of the Roman marriage, but the following short dialogue concerning Antony and Octavia is suggestive. Enobarbus is brooding about Antony's engagement to Caesar's sister:

> ENOBARB: Octavia is of a holy, cold, and still conversation.
> MENAS: Who would not have his wife so?   (II. vi. 121–23)

Menas' answer is typically Roman; but Enobarbus knows that Antony is not simply the typical Roman. So when he responds to Menas' question with "Not he that himself is not so; which is Mark Antony" (II. vi. 124–25), he is drawing both on his knowledge of the scope of Antony's own character and on his own perception that a true marriage for a man like Antony is founded on full and real mutuality and satisfaction between two human beings, not form nor even *goodness*, taken in its rather narrow and conventional Roman sense, the sense of a Menas, for instance.

Set against the narrow Roman view of eros and in competition with it is the vivid and large conception of eros that we identify with Egypt. This is, of course, summed up most ideally in the rich magnificence,

> The barge she sat in, like a burnisht throne
> Burned on the water: the poop was beaten gold;
> Purple the sails, and so perfuméd that
> The winds were love-sick with them;   (II. ii. 191–94)

the unembarrassed life,

> I saw her once
> Hop forty paces through the public street;
> And having lost her breath, she spoke, and panted,
> That she did make defect perfection,
> And, breathless, power breathe forth.   (II. ii. 228–32)

the inexhaustible wonder, "Age cannot wither her, nor custom stale/Her infinite variety:" (II. ii. 235–36) of Cleopatra herself. Volatile, imaginative, sensual, emotional: these are central values in the romantic consciousness. The Roman world, then, is strong on institutional virtues such as military organization and political manipulation; the Egyptian world is weak in these but strong where the Romans are weak, in the personal virtues of love, pleasure, and fidelity.

Antony's problem is a complex one. He in himself appears to unite both sides of this psychological and sociological opposition. He is a great Roman soldier (whose greatness appears in part to be founded on his ability to evoke a highly emotional response from his own soldiers) and he is the paragon of lovers. Nevertheless, the marriage of oppositions is by no means a stable one. It seems clear that as the pressure of events becomes greater a fundamental conflict between his role as lover (the world of eros and the allegiance to Cleopatra) and his role as Roman leader (the world of rule and the allegiance to empire and the interests of Caesar) becomes more and more pronounced. And, of course, more and more damaging.

Even at the first act of the play a strain is felt. The Antony of I. i is the romantic Antony, to the point of hyperbole. "Let Rome in Tiber melt," he says to Cleopatra when pressed to hear Caesar's messengers. The passage goes on to define true glory, true value as that created by love and the act of love—under a certain condition:

> Here is my space.
> Kingdoms are clay: our dungy earth alike
> Feeds beast as man: the nobleness of life
> Is to do thus; when such a mutual pair [*embracing*]
> And such a twain can do't, . . .   (I. i. 34–38)

The condition is that they be "such a mutual pair." It is precisely this mutuality that is most threatened by the instability of Antony's attitude towards the rival pull of Rome and Egypt. For in the next scene, Antony does listen to messages concerning activities of his wife Fulvia. Then he hears of new incursions by Asian enemies. This provokes in Antony a state of extreme self-consciousness and chagrin:

> ANT: Antony, thou wouldst say—
> MESSEN: O, my lord!
> ANT: Speak to me home, mince not the general tongue,
>   Name Cleopatra as she is called in Rome:
>   Rail thou in Fulvia's phrase, and taunt my faults
>   With such full license as both truth and malice
>   Have power to utter. O, then we bring forth weeds
>   When our quick minds lie still, . . .   (I. ii. 105–11)

The specific form this chagrin takes is antiromantic, anti-Egyptian. It is also self-serving, for he sees no real flaw or failure in himself, except inasmuch as he has been entrapped by a conniving female. The entrapment motif dominates Antony's language for the remainder of this scene, that is, as long as Antony is talking to a fellow Roman, out of Cleopatra's presence:

a) These strong Egyptian fetters I must break,
    Or lose myself in dotage.   (I. ii. 117–18)

b) I must from this enchanting queen break off: (I. ii. 129)

c) She is cunning past man's thought.   (I. ii. 146)

Shakespeare is, of course, exercising a fair measure of irony in all this. This sudden self-serving misogyny is as much a failure of intelligence as his earlier short-lived hyperbolic romanticism. And when Shakespeare has him exclaim "Would I had never seen her!" (I. ii. 153), he is invoking for our recollection the equal overreaction of, for instance, Brabantio ("Who would be a father!") and Othello ("Why did I marry?").

The return of Cleopatra, despite the mutual sparring, does see a return to reason, a reconciliation, and the mutual generosity and understanding that is crucial to Shakespeare's conception of romantic eros:

CLEO: Your honour calls you hence;
         Therefore be deaf to my unpitied folly,
         And all the gods go with you! Upon your sword
         Sit laurel victory! and smooth success
         Be strewed before your feet!
ANT: Let us go. Come;
         Our separation so abides and flies,
         That thou, residing here, goes yet with me,
         And I, hence fleeting, here remain with thee.
                                    (I. iii. 97–104)

But, more important at this point of the analysis is the fact that there is in these first three scenes a foreshadowing of the dominant rhythm of the play: that is—the movement from mutual love and trust, to vacillation on Antony's part as his *Roman* frame of mind dominates, to near destruction of the bond with Cleopatra (the death of love motif familiar from previous chapters), and—again—affirmation and union.

Within this overall rhythm, however, we may trace three smaller cycles of the same kind and these may be justly said to be the primary structural elements in the action of the play. The first is the action that centers around Antony's marriage to Octavia. It is plain that although Antony responds powerfully to the Egyptian vision of eros, he retains among other traces of the Roman view of life a Roman attitude towards marriage. His reaction to the death of Fulvia, indeed, his persistent need to live apart from her despite his grudging admiration for her boldness of spirit, indicates that this was not a marriage with much erotic content, not, in other words, a *romantic marriage* in the sense defined by the plays of the early romantic period. Nevertheless, it is also plain that marriage with Cleopatra, the woman for whom he has a most powerful erotic and spiritual attraction, has not really occurred to him as an acceptable alternative to enjoyment of her as a paramour. This fact does seem to rankle Cleopatra; for while she herself never raises the question of marriage, her references to Fulvia and Antony's marriage are full of barely suppressed envy and resentment (I. i. 28–32; I. i. 41; I. iii. 20–23). Antony, however, is at one with the Romans in their view that marriage is primarily a contract in which political reasons are the dominant ones. Near the end of the first tense meeting between Caesar and Antony, during which each man is trying to establish some slight edge on the other, Caesar twits Antony on his erotic proclivities by slyly suggesting that he has slipped so far as to make his paramour his wife. The dialogue goes thus:

AGRIPPA: . . . great Mark Antony
            Is now a widower.
CAESAR: Say not, so, Agrippa:
            If Cleopatra heard you, your reproof
            Were well deserved of rashness.
   ANT: I am not married, Caesar: let me hear
            Agrippa further speak.   (II. ii. 119–24)

One can hear, I believe, in Caesar's irony and the stuffy dignity of Antony's terse response, their Roman prejudice working to devalue the romantic vision and enforce the Roman. The next stage of this conversation is in fact the proposal to marry Antony to Octavia, which is the same devaluation translated into real action. The Agrippa who proposes the idea is a dry, rational man. He speaks of love, but it is political accord he means:

            To hold you in perpetual amity,
            To make you brothers, and to knit your hearts
            With an unslipping knot, take Antony
            Octavia to his wife; . . .   (II. ii. 125–28)

The marriage is, in other words, not between Antony and Octavia but between Antony and Octavius. And despite this marriage's stormy conclusion, the feelings generated by it are as seer and dry as the mind of its inventor:

> Pardon what I have spoke,
> For 'tis a studied, not a present thought,
> By duty ruminated.   (II. ii. 137–39)

We can best see what Antony has done to himself by once more recalling the ideal of the romantic marriage that is the crucial center of so many Shakespeare plays and of the early tradition of romantic tragedy. The young lovers of plays like *The Spanish Tragedy* and *Romeo and Juliet* had dominating fathers to try to force them into loveless marriages. Antony has no such excuse, unless we see Antony's Roman image of himself as a Freudian superego, in which case Antony (or one side of him) becomes his own father figure. Be that as it may, however; Antony, by making a loveless union with Caesar's family, has—as Enobarbus immediately sees—made a marriage that will be the death of love between Caesar and Antony rather than the protector of it: "you shall find, the band that seems to tie their friendship together will be the very strangler of their amity" (II. vi. 119–21). Antony has also intensified the scope and significance of the split in his own psyche. For immediately upon contracting himself to Octavia, he makes a choice that dramatizes the nebulousness of the contract:

> I will go to Egypt:
> And though I make this marriage for my peace,
> I'th'East my pleasure lies.   (II. iii. 38–40)

This Roman marriage is for political peace; in the East, however, is "pleasure." But by "pleasure" Shakespeare means (the rich portrayal of Cleopatra leads us to understand) not just sexual obsession, but a whole range of intellectual, emotional, even spiritual life. Antony's subsequent return to Cleopatra completes the first cycle of union-abandonment-reunion. And it points up the basic weakness of his compromise. His marriage lacks the bond of eros; his love lacks the public strength and private commitment of a real marriage.

From this point on, the cycle is to be measured in psychological distance rather than physical. Antony's humiliating failure at Actium begins one such cycle. It has, for one thing, placed him in a position where he must "dodge/And palter in the shifts of lowness" (III. xi. 62–63), *i.e.*, sue for mercy "to . . . breathe between the heavens and earth,/A private man in Athens" (III. xii. 14–15). This is not a position natural to Antony, and the misery of it plainly unhinges him. One sign of temporary derangement is his treatment of Caesar's messenger Thidias. The Antony who early in the play said "Who tells me true, though in his tale lie death,/I hear him as he flattered" (I. ii. 99–100) now sadistically takes out his own frustrations on Caesar's surrogate:

> Whip him, fellows,
> Till like a boy you see him cringe his face,
> And whine aloud for mercy. Take him hence.
>
> (III. xiii. 99–101)

It is not one of Antony's finest moments. But another form which derangement takes is the morbid, paranoid suspicion of female wiles. He sees Cleopatra allowing her hand to be kissed by Caesar's messenger (in effect, dodging and paltering in shifts of lowness, just as Antony has been), and is immediately provoked into the self-serving Roman frame of mind:

> You were half blasted ere I knew you . . . Ha!
> Have I my pillow left unpressed in Rome,
> Forborne the getting of a lawful race,
> And by a gem of women, to be abused
> By one that looks on feeders?
>
> (III. xiii. 105–109)

The root of this outburst is insecurity and failure of confidence. The form it takes is morbidly jealous erotic fantasying:

> I found you as a morsel cold upon
> Dead Caesar's trencher; nay, you were a fragment
> Of Gnaeus Pompey's; besides what hotter hours,
> Unregistered in vulgar fame, you have
> Luxuriously picked out: for I am sure,
> Though you can guess what temperance should be,
> You know not what it is.   (III. xiii. 116–22)

In imagining the "hotter hours" he speaks of, his mind is working the same sterile ground as Othello's or Leontes'. And the irony of an Antony rebuking anyone for intemperance is palpable and gross. The scene is, in other words, a severe test of the bond that they both value a great deal. The enemy to the bond here is the self-serving side of the Antony ego. What saves it is the other side of that ego, the one that is open to Cleopatra's appeals to the integrity of the bond. And, of course, with their reunion comes a renewal of Antony, who calls for wines and viands and goes the next day to a notable victory. Shakespeare's subtle use of life imagery here underscores his point:

> CLEO: It is my birth-day,
> I had thought t'have held it poor. But since
>   my lord
> Is Antony again, I will be Cleopatra.
>   (III. xiii. 185–87)

To reestablish the bond is to be truly born again, for it means the return to a true identity.

The final sequence of estrangement-reconciliation begins after the third and final battle. Faced with this final failure, Antony again descends to the rhetoric of egoistic misogyny to save self-respect. Cleopatra becomes the "foul Egyptian," the "triple-turned whore." Antony himself is persuaded that love has been killed by betrayal:

>   Betrayed I am.
> O this false soul of Egypt: this grave charm—
> Whose eye becked forth my wars and called them home,
> Whose bosom was my crownet, my chief end—
> Like a right gipsy hath at fast and loose
> Beguiled me to the very heart of loss.
>   (IV. xii. 24–29)

This time anger and absurd jealousy carry Antony nearly to the extremes of an Othello, to the brink of murder:

>   The witch shall die.
> To the young Roman boy she hath sold me, and I fall
> Under this plot: she dies for't.   (IV. xii. 47–49)

Later it is "She hath betrayed me, and shall die the death" (IV. xiv. 26). And to answer his betrayal of faith, she does in fact betray him with the lie that provokes his suicide:

> Mardian, go tell him I have slain myself;
> Say that the last I spoke was 'Antony,'
> And word it, prithee, piteously.   (IV. xiii. 7–9)

We see again the nearly total breakdown of a love relationship, the death of romantic faith. But Shakespeare gives to Antony and Cleopatra the moment that is absent in the great middle tragedies and so important in the late plays and romances—still one more chance at union, reconciliation and reaffirmation. Thus, from the point that Mark Antony is pulled up into Cleopatra's tower, the love-death imagery has an exclusively romantic tone, romantic both in the sense of things lost and the celebration of what has been. Death has—as in *Romeo and Juliet*—been kept from subverting love and put to serving it.

The crucial issue here is that of love and the romantic faith, love and human bonds. To place what happens finally between Antony and Cleopatra, we need to carefully study Shakespeare's treatment of Enobarbus. Enobarbus is a classic example of the rationalist gone wrong. From the beginning he has understood and appreciated as well as anyone Cleopatra's beauty and her attraction. His descriptions of her arrival at Cydnus are among the great passages in English drama. But the ironic wit which gives his remarks on Cleopatra's tears and the death of Fulvia (I. ii. 132ff) their attractive saltiness turns sour when the times turn bad for them all. The crucial issue is—will he remain with Antony, keeping whole the bond, or will he desert him, breaking it? The force that demands that he break the bond is "reason." After Actium love is still stronger than reason, but it is plain that the latter is gaining influence:

> I'll yet follow
> The wounded chance of Antony, though my reason
> Sits in the wind against me.   (III. x. 35–37)

Among Antony's reactions to his humiliating defeat at Actium are various attempts to cheer himself up, to restore his good spirits and morale. Among these is a challenge to Caesar to fight him in single combat. Enobarbus, who is becoming increasingly distant from Antony, takes a serious view of this harmless bravado, however:

> I see men's judgements are
> A parcel of their fortunes, and things outward
> Do draw the inward quality after them,
> To suffer all alike. That he should dream,
> Knowing all measures, the full Caesar will
> Answer his emptiness! Caesar, thou hast subdued
> His judgement too.   (III. xi. 31–37)

There is some Shakespearean irony here. For Enobarbus' words could as well apply to himself. Enobarbus' "judgement" is a parcel of what he sees to be a declining fortune. And Caesar is well on the way to subduing Enobarbus' judgment to the point that he will do what Cleopatra (though offered the chance [III. xii. 20ff]) would never do—betray Antony for Caesar.

At this point Enobarbus' meditations become quite complex. At first, he seems to make a distinct movement towards abandonment:

> Mine honesty and I begin to square.
> The loyalty well held to fools does make
> Our faith mere folly: . . .   (III. xiii. 41–43)

Antony is now a "fool" and Enobarbus feels himself demeaned by the association. But Shakespeare makes him aware also of a more heroic, *romantic* response to the situation:

> . . . yet he that can endure
> To follow with allegiance a fall'n lord
> Does conquer him that did his master conquer,
> And earns a place i'th'story.   (III. xiii. 43–46)

The crucial terms here then are *faith* and *conquer*. To keep the "faith" is a way of conquering. But it is not a way that Enobarbus will choose. His next action is to misinterpret Cleopatra's excessively courtly welcome to Thidias as an indication that she is about to abandon Antony:

ENOBARB: Sir, sir, thou art so leaky
> That we must leave thee to thy sinking, for
> Thy dearest quit thee.   (III. xiii. 63–65)

It is interesting that the misinterpretation is so unconsciously self-serving. "We must leave thee" really means here "I must leave thee." And the "dearest" who will quit Antony is not, of course, Cleopatra but Enobarbus himself.

The conflict in Enobarbus is clear. And so is the direction of his thinking. Enobarbus will stake his all on his "reason," and the final stage of the process of disengagement from Antony comes as he watches Antony—now growing increasingly like the Antony of old—order feasting and drinking on the eve of the second battle:

> Now he'll outstare the lightning. To be furious
> Is to be frighted out of fear, and in that mood
> The dove will peck the estridge; and I see still
> A diminution in our captain's brain
> Restores his heart: when valour preys on reason,
> It eats the sword it fights with. I will seek
> Some way to leave him.   (III. xiii. 195–201)

This again is the death of love, the breaking of a bond, now between man

and man. And in such a context I believe we must see Enobarbus' melan-
cholic collapse as a Shakespearean judgment:

> This blows my heart:
> If swift thought break it not, a swifter mean
> Shall outstrike thought: but thought will do't, I feel.
>
> (IV. vi. 34–36)

His mind has led him against his heart, and his heart turns bitterly on itself.
His last phrase in this scene is interesting:

> No, I will go seek
> Some ditch wherein to die; the foul'st best fits
> My latter part of life.   (IV. vi. 37–39)

It links the antiromantic Enobarbus to a later antiromantic rationalist—
Webster's Bosola. But Bosola, moving in the opposite direction from Enobarbus (from reason to love instead of love to reason), could say "The last
part of my life/Hath done me best service" (*DM*. V. v. 64–65). Antony and
Cleopatra have this affirmation too, despite all the fluctuations of feeling,
and since they have much more to build on, the affirmation is consequently
much more powerful.

The last hours of Antony and Cleopatra recapture—despite the pair's
military reverses—the mood of their prime. When Antony is brought to
Cleopatra's tower it is not with reproach or self-reproach he comes but with
love:

> I here importune death awhile, until
> Of many thousand kisses the poor last
> I lay upon thy lips.   (IV. xv. 19–21)

Love is no longer seen as a spell or a poison but as the very essence of life:

> O, come, come, come;
> And welcome, welcome! Die when thou hast lived,
> Quicken with kissing: had my lips that power
> Thus would I wear them out.   (IV. xv. 37–40)

And even if Cleopatra's kisses cannot do in actuality what she wishes they
could—bring Antony back to life—they do restore the primary metaphoric
equation between eros and life. Death becomes what it was in *Romeo and
Juliet*, a moment where the important thing in the characters' lives—the
bond of love between them—is restored and paradoxically affirmed. Enobarbus dies alone, unreconciled and miserable. Antony and Cleopatra die

with a serenity founded on the final knowledge that the bond between them is something truly of value:

1) ANT: . . . but I will be
   A bridegroom in my death, and run into't
   As to a lover's bed.   (IV. xiv. 99–101)

2) CLEO: Peace, peace!
   Dost thou not see my baby at my breast,
   That sucks the nurse asleep?   (V. ii. 307–309)

The feeling in both cases is that of completion, the completion of lives lived fumblingly and foolishly at times but to the full. "Ripeness is all," is a key phrase in *King Lear*. The feeling at the end of *Antony and Cleopatra* is one of ripeness: love completed by death, not undermined—drawing the lovers in metaphor and image to the love marriage that they never gave each other in life.

2. *The Winter's Tale:* Conclusion

I am merging my conclusion with a brief discussion of *The Winter's Tale* because this play—though not a tragedy—seems to me an allegory of love that sums up Shakespeare's mature dramatic thought on the subject. It is also a *romance*, and therefore a gesture of faith in romantic love as chief source of good in life.

The structure of *The Winter's Tale* plainly embodies two motifs central to Renaissance tragedy and this study. First, the motif of the death of love is embodied in Leontes' tragic jealousy. Then, however, the second chance is given, leading to the reestablishment of a broken bond. The specific vehicle of this last movement is the idea of love-rebellion in two Romeo and Juliet-like young lovers. Thus the theme of youth redeeming age is allowed to evolve to completion instead of being cut off by the deaths of the lovers.

Shakespeare sees the theme of the death of love in terms of a seizure of the irrational—specifically the irrational and paranoid fear of the sexual nature of woman that lies at the heart of the antiromantic tradition. So— when we read a speech such as the following:

                    There have been
(Or I am much deceived) cuckolds ere now,
And many a man there is (even at this present,
Now, while I speak this) holds his wife by th'arm,
That little thinks she has been sluiced in's absence,
And his pond fished by his next neighbour (by
Sir Smile, his neighbour): nay, there's comfort in't,
Whiles other men have gates, and those gates opened,

290 Love and Death in Renaissance Tragedy

> As mine, against their will. Should all despair
> That have revolted wives, the tenth of mankind
> Would hang themselves. (I. ii. 190–200)

we think immediately of Vindice, Heywood's young Geraldine, Webster's Ferdinand, Middleton's Leantio, Shakespeare's Hamlet and Othello. Not every tone of misogynous obsession is comprehended in Leontes, but the central ideas, the fantastic imaginings, the wild generalizations on universal female evil, and the vividly expressed disgust with the body are all to be found in plays both before and after this one. And, in *The Winter's Tale* as in *The Revenger's Tragedy*, the world created by such a vision is closed, phantasmagoric, only partially representing nature. I call on Eliot again: "The cynicism, the loathing and disgust of humanity, expressed consummately in *The Revenger's Tragedy*, are immature in the respect that they exceed the object. Their objective equivalents are characters practising the grossest vices; characters which seem merely to be spectres projected from the poet's inner world of nightmare, some horror beyond words."[4] I believe that this is equally true of Leontes and, furthermore, that Shakespeare shows his disaffiliation from antiromanticism by identifying it with death —the death of Mamillius, the supposed death of Hermione, the near death of Perdita.

But Shakespeare also goes beyond this. Not only is the antiromantic vision linked to death, but life is embodied in the classic figures and actions of the early romantic tradition. The story of Florizel and Perdita is the *Romeo and Juliet* motif all over again, with one exception. This time the parental opposition comes from the father of the hopeful bridegroom instead of the bride. But the opposition is no less extreme for all that. It too issues out in images of alienation, pain, death:

POLIX: Mark your divorce, young sir,
      Whom son I dare not call; thou art too base
      To be acknowledged. . . . Thou a sceptre's heir,
      That thus affects a sheep-hook! Thou, old traitor,
      I am sorry, that by hanging thee, I can
      But shorten thy life one week. . . . And thou, fresh
            piece
      Of excellent witchcraft, who, of force, must know
      The royal fool thou cop'st with—
SHEP: O, my heart!
POLIX: I'll have thy beauty scratched with briars, and
            made
      More homely than thy state.   (IV. iv. 414–23)

4. Eliot, "Cyril Tourneur," 189–90.

In this play, however, life is not to be stifled. Perdita especially has from the play's beginning been the symbolic embodiment of the primal energies of life. Nature itself is the force behind her birth:

> This child was prisoner to the womb, and is
> By law and process of great nature thence
> Freed and enfranchised— . . .   (II. ii. 59–61)

And to the shepherds who find her she seems almost a miraculous image of life found at a point when death seemed to triumph almost entirely: "Heavy matters, heavy matters. . . but look thee here, boy. Now bless thyself; thou met'st with things dying, I with things new-born" (III. iii. 107–109). When she is grown, these identifications become still stronger. There is this exchange between Perdita and Florizel:

> PERD: O, these I lack,
>   To make you garlands of—and my sweet friend,
>   To strew him o'er and o'er.
> FLOR: What, like a corse?
> PERD: No, like a bank, for love to lie and play on;
>   Not like a corse: or if. . . not to be buried,
>   But quick, and in mine arms.   (IV. iv. 127–32)

In it the death term ("like a corse") is countered immediately and convincingly by the terms of love, play, life, eros. The summary phrase in defining the meaning of Perdita is probably "great creating nature." She uses it herself when arguing from a position so uncompromising on the side of natural fertility that she will not even allow grafted flowers in her garden despite the fact that

>   . . . [she has] heard it said
>   There is an art which in their piedness shares
>   With great creating nature.   (IV. iv. 86–88)

If—I speak most diffidently about his almost unknowable intellectual and spiritual biography—Shakespeare did go through a period in which he questioned the value of sexuality, then I should say it was just this intimate link between sexual love and creative nature that drew him out of it. For to love life and hate sexuality is to do something profoundly contradictory.

It is important to point out that there is nothing passive about these natural sexual energies. Unlike Ford's stoical yet suffering young lovers, Florizel and Perdita do rebel against the suppression of love. The elopement is impulsive, but as in the case of Romeo and Juliet, it opens the door to larger and truer concord, this time for young lovers as well as the long-divorced older ones. When Leontes looks on the fled pair and says

What might I have been,
Might I a son and daughter now have looked on,
Such goodly things as you?   (V. i. 176–78)

he does not realize what he soon will know: that he has been given again the gift of son and daughter, of friend, and of wife. What we the audience or readers realize is that to complete this circle of loved ones Shakespeare has reached back full circle to the structure and thought of *Romeo and Juliet*, the first truly great romantic tragedy.

One final point: this study has been concerned with love and death, with the cycle of nature in Elizabethan drama. It can be seen, I think, that one of the greatest effects resulting from concentration on this theme, and on these earthly boundaries, was the secularization of dramatic literature. A divine literature (*Everyman* seems an archetype of what was superseded) inevitably looks beyond the earth for its values. In a sense it could even be said to begin where a secular literature leaves off, and at the very least it presupposes a lesser status for earthly experience. The opposite is true of a literature of love and death. Death marks the end of life; love (and its re-lated opposites—hatred, envy, jealousy) composes the high and low mo-ments of life's substance. The focus is therefore resolutely on the temporal. In Elizabethan and Jacobean drama this means—even in those dramatists most attached to the older values—a consistent sharpening of the poetic and dramatic tools for representing the texture of human life and its basis in human relationship. It also often meant the refounding of values them-selves within an earthly context, often with some dislocation of the old. Politics had long been captive to medieval monkish conceptions, particu-larly the pattern of the rise and fall of princes; eros, being a potent force not so easily brought into these patterns of pride and decline, struggled—as we have seen in this study—to impose its own patterns and values within an earthly context. Out of the tensions created between these two forces—divine and secular—comes much of the power of Elizabethan and Jacobean literature.

I recall a remark of Wallace Stevens: "The great poems of heaven and hell have been written and the great poem of the earth remains to be writ-ten."[5] But, remembering such moments of earthly hell as that in Hamlet's mind or Lear's as he wanders on the heath, and such moments of earthly heaven as that when Lear is reunited with Cordelia, Antony with Cleo-patra, or Leontes with Hermione, I would suggest that the poetry of earth has indeed been written, by Shakespeare and his contemporaries.

5. Wallace Stevens, *The Necessary Angel* (London: Faber and Faber, 1942), 142.

Bibliography

Wherever reprints are used, the date of original publication is in parenthesis.

Anderson, Donald K., Jr. "The Banquet of Love in English Drama (1595–1642)." *Journal of English and Germanic Philology*, LXIII (1964), 422–32.

Babb, Lawrence. *The Elizabethan Malady*. East Lansing: Michigan State College Press, 1951.

Barber, C. L. *Shakespeare's Festive Comedy*. Meridian Books. Cleveland, Ohio: The World Publishing Co., 1966 (1959).

Bayley, John. *The Characters of Love*. London: Constable & Co. Ltd., 1960.

Boccaccio, Giovanni. *The Decameron*. Translated by J. M. Rigg. Vol. I. London: J. M. Dent & Sons Ltd., 1960 (1930).

Bogard, Travis. *The Tragic Satire of John Webster*. Los Angeles: University of California Press, 1955.

Boklund, Gunnar. *The Duchess of Malfi: Sources, Themes, Characters*. Cambridge: Harvard University Press, 1962.

———. *The Sources of The White Devil*. Cambridge: Harvard University Press, 1957.

Bowers, Fredson T. *Elizabethan Revenge Tragedy, 1587–1642*. Princeton: Princeton University Press, 1940.

Bradbrook, M. C. *Themes and Conventions of Elizabethan Tragedy*. Cambridge: The University Press, 1964 (1935).

Bradley, A. C. *Shakespearean Tragedy*. 2nd ed. London: Macmillan & Co. Ltd., 1905.

Brissenden, Alan. "Impediments to Love: A Theme in John Ford," *Renaissance Drama*, VII (1964), 95–102.

Broadbent, J. B. *Poetic Love*. London: Chatto & Windus, 1964.

Brodwin, Leonora Leet. *Elizabethan Love Tragedy 1587–1625*. New York: New York University Press, 1971.

Brooke, Nicholas. *Shakespeare's Early Tragedies*. London: Methuen & Co. Ltd., 1968.

Brown, John Russell. *Shakespeare and His Comedies*. London: Methuen & Co. Ltd., 1957.

Caputi, Anthony. *John Marston, Satirist*. Ithaca, N.Y.: Cornell University Press, 1961.

Charlton, H. B. *Shakespearian Comedy*. London: Methuen & Co. Ltd., 1966 (1938).

293

Clemen, Wolfgang H. *The Development of Shakespeare's Imagery*. London: Methuen &
Co. Ltd., 1951.
———. *English Tragedy Before Shakespeare*. Translated by T. S. Dorsch. London:
Methuen & Co. Ltd., 1961.
Coleridge, Samuel Taylor. *Shakespearean Criticism*. Edited by Thomas Middleton
Raysor. Everyman Library. Vol. I. 2nd ed. London: J. M. Dent & Sons Ltd.,
1960.
Cunliffe, John W., ed. "Introduction," *Early English Classical Tragedies*. Oxford:
Clarendon Press, 1912.
Danby, John F. *Poets on Fortune's Hill: Studies in Sidney, Shakespeare, Beaumont and
Fletcher*. London: Faber and Faber, 1952.
D'Arcy, M. C. *The Mind and Heart of Love*. The Fontana Library. London: Collins,
1962 (1945).
Dean, Leonard F., ed. *Shakespeare: Modern Essays in Criticism*. Rev. ed. New York:
Oxford University Press, 1967.
Dickey, F. M. *Not Wisely but Too Well*. San Marino, Calif.: Huntington Library, 1957.
Donne, John. *John Donne: Complete Poetry and Selected Prose*. Edited by John Hay-
ward. London: The Nonesuch Press, 1962.
Donoghue, Denis. *The Ordinary Universe: Soundings in Modern Literature*. London:
Faber and Faber, 1968.
Doran, Madeleine. *Endeavors of Art: A Study of Form in Elizabethan Drama*. Madison:
University of Wisconsin Press, 1954.
Edwards, Philip, ed. "Introduction," *The Spanish Tragedy*, by Thomas Kyd. The
Revels Plays. London: Methuen & Co. Ltd., 1959.
———. *Shakespeare and the Confines of Art*. London: Methuen & Co. Ltd., 1968.
———. *Thomas Kyd and Early Elizabethan Tragedy*. London: Longmans, Green & Co.,
1966.
Ekeblad, Inga-Stina. "The 'Impure Art' of John Webster." *Review of English Studies*,
IX (1958), 253–67.
———. "*The Love of King David and Fair Bethsabe*: A Note on George Peele's Biblical
Drama." *English Studies*, XXXIX (April, 1958), 57–62.
Eliot, T. S. *Selected Essays*. 3rd enlarged ed. London: Faber and Faber, 1951.
Ellis-Fermor, Una M. *Christopher Marlowe*. London: Methuen & Co. Ltd., 1927.
———. *The Jacobean Drama: An Interpretation*. 5th ed. London: Methuen & Co. Ltd.,
1965.
Empson, William. "*The Spanish Tragedy*." *Nimbus*, III (Summer, 1956). Reprinted in
Elizabethan Drama. Edited by R. J. Kaufmann.
Farnham, Willard. "Troilus in Shapes of Infinite Desire." *Shakespeare 400*. Edited by
James G. McManaway. New York: Holt, Rinehart and Winston, 1964.
Ford, John. *The Broken Heart*. Edited by Donald K. Anderson, Jr. Regents Renais-
sance Drama Series. Lincoln: University of Nebraska Press, 1968.
———. *John Ford (Five Plays)*. Edited by Havelock Ellis. A Mermaid Dramabook.
New York: Hill and Wang, 1957.
———. *'Tis Pity She's a Whore*. Edited by N. W. Bawcutt. Regents Renaissance
Drama Series. Lincoln: University of Nebraska Press, 1966.
Freud, Sigmund. Fourth Lecture. *Five Lectures on Psycho-Analysis* (1910). Vol. XI of
The Standard Edition of the Complete Psychological Works of Sigmund Freud. Trans-
lated under the general editorship of James Strachey. London: Hogarth Press
and the Institute of Psycho-Analysis, 1957.

———. *Three Essays on the Theory of Sexuality* (1905). Translated and edited by James Strachey. The International Psycho-Analytical Library, No. 57. Rev. ed. London: Hogarth Press, 1962.

Frye, Northrop. *Anatomy of Criticism: Four Essays*. Princeton: Princeton University Press, 1957.

———. "The Argument of Comedy." *English Institute Essays* (1948). Reprinted in *Shakespeare's Comedies: An Anthology of Modern Criticism*. Edited by Laurence Lerner.

———. *Fools of Time: Studies in Shakespearean Tragedy*. Toronto: Toronto University Press, 1967.

———. *A Natural Perspective*. New York: Columbia University Press, 1965.

Frye, Roland Mushat. *Shakespeare and Christian Doctrine*. Princeton: Princeton University Press, 1963.

———. "The Teachings of Classical Puritanism on Conjugal Love." *On Milton's Poetry*. Edited by Arnold Stein. Greenwich, Conn.: Fawcett Publications, Inc., 1970.

Gardner, Helen. "*Hamlet* and the Tragedy of Revenge." Reprinted in *Shakespeare: Modern Essays in Criticism*. Edited by Leonard F. Dean.

———. "The Noble Moor." British Academy Shakespeare Lecture (1955). Reprinted in *Shakespeare Criticism 1935–1960*. Selected by Anne Ridler. London: Oxford University Press, 1963.

———. "The Tragedy of Damnation." *Essays and Studies*, I (1948), 46–66. Reprinted in *Elizabethan Drama*. Edited by R. J. Kaufmann.

Griffin, Ernest G. "'Gismond of Salerne': A Critical Appreciation." *A Review of English Literature*, IV (April, 1963), 94–107.

Harbage, Alfred. *Annals of English Drama, 975–1700*. Revised by S. Schoenbaum. Rev. ed. London: Methuen & Co. Ltd., 1964.

———. *Shakespeare and the Rival Traditions*. New York: Macmillan, 1952.

Heilman, Robert B. *Magic in the Web: Action and Language in Othello*. Lexington: University of Kentucky Press, 1956.

Heywood, Thomas. *The English Traveller. Thomas Heywood*. Edited by A. Wilson Verity. The Mermaid Series. London: Vizetelly & Co. Ltd., 1888.

———. *A Woman Killed with Kindness*. Edited by R. W. Van Fossen. The Revels Plays. London: Methuen & Co. Ltd., 1961.

Holloway, John. *The Story of the Night*. London: Routledge and Kegan Paul, 1961.

Hunter, G. K., ed. "Introduction to John Marston," *Antonio and Mellida*, by John Marston. Regents Renaissance Drama Series. London: Edward Arnold Ltd., 1965.

Kaufmann, R. J., ed. *Elizabethan Drama: Modern Essays in Criticism*. Galaxy Books. New York: Oxford University Press, 1961.

———. "Ford's Tragic Perspective." *Texas Studies in Literature and Language*, I (1960), 522–37. Reprinted in *Elizabethan Drama*. Edited by R. J. Kaufmann.

Kimbrough, Robert. *Shakespeare's Troilus and Cressida and Its Setting*. Cambridge: Harvard University Press, 1964.

Knight, G. Wilson. *The Crown of Life*. London: Methuen & Co. Ltd., 1965 (1947).

———. *The Imperial Theme*. London: Methuen & Co. Ltd., 1968 (3rd ed., 1951).

———. *The Wheel of Fire*. University Paperbacks. London: Methuen & Co. Ltd., 1965 (4th ed., 1949).

Knights, L. C. *An Approach to "Hamlet."* London: Chatto & Windus, 1960.

——. *Some Shakespearean Themes and An Approach to Hamlet*. Peregrine Books. Harmondsworth: Penguin Books Ltd., 1966.

Kott, Jan. *Shakespeare Our Contemporary*. Translated by Boleslaw Taborski. London: Methuen & Co. Ltd., 1964.

Kraus, Henry. *The Living Theatre of Medieval Art*. London: Thames and Hudson, 1967.

Kyd, Thomas. *The Spanish Tragedy*. Edited by Philip Edwards. The Revels Plays. London: Methuen & Co. Ltd., 1959.

Lawlor, John. *The Tragic Sense in Shakespeare*. London: Chatto & Windus, 1960.

Leavis, F. R. "Diabolic Intellect and the Noble Hero," (1937) in *The Common Pursuit*. London: Chatto & Windus, 1952.

Leech, Clifford. *John Ford and the Drama of His Time*. London: Chatto & Windus, 1957.

——. *John Webster: A Critical Study*. London: Hogarth Press, 1951.

——. *Webster: The Duchess of Malfi*. Studies in English Literature, No. 8. London: Edward Arnold Ltd., 1963.

Lerner, Laurence, ed. *Shakespeare's Comedies: An Anthology of Modern Criticism*. Harmondsworth: Penguin Books Ltd., 1967.

Lewis, C. S. *The Allegory of Love*. Galaxy Books. New York: Oxford University Press, 1958 (1936).

Levin, Harry. *Christopher Marlowe: The Overreacher*. London: Faber and Faber, 1965 (1954).

——. "Form and Formality in *Romeo and Juliet*." *Shakespeare Quarterly*, XI (Winter, 1960), 3–11.

——. *The Question of Hamlet*. New York: Oxford University Press, 1959.

Lyons, Charles R. *Shakespeare and the Ambiguity of Love's Triumph*. The Hague: Mouton, 1971.

McGinn, Donald J. "A New Date for *Antonio's Revenge*." *PMLA*, LIII (March, 1938), 129–37.

Mahood, M. M. *Shakespeare's Wordplay*. London: Methuen & Co. Ltd., 1968 (1957).

Marlowe, Christopher. *The Tragedy of Dido Queen of Carthage*. *The Complete Plays of Christopher Marlowe*. Edited by Irving Ribner. New York: The Odyssey Press, 1963.

Marston, John. *Antonio and Mellida*. Edited by G. K. Hunter. Regents Renaissance Drama Series. London: Edward Arnold Ltd., 1965.

——. *Antonio's Revenge*. Edited by G. K. Hunter. Regents Renaissance Drama Series. Lincoln: University of Nebraska Press, 1965.

Meredith, George. "An Essay on Comedy." Reprinted in *Comedy*. Edited by Wylie Sypher. Garden City, N.Y.: Doubleday Anchor Books, 1956.

Middleton, Thomas. *Women Beware Women*. Edited by Roma Gill. A Mermaid Dramabook. New York: Hill and Wang, 1969.

——, and William Rowley. *The Changeling*. Edited by N. W. Bawcutt. The Revels Plays. London: Methuen & Co. Ltd., 1961.

Moore, Don D. *John Webster and His Critics 1617–1964*. Baton Rouge: Louisiana State University Press, 1966.

Murray, Peter B. *A Study of Cyril Tourneur*. Philadelphia: University of Pennsylvania Press, 1964.

Oliver, H. J. *The Problem of John Ford*. Carlton, Victoria: Melbourne University Press, 1955.

Ornstein, Robert. "*The Atheist's Tragedy* and Renaissance Naturalism." *Studies in Philology*, LI (April,1954), 194–207.
———. "The Ethic of the Imagination: Love and Art in *Antony and Cleopatra.*" *Later Shakespeare*. Edited by T. R. Brown and Bernard Harris. Stratford-upon-Avon Studies. London: Edward Arnold Ltd., 1966. Reprinted in *Shakespeare: Modern Essays in Criticism*. Edited by Leonard F. Dean.
———. *The Moral Vision of Jacobean Tragedy*. Madison: University of Wisconsin Press, 1960.
Ortega y Gasset, José. *On Love . . . Aspects of a Single Theme* (1941). Translated by Tony Talbot. London: Jonathan Cape Ltd., 1967.
Parrott, Thomas M. and Robert H. Ball. *A Short View of Elizabethan Drama*. New York: Charles Scribner's Sons, 1958 (1943).
Peele, George. *The Love of King David and Fair Bethsabe. Minor Elizabethan Drama*. Edited by Ashley Thorndike. Everyman Library. Vol. I. Rev. ed. London: J. M. Dent & Sons Ltd., 1958 (1910).
Peter, John. *Complaint and Satire in Early English Literature*. Oxford: Clarendon Press, 1956.
Pettet, E. C. *Shakespeare and the Romance Tradition*. London: Staples Press Ltd., 1949.
Prior, Moody E. *The Language of Tragedy*. New York: Columbia University Press, 1947.
Ribner, Irving, ed. "Introduction," *The Atheist's Tragedy*, by Cyril Tourneur. The Revels Plays. London: Methuen & Co. Ltd., 1964.
———. *Jacobean Tragedy*. London: Methuen & Co. Ltd., 1962.
———. *Patterns in Shakespearean Tragedy*. London: Methuen & Co. Ltd., 1960.
———. "Then I Denie You Starres." *Studies in the English Renaissance Drama in Memory of Karl Julius Holzknecht*. Edited by J. W. Bennett, Oscar Cargill, and Vernon Hall, Jr. New York: New York University Press, 1959.
Ricks, Christopher. "The Moral and Poetic Structure of *The Changeling.*" *Essays in Criticism*, X (July, 1960), 290–306.
———. "Word-Play in *Women Beware Women.*" *Review of English Studies*, XII (1961), 238–50.
Righter, Anne. *Shakespeare and the Idea of the Play*. London: Chatto & Windus, 1962.
Rougemont, Denis de. *Passion and Society*. Translated by Montgomery Belgion. Rev. ed. London: Faber and Faber, 1962.
Salingar, L. G. "*The Revenger's Tragedy* and the Morality Tradition." *Scrutiny*, VI (March, 1938), 402–24.
Sargeaunt, M. Joan. *John Ford*. Oxford: Basil Blackwell, 1935.
Schoenbaum, Samuel. *Middleton's Tragedies: A Critical Study*. New York: Columbia University Press, 1955.
———. "The Precarious Balance of John Marston." *PMLA*, LXVII (December, 1952), 1069–78.
Seneca. *Thyestes. Tragedies*. Translated by Frank Justus Miller. Vol. II. Rev. ed. The Loeb Classical Library. London: William Heinemann, 1929.
Sensabaugh, G. F. *The Tragic Muse of John Ford*. Stanford, Calif.: Stanford University Press, 1944.
Shakespeare, William. *Shakespeare's Sonnets*. Edited by W. G. Ingram and Theodore Redpath. London: University of London Press Ltd., 1964.
———. *The Works of Shakespeare*. Edited by J. Dover Wilson and Arthur Quiller-Couch. New Cambridge Edition. Cambridge: The University Press, 1921–66.

298   Bibliography

Siegel, P. N. "Christianity and the Religion of Love in *Romeo and Juliet*." *Shakespeare Quarterly*, XII (1961), 371–92.
Smith, Hallett D. "*A Woman Killed With Kindness*." *PMLA*, LIII (March, 1938), 138–47.
Smith, James. "The Tragedy of Blood." *Scrutiny*, VIII (December,1939), 265–80.
Spencer, Theodore. *Death and Elizabethan Tragedy*. Cambridge: Harvard University Press, 1936.
————. *Shakespeare and the Nature of Man*. New York: The Macmillan Company, 1942.
Spivack, Bernard. *Shakespeare and the Allegory of Evil*. New York: Columbia University Press, 1958.
Spurgeon, Caroline F. E. *Shakespeare's Imagery and What It Tells Us*. Cambridge: The University Press, 1935.
Steane, J. B. *Marlowe: A Critical Study*. Cambridge: The University Press, 1964.
Stevens, Wallace. *The Necessary Angel*. London: Faber and Faber, 1942.
Stewart, J. I. M. *Character and Motive in Shakespeare*. London: Longmans, Green and Co. Ltd., 1949.
Stoll, Elmer Edgar. *Art and Artifice in Shakespeare*. Cambridge: The University Press, 1933.
————. *Shakespeare's Young Lovers*. The Alexander Lectures at the University of Toronto, 1935. New York: AMS Press, Inc., 1966.
Tillyard, E. M. W. *Shakespeare's Last Plays*. London: Chatto & Windus, 1938.
Tomlinson, T. B. *A Study of Elizabethan and Jacobean Tragedy*. Cambridge: The University Press, 1964.
Tourneur, Cyril. *The Atheist's Tragedy*. Edited by Irving Ribner. The Revels Plays. London: Methuen & Co. Ltd., 1964.
————. *The Revenger's Tragedy*. Edited by R. A. Foakes. The Revels Plays. London: Methuen & Co. Ltd., 1966.
Traversi, D. A. *An Approach to Shakespeare*. 3rd ed. rev. 2 vols. Garden City, N.Y.: Doubleday & Company, Ltd., 1969.
————. *Shakespeare: The Last Phase*. London: Hollis and Carter, 1954.
————. *Shakespeare: The Roman Plays*. London: Hollis and Carter, 1963.
Ure, Peter. "Marriage and the Domestic Drama of Heywood and Ford." *English Studies*, XXXII (1951), 200–16.
Van Fossen, R. W., ed. "Introduction," *A Woman Killed With Kindness*, by Thomas Heywood. The Revels Plays. London: Methuen & Co. Ltd., 1961.
Vyvyan, John. *Shakespeare and the Rose of Love*. London: Chatto & Windus, 1960.
Wadsworth, Frank W. "Webster's *Duchess of Malfi* in the Light of Some Contemporary Ideas on Marriage and Remarriage." *Philological Quarterly*, XXXV (October, 1956), 394–407.
Watson, Curtis Brown. *Shakespeare and the Renaissance Concept of Honor*. Princeton: Princeton University Press, 1960.
Webster, John. *The Duchess of Malfi*. Edited by John Russell Brown. The Revels Plays. London: Methuen & Co. Ltd., 1964.
————. *The White Devil*. Edited by John Russell Brown. The Revels Plays. London: Methuen & Co. Ltd., 1960.
Whittick, Arnold. *Symbols, Signs and Their Meaning*. Newton 59, Mass.: Charles T. Branford Company, 1961.

Wilkins, George. *The Miseries of Enforced Marriage. A Select Collection of Old English Plays*. Edited by Robert Dodsley. Revised and enlarged by W. Carew Hazlitt. IX, 4th ed. London, 1874–1876.

Wilmot, R., *et al*. *Gismond of Salern: in Love. Early English Classical Tragedies*. Edited by John W. Cunliffe. Oxford: Clarendon Press, 1912.

Wilson, J. Dover. *What Happens in Hamlet*. 3rd ed. Cambridge: The University Press, 1951.

Wright, Louis B. *Middle-Class Culture in Elizabethan England*. Chapel Hill: University of North Carolina Press, 1935.

Index

Adultery and erotic betrayal as antiromantic theme, 4–6, 112–14, 124, 149, 166–69, 173–75, 192, 195, 199, 217–19, 224, 225–27, 259–61, 289, 290

Antonio and Mellida, 4, 82–89, 213; romantic marriage, idealization of, 83–87, 89; Piero as domineering father, 83, 84; Arranged Marriage, 86, 87; Deadly Nuptial motif, 86; courtly love, satiric rejection of, 87–89

Antonio's Revenge, 4, 89–96, 97, 242; mingling of eros and death motives in Piero, 89, 90, 92, 93; second marriage, threat of, 92, 93; eros and death motives in Antonio's vengeance, 93–96; Seneca, influence on Marston, 94–96

Anthony and Cleopatra, 2, 41, 233, 247, 277, 278–89; romantic and antiromantic visions of woman and eros, Antony's vacillations between, 278–86; Enobarbus, the significance of his fate, 277, 278, 286–88; love bond, the reestablishment of, 288, 289

Arranged Marriage motif. *See* Enforced Marriage

Atheist's Tragedy, The, 197, 212–23, 232, 267; inappropriate borrowings from early romantic love tragedies, 213–15, 219, 222, 223; equation of eros and death, 215–19; negation of theme on erotic rebellion, 220–23

Broken Heart, The, 2, 271–76; romantic marriage theme and influence of *Romeo and Juliet*, 272, 276; Enforced Marriage, hatred of, 275, 276

Changeling, The, 2, 6, 190, 248–56, 257; romantic marriage pattern, subversion of, 248 –

51; language of love, the ambiguities of, 251–54; courtly "service," 252–54; Deadly Nuptial motif, 254, 255; male response to the destructive female, 255, 256

Coleridge, Samuel Taylor, 33, 75

Courtly love patterns, interpretated by dramatists, 5, 23, 28, 29, 30, 61, 66, 76, 87–89, 123, 131, 132, 141, 176–78, 188, 201, 252–54

Deadly Nuptial motif, 37, 38, 72–74, 86, 87, 94, 97, 98, 163–65, 183, 215, 234, 235, 243–45, 254, 255, 264, 269

Death scenes, merging of love and death motifs in, 16, 20, 21, 24, 25, 31–34, 54, 55, 72–74, 164, 165, 183, 210, 212, 242–45, 255, 256, 271, 272, 288, 289

Decameron, The, 12–16

Doctor Faustus, 42

Donne, John, 50

Duchess of Malfi, The, 2, 6, 217, 235–46, 247; celebration of marriage, 236–39; Ferdinand and the Cardinal and the principle of masculine dominance run wild, 239–46; woman, antiromantic images of, 241, 242; second marriages for widows, as issue, 239–41; Deadly Nuptial motif, 241, 243–45; rejection of antiromantic vision, 246

Dutch Courtesan, The, 83

Edward IV, 179

Edwards, Philip W., 26, 122

Eliot, T. S., 82, 169, 175, 178, 182*n*, 183, 184, 247, 248, 259, 267

Empson, William, 34

Enforced (or Arranged) Marriage, as theme, 34–36, 71, 72, 73, 86, 87, 97, 98, 130, 215, 220–23, 250, 251, 269, 274, 275